"Michael's ideas on user adoption are action-oriente[d]
There is very little abstract 'consultant speak' about
idea of his I like a lot is 'Facilitated Group Re-Imagini[ng]
getting groups or teams together to discover how they work today, then define—with
them—how they can work in the new collaboration context. This lets teams define their
way of working together. Getting an intact group to agree on working in a different way is
critical to success."

Jane McConnell
Intranet and Portal Strategist, NetJMC
France
www.netjmc.com

"Michael has been a 'collaboration strategist' for 15 years—well before 'workplace
collaboration' entered mainstream business vernacular. All his thoroughly researched,
expertly written, and accessible books and articles attest to his deep experience and
abiding interest in effective team work and the various technologies produced over the
last decade or so to support collaboration. In this latest publication, Michael focuses on the
user—the key to achieving success from collaboration technologies, regardless of the
product. Providing a wealth of insight and guidance, *User Adoption Strategies* is a must-
read for anyone planning a technology implementation or seeking practical means of
helping users make effective use of today's technologies to improve their workplace
collaboration."

Lynn Warneke
Information Management & SharePoint Consultant
Melbourne, Australia
au.linkedin.com/in/lwarneke

"Michael's book provides a comprehensive toolkit which you can put to good use when you
need to get people to use the new stuff you have developed. Obviously the book is centered
around online tools, but most of the approaches work equally well with many other kinds
of projects—and not only things online. Michael has written a book for everyone who is
working with change management and adoption. Whether you're an experienced change
agent or you're coming to terms with your first project, I'm sure that you will find many
useful tips and strategic approaches, and that you'll find yourself reaching for the book
again and again."

Martin Risgaard Rasmussen
Application Consultant, Grundfos Holding A/S
Denmark
www.linkedin.com/in/martinrisgaard

"Michael Sampson's book *User Adoption Strategies* is a must-read. In it, he compellingly outlines the need for behavioural change if collaboration tools are going to succeed within organisations, and provides a simple four-stage model for planning this transformation. Most importantly, he outlines 20 different change strategies that can be applied to gain adoption of collaboration tools. These range from quick-and-easy activities to major enterprise initiatives; all are worth considering. This is a masterwork, and it highlights what organisations must do to make collaboration tools work."

> James Robertson
> Managing Director, Step Two Designs
> Australia
> www.steptwo.com.au

"What I enjoyed most from the book is the way Michael explains these strategies. Not only do you get to know how they work, but also when to apply them (in which situation), and why they actually help you. All this is written in very understandable language filled with lots of examples, making it easy for you to grasp the concepts immediately. While reading, a few times I thought 'why didn't I think about this before?' These aren't complex frameworks for which you need to read and think a lot beforehand to understand them, and neither does it take a lot of time to apply them."

> Rene Modery
> Web Program Manager
> Author, "Chapter 6. Exploring Different Options for Implementing SharePoint Solutions" in *The SharePoint 2010 Handbook* (2011)
> Singapore
> www.modery.net

"Although most of us work on the technology end of collaborative software, we almost always get involved in the discussions surrounding the age-old question ... 'Why aren't people using <insert-vendor-software-name-here>?' The easy knee-jerk answer (and one I've used a number of times myself) is that it's not the technology, it's the culture. While true at a certain level, there's so much more behind getting people to adopt collaborative software so that it delivers on the promises that were made. Michael Sampson, a well-known expert on the topic of collaboration, dives deeply into what makes for successful user adoption in his book *User Adoption Strategies: Shifting Second Wave People to New Collaboration Technology*. This should be one of the first books that is read and studied before launching your SharePoint/Connections/etc. rollout. And since the book is vendor-agnostic, it really doesn't matter what platform you're rolling out. These problems are common to all of them."

> Thomas Duff
> Developer, Regence
> Author, *IBM Lotus Sametime 8 Essentials: A User's Guide*, with Marie Scott
> www.duffbert.com

User Adoption Strategies (2nd Edition)

Shifting Second Wave People to New Collaboration Technology

Michael Sampson

PUBLISHED BY
The Michael Sampson Company Limited
33 Bridge Road, Greendale
RD1
Christchurch 7671
New Zealand

ISBN 978-0-473-21121-9

Printed and bound in New Zealand, with thanks to The Caxton Press.

Product and company names mentioned herein may be the trademarks of their respective owners.

This book expresses the author's views and opinions. The information contained in this book is provided without any express, statutory, or implied warranties. Neither the author, The Michael Sampson Company Limited, nor its resellers or distributors will be held liable for any damages caused or alleged to be caused either directly or indirectly by this book.

Editors: Kingsley Sampson and Barbara Sampson
Editorial Production: Michael Sampson
Cover Design: Michael Sampson

First printing, July 2012

To Matthew, my second-born son,
an avid reader and budding author of great books.
I'm looking forward to reading your books in the years ahead.

—MICHAEL SAMPSON

Acknowledgements

The acknowledgements section of a book is one of the best sections, and as I have started to write my own books, I've begun to pay more attention to the acknowledgements section in other people's books. It is "one of the best" because you get an insight into the support network behind the author—and as has been said many times before, it takes more than one person to write a book.

This book has benefitted greatly from the input and support of many people, including:

- Lee Reed, Jane McConnell, Paul Culmsee, and others for their feedback on earlier iterations of these ideas in my first two books, *Seamless Teamwork* and *SharePoint Roadmap for Collaboration*.

- Kurt Kragh Sørensen for an invitation to present a half-day workshop on user adoption strategies at the IntraTeam conference in Copenhagen in March 2010. I wrote most of the first edition of this book in advance of that workshop.

- Samuel Driessen and his colleagues at Entopic invited me to speak on collaboration and user adoption in the Netherlands in March 2012. Facing a rapidly dwindling supply of the first edition of the book, I started writing this second edition in advance of visiting the Netherlands. While it wasn't finished for the visit, the pending trip provided sufficient motivation to get started.

- Jed Cawthorne (Canada), Catherine Grenfell (Australia), Michelle Lambert (Australia), Gavin Knight (New Zealand), and Martin White (United Kingdom) for their feedback and editorial input. After reading a draft of the first edition, Martin said I needed to address the topic of measuring user adoption. I could not take his feedback on board for the first edition, but there's a whole chapter in this edition on that topic.

- Kingsley and Barbara Sampson—my parents—for editorial assistance in getting the book ready to go—both the first and second editions. The accepted wisdom is to engage a professional editor for your book and to not "ask your mother" to do it. Clearly the people who say such things have not met my mother or father.

I have the privilege of working with great clients—you can see the type of engagements at michaelsampson.net/clients.html. I have learnt a lot through these projects, and while the names of my clients are not emblazoned in these pages, the lessons shine through. I am very grateful for the opportunities afforded me by my clients to serve them directly while learning principles and lessons for wider benefit.

For an author, in one sense, you could argue that acknowledging "my family" is kind of blasé. I'm the sole breadwinner at home, so writing a book to sell could be seen as "merely a way of winning the bread." But I'd argue that authoring a book takes more than that, and can't be neatly left behind in my writing den. An in-progress book goes with the author wherever they go, and even intrusions like getting up from the dinner table to capture an idea for a current chapter have an impact on one's family. So it isn't blasé to say "thank you" to my family, and to acknowledge that they have had to live with someone who has their head in a book and their body in the home. I've tried to drive a wedge between these two aspects, but it hasn't always worked.

Teaching the concepts and ideas in my books through public seminars has brought me into contact with many people around the world. Beginning with the publication of *Seamless Teamwork* in late 2008, and picking up significantly with the release of *SharePoint Roadmap for Collaboration* in 2009 and *User Adoption Strategies* in 2010, I have presented day-length seminars in many places. Throughout the course of these seminars there are many opportunities for discussion and contextualization, and I have learnt as much from these discussions as the attendees. My thanks to all the public seminar attendees for their questions and input.

Many of the newer concepts in this book can trace their genesis to specific conference keynotes.

Writing books has also brought a raft of invitations to keynote at conferences, especially on the international scene. Whether attendees have known it or not, I try to bring my latest material to life during these conference keynotes, rather than merely repeating older material. Many of the newer concepts in this book can trace their genesis to specific conference keynotes. Hence my very real thanks to the conference organizers for the invitations to speak—even those I turned down due to prior commitments—and equally, thanks to the conference attendees for the post-keynote discussions.

The most delightful result for me from writing and publishing books has been the people I've met. A book becomes many things once it is released—an orchestrator of new relationships, a doorway to new conversations, and a lightning rod for new experiences. I'm very grateful for the opportunity to have met new people through my previous books, and I look forward to the new people I will meet through this second edition of *User Adoption Strategies*. Ultimately, this is what it's all about for me—meeting new people and having an opportunity to help them in their collaboration journey.

Michael Sampson
July 2012

Visual Overview of User Adoption Strategies

**About User Adoption Strategies –
this book and what it talks about**
OVERVIEW, FOREWORD

**Focusing on user adoption is
critical to success**
CHAPTER 1, Page **17**

↓

Setting the Scene

User adoption occurs within an organizational and process context CHAPTER 2, Page **31**	**User adoption implies changing the way we work; let's discuss** CHAPTER 3, Page **47**	**New technology provides new ways of approaching work** CHAPTER 4, Page **77**

↓

The Model and the Strategies

**We can think about user adoption
happening in four stages**
CHAPTER 5, Page **95**

Winning Attention CHAPTER 6, Page **109**	Cultivating Basic Concepts CHAPTER 7, Page **141**	Enlivening Applicability CHAPTER 8, Page **163**	Making It Real CHAPTER 9, Page 203

↓

User Adoption at Your Organization

Crafting an approach to user adoption for your organization CHAPTER 10, Page **235**	**Measuring user adoption, and how to think about value** CHAPTER 11, Page **255**	**Working with the advocates of the old way; some thoughts** CHAPTER 12, Page **275**

↓

**Enjoy your user adoption journey
– here are some other resources**
CHAPTER 13, Page **281**

Detailed Table of Contents APPENDIX 1 Page **291**	**Table of Figures** APPENDIX 2 Page **301**

Table of Contents

Here's the brief Table of Contents. See page 291 for the detailed version.

Overview

Here's the question: What is the biggest complaint around the introduction of new collaboration technologies into a team, group, or organization?

The answer: No one uses them.

The new tools are barely used for five minutes before being rejected, if they're used at all. The very people who are supposed to use them don't do so—they keep going with earlier ways of working.

Sometimes "culture" is blamed for this failure (see Chapter 3 for more), but I believe it is more accurate to point to lack of intentional effort on user adoption.

Overview of User Adoption Strategies

This book aims to help rectify the lack of intentional effort on user adoption at your organization. It greatly expands on my previous work on user adoption in *Seamless Teamwork* and *SharePoint Roadmap for Collaboration*, by adding three main contributions:

- *Theory of Change.* There is an extended discussion about the theory of individual and group change, which forms a vital backdrop for the specific user adoption strategies discussed in Chapters 5-9. Although we don't delve deeply into the theory of change, having an appreciation of what motivates people to change is helpful when formulating a user adoption approach for a specific organization.

- *Model of Adoption.* The Four-Stage Model of User Adoption, a new framework for the user adoption process, is introduced in Chapter 5, and discussed in chapters 6-9. There are multiple strategies that can apply within each stage, and these are covered in the four subsequent chapters. I give examples about how each strategy can be applied, and include data from a recent survey on the use and effectiveness of user adoption strategies.

- *Broad Applicability.* This book includes discussion of collaboration technologies beyond SharePoint. Two of my previous books focused exclusively on helping organizations embrace the technology of SharePoint to enhance business collaboration, those being *Seamless Teamwork* (Microsoft Press, 2009), and *SharePoint Roadmap for Collaboration* (2009). This book moves on to a broader discussion.

My intent is that you can read this book quickly and apply its ideas rapidly. While the book should be read straight through (because each chapter builds on what came before), once you have set your User Adoption Approach, come back to it often and use it as a reference guide for your work.

A Toolkit for User Adoption

There are over 20 strategies for user adoption profiled in this book. Although I state clearly in Chapter 5 that the intention is not that you embrace them all, don't wait until then before figuring that out. I'll say it now: Don't do them all.

I have developed a toolkit for you to take and use in your user adoption work. This toolkit includes the material on change (Chapter 3), the Four-Stage Model (Chapter 5), the various strategies (in Chapters 6-9), and the User Adoption Jigsaw (Chapter 10). But you have to do the hard work of using the toolkit appropriately in your organization—which means selecting which tools to apply to your user adoption challenge at the right time.

A Doing Book

This is a "doing book." Perhaps you feel you are stuck at the traffic lights in relation to the adoption of collaboration technologies at your organization. The light is currently on red, and so it's fine for you to sit there and wait. But once it changes to green, you have to go. Not doing so will result in a rear fender-bender, a ticket from a police officer, or a fist in the face from an angry driver. Green signals that action is required—you can't sit any more and wait—you've got to go!

That's no different to the principles in this book. You will come to a point in your collaboration journey when you get pushback from the people you are trying to help. That's the red light. This is the place where it suddenly gets hard. It's okay to sit there for a while and contemplate why you are getting pushback, but with the coaching of this book, don't sit there for too long. The ideas and principles in here are not mere theory. Wisely implemented, they contain the power to transform the way people work.

> This is a "doing book." The ideas and principles in here are not mere theory. Wisely implemented, they contain the power to transform the way people work.

A Few Words on Independent Advice

Let's be very clear about something at the beginning of this book. I'm not vendor aligned. I'm independent—as an analyst, strategist, consultant, and thinker. The intent of my work is to help end-user organizations prosper and do better. I don't serve the vendors—be that Microsoft, IBM, Jive, Socialtext, Central Desktop, Huddle, or anyone else. If you spend money with vendors as a consequence of something you read in this book, I receive no financial kick back. And I want it that way. To state the intent of my work in a different way, while I'm deeply interested in what vendors have to offer because these offerings create opportunities for end-user organizations, it's what end-user organizations do with the technology that interests me. In summary, my "three no's" with respect to vendors are:

- I have no business partnership with any vendors.

- I have no financial stakes in vendor companies.

- I receive no commission from product or service sales.

I believe my approach has a huge benefit for you (and one that my current clients greatly value)—you get truly independent advice. Because my firm doesn't do technical implementations of collaboration technology, nor custom development, my recommendations aren't about driving extra work for the rest of my firm. They are focused on making the best of collaboration technology for you.

Why Write User Adoption Strategies?

Why write this book? Here's my top five reasons:

1. The topic needs a book. I feel as though I'm short-changing people when the topic of user adoption strategies is handled in a paragraph long conversation ("Yes, it's really important"), or even in a 30-minute presentation. There is much that needs to be said, and much context that needs to be communicated. A book is the best mechanism for delivering the greater message.

2. People who work with new collaboration technologies need the guidance in this book to make their work successful. With no adoption, the organization gets no value—and that's both costly and sad.

3. There is a dearth of coherent guidance around user adoption strategies for collaboration technology, and this book aims to fill the gap. Too many people are running blind—and scared—and it's time to offer some direction.

4. There is a lot of noise about user adoption at the present time. It fascinates me to see the current level of interest in this topic coming through in blog posts, articles, white papers, and Twitter. What's missing is something that pulls it all together and provides an end-to-end approach. That's the intent of this book.

5. This is my topic. I feel as though all the work I have done around the design and use of collaboration technologies in organizations comes together in this topic. This is where it really matters.

With respect to this second edition, I wrote it because the first edition was almost out-of-print, I wanted to put the book into the bigger size of *Collaboration Roadmap* (my 2011 book), and I had a whole lot of extra ideas and updates to share. Merely reprinting the book as written in mid-2010 didn't seem good enough. I also wanted to add a chapter on measuring user adoption, and couldn't include that without doing other updates.

Intended Audience

Who are you? Based on the people I work with, I know some of you by name, and the roles you play. I have written this book for:

- *Project Managers.* It is your responsibility to ensure the new collaboration technology is implemented. This book is a resource for you to use in guiding your team in the effective delivery of the project—not just the technical details, though, but the critical issue of user adoption.

- *Business Analysts.* You work between the IT function and the people in the business, trying to understand and communicate needs and requirements in two languages. This book will help you in looking deeper at the challenges of introducing new collaboration technologies into existing work groups and teams.

- *Collaboration Strategists.* Your mandate is to explore opportunities for applying new collaboration philosophies and technologies to improve the way work is done. This book will assist you in bringing the wider organization along on the journey you have in mind.

- *Change and Training Managers.* You are charged with ensuring the people in the organization have the capability to carry out their work, but struggle with making change stick. The traditional classroom training approach has some validity for new collaboration technologies, but must be complemented by other strategies. This book offers the opportunity to up-skill in your work.

Let's Talk

I'd love to speak with you about your work with user adoption strategies for collaboration technologies. What you're up to. What you're thinking about doing. What your dream is for your organization if it embraces collaboration technology to its maximum potential. So let's talk, and I really mean that. I answer my own phone (+64 3 317 9484)—you're calling New Zealand—and personally answer my email (michael@michaelsampson.net).

With that introduction stated, and the reasons for writing this book clearly outlined, let's begin. There is work to do.

Michael Sampson
The Michael Sampson Company Ltd.
michaelsampson.net
July 2012

Foreword—by Nancy White, Full Circle Associates

Collaboration shouldn't be an elusive practice. We recognize we can and must work together. We recognize that technology has changed what it means to work together, both when we are in the same place or scattered across the globe. We have the business imperatives. We have the technology. Yet why does it remain so hard?

Let me tell you a story.

A research organization had a support team who recognized early on the possibilities of the use of social media for their scientists. So they installed blog and wiki software, created training sessions and thought that it would be a quick and obvious adoption. It was SO clear to these smart individuals. Their scientists were clever. Easy.

Not so. After some missteps, the team changed their strategy. They were not scientists. They needed the scientists to define the rules of the game. Instead of training sessions, they convened conversations about research, not about social media. As real collaboration needs surfaced, they offered suggestions and experiments between them. The technology folks created prototypes for experimentation, taking a page from the very practices the scientists used on a daily basis. Prototypes were set up, feedback offered and applied and tools and practices subsequently adjusted.

> Instead of training sessions, they convened conversations about research, not about social media. As real collaboration needs surfaced, they offered suggestions and experiments between them. The technology folks created prototypes for experimentation, taking a page from the very practices the scientists used on a daily basis.

What happened? Practices to enhance collaborative research emerged. They just happened to use technology as part of the process. The scientists did science, not "blog and wiki" classes that they felt were a waste of time.

To follow up, the technology team readjusted their roles to stewarding the technology—keeping an eye on how the scientists were using the tools, making adjustments and looking out for new options. They were careful not to define the conversation, instead listening and contributing. They lived the words Michael shares with us on page 250, "Go! Learn! Adjust! And then go some more!"

Through the process these "technology stewards" redefined their roles. What about the scientists? Think about it. Are scientists "second wave adopters?" In reality, the scientists are first wave adopters in their fields of research, but second wave technology adopters. It took seeing the collaboration from their context to bring them on board, but without making them feel like second-class citizens and by respecting their way of working.

I'm attracted to the idea of second wave adopters—that large group of people Everett Rogers writes about in *Diffusion of Innovations*. They are the people who are out there getting work done. If we as leaders are about creating the conditions for that work to happen, then this should be a group we pay attention to and support. When we did our research about technology for communities of practice for our book *Digital Habitats: Stewarding Technology for Communities*, we recognized that people use technology creatively, often in ways the designers or IT never expected. We realized there is a role that is different from IT, a role that requires both knowledge of technology and knowledge of the people. In this dynamic interplay, we have the issue of technology adoption.

Waves are funny things. Think of ocean waves. They go up and down, they can be gentle or pound us into the sand. Just when we think we have their rhythm, the next wave changes and surprises us. The key is staying alert, knowing how to swim, and being ready for the unexpected.

Michael Sampson is about to take you surfing on the ocean of collaboration technology adoption. In clear, practical language, he offers us insights that can reduce the pain and increase the benefits of collaboration software adoption. Come on, catch the wave!

Nancy White
Full Circle Associates, www.fullcirc.com
Author, *Digital Habitats: Stewarding Technology for Communities*, with Etienne Wenger and John D. Smith

Chapter 1.
Focusing on User Adoption is Critical

 Adoption can be hard ... particularly with broad-brushed tools that can do so much. [1]

Scott Jamison, Jornada

The world is filled with groovy technology to support people working together. There's no shortage of it. During the decade that I tracked all new product and service announcements in the "collaboration" space, hardly a day went by without at least one existing vendor releasing new features, if not a new entrant vendor making a splash on the global stage. My contention is that the technology to support collaboration is no longer the limiting factor. User adoption is.

In this chapter, we will:

- Consider the evidence on the importance of user adoption.

- Contemplate the cost and risk of not developing a user adoption approach for your organization.

- Define the term "user adoption strategies" and its derivatives, as used in this book.

- Learn the difference between first and second wave people.

The "Why" of User Adoption Strategies

The user adoption "problem" is a refrain I hear all over the world when I'm working with organizations on collaboration strategy—in Singapore, in Australia, in the United States, in Europe, and yes, even in my home country of New Zealand. But it's not just what I'm hearing. There is growing agreement among multiple groups of people involved with collaboration technology—the vendors, the consultants, the internal evangelists, the end-user organizations—that an intentional focus on user adoption is essential. I'd go as far as saying that many are coming to the view that this is the main game.

> There is growing agreement among multiple groups of people involved with collaboration technology that an intentional focus on user adoption is essential.

The basic thinking goes like this:

- It is important to choose the right collaboration technology for your group, organization or community —not too much to confuse them, and not too little to annoy them. For this you need to know certain things (e.g. how the people within the target group work), you need to get various things right (e.g. vendor selection, risk mitigation, and technology integration), and you need to have the right people in place to make it work well (e.g. business-focused IT administrators). I talk about this in depth in *Collaboration Roadmap*.

- There will be a group of people in any organization who quickly and actively embrace the new collaboration technology. These are people we have traditionally called "early adopters," but in this book are called "first wavers." They are the people for whom getting to use the new technology is sufficient reward to experiment and try things out. They don't need someone else to actively advocate how new technology will help them, make their lives better, or be better than the current technologies they are using today—they're able to intuit it for themselves.

- There are only a few first wave adopters within any group, organization or community. Getting beyond them to the second wave adopters is essential to driving better business performance. This is because second wave people are carrying out vital business activities, there are many more of them numerically within any group, organization or community, and as a consequence they have a much greater impact on business performance.

- Second wave people, however, are different from first wave people. They don't easily make the intuitive leap from what the technology does to how they could use it to do their work better; they need help from others to adopt new ways of working.

This book is about how to help second wave people do this.

User Adoption Problems in SharePoint Land

I have done a lot of work with SharePoint during the past six years, resulting in two SharePoint-focused books. One of the problems I have frequently observed involves the "IT-department-led" implementation of SharePoint. This isn't a problem with the technology of SharePoint as such, but rather a problem of how specific organizations approach the use and adoption of SharePoint.

By the time IT professionals have SharePoint ready to go for everyone else, they have forgotten the pain and frustration they experienced when learning SharePoint. In addition, while SharePoint is "the job" for IT professionals, it's definitely not the job for business end users. Business end users have a job to accomplish, and SharePoint is merely a means to an end. These factors create two problems for IT professionals when working with business users on SharePoint adoption:

> An "IT-department-led" implementation of SharePoint creates problems when working with business users on adoption.

1. They think all business users know what they know— SharePoint has become second nature to them, and they can't understand the "big deal" users are making about changing their work and embracing SharePoint.

2. They don't share a common motivation or language with the business users, and so talk at cross-purposes. Both sets of people may be speaking English (or French, or German, or Danish), but for all intents and purposes, there is no common ground on which a conversation can be held.

Again, this isn't a technology problem—it can happen regardless of the specific collaboration technology your organization embraces. The problem is the approach taken by the organization (or part of it), and its effects can be very damaging.

Other people who work with organizations on SharePoint have commented on the same phenomena. For example:

*   Lee Reed frequently presents on the user adoption challenge with SharePoint at conferences and events in the United States.[2] Lee says, *Oftentimes, SharePoint is rolled out with great fanfare and is lauded as a fantastic solution to a huge number of business challenges. "We're transforming our organization through collaboration," the mass e-mail notification might say. Well, your users have heard that before, haven't they?*

    Users have a hard time believing such pontifications, and their skepticism can quickly undermine any efforts to roll out SharePoint.

- Kim Lund from Mindsharp wrote a blog post in late 2009 entitled *How to Increase SharePoint End User Adoption.*[3] Kim writes, *If you find that user adoption of SharePoint is avoided or slower than anticipated in your working environment, you are not alone. Many students that I have trained, consulted [with], and listened to have expressed their pain points for SharePoint adoption.*

- Clare Stone from Pentalogic Technology wrote a white paper on barriers to end user adoption on SharePoint in October 2009.[4] Clare starts the white paper with this statement: *It's easy to deploy an application like SharePoint within an organization; the hard part is getting people to use it in a way which makes them more productive.*

  Many people I talk with disagree that deploying SharePoint is "easy," but fully agree that user adoption is the "hard part."

Various research reports on SharePoint during 2011 also highlighted the same issue— adoption is a major challenge.[5]

User Adoption Problems with Collaboration Technology

I wrote above that many people are coming to see that an intentional focus on user adoption is essential. While it's definitely a problem for organizations with SharePoint, it's not exclusively a SharePoint problem. For example:

- Socialtext (www.socialtext.com), an enterprise collaboration software and professional services company, released a white paper on user adoption in 2009.[6] In the opening section, the white paper states: *The success or failure of any social software solution ... [is] a direct result of its adoption rate .... There are plenty of examples of failed social software projects. Why did they fail? Because they were not embraced by users.*

- NewsGator (www.newsgator.com), a software company focused on enterprise social computing extensions for SharePoint, also released a white paper on user adoption in 2009.[7] In the opening remarks, NewsGator says: *This paper presents a model for proactive analysis that should be undertaken prior to or during the early phases of deploying an enterprise social computing initiative. Investing the time and effort to complete the analysis should greatly increase the opportunity for successful adoption and active ongoing participation.* In other words, how you approach social software in the enterprise has a big impact on adoption.

> NewsGator: how you approach social software in the enterprise has a big impact on adoption.

- The UC View (www.theucview.com) published an article I wrote on user adoption and Lotus Connections in April 2009.[8] I started with, *Increasing user adoption is a common challenge for organizations that introduce collaboration and social software tools such as IBM Lotus Connections. Administrators often find it difficult to teach business users how new tools can help them in their work. People are busy, and in today's economic maelstrom, people are scared. In such times, the safe approach is to stay with what you know given the inherent productivity and efficiency of this option.*

User Adoption Problems with Other Technologies

Vendors outside the collaboration camp are also advocating the importance of user adoption, thereby illustrating that it's a broad and general issue.

- In a March 2005 white paper from Business Intelligence (BI) vendor Business Objects, the author writes: *A typical BI project has a return on investment (ROI) of 430%—assuming proper implementation and organization-wide user adoption. Failure to achieve user adoption results in missed deadlines and compromised business performance. Despite today's pressures, proactive organizations with an eye to business advantage can enjoy unprecedented benefits. New thinking suggests that user adoption is a key determinant of success.*[9]

> Lack of understanding of how to use analytics to improve the business is the top obstacle to widespread adoption of business analytics technology.

- In late 2010, a study from IBM and MIT commented on the difficulties with gaining acceptance of business analytics inside organizations, and pointed the finger at user adoption issues. *Business analytics is atop most companies' apps wish lists. The business goal, of course, is to make sense of the enormous amount of data and information housed in their servers—and stop making critical decisions from the gut. The problem, however, is that the adoption of analytics is being hindered not by technology but by age-old people problems: change management and cultural resistance.*[10] The research cited four main obstacles to widespread adoption: lack of understanding of how to use analytics to improve the business, lack of bandwidth due to competing priorities, lack of skills internally in the line of business, and an existing culture that does not encourage the sharing of information.

This book does not contextualize user adoption within these other areas, but the approach and strategies outlined in the book can be applied to mitigate the problems noted above.

What's Going On?

Why all this discussion and interest in user adoption strategies? Here's what I see:

- *The technology is easy to buy and install.* It's easy to get the latest and greatest technology; it's fairly cheap, it's widely accessible, and it's available from many different vendors. When Nicholas Carr said that IT doesn't matter, part of his argument was that the widespread availability of mature technology to any purchaser eliminates opportunities for competitive differentiation. It's not the IT that matters—it's what you do with it.

- *"Just because" isn't enough.* Having "cool" stuff is directly appealing to some people, and unappealing to others. Even the latest and greatest SharePoint or Enterprise 2.0 technology lacks the punch required to get everyone to shift "just because." Something more—an intentional approach to encouraging user adoption—is required.

What's the Cost of Not Doing It?

Have you heard the saying, "Hope is not a strategy"? Unfortunately, hope is the "strategy" in which many organizations put their trust when rolling out new collaboration technology. The IT department builds it, makes it available, and then "hopes" that the target people in the organization will make good use of it. While hope is not an upfront strategy, it's a frequently embraced surrogate.

What's the cost of embracing this surrogate approach? Consider the following three stages:

> The IT department builds it, makes it available, and then "hopes" that the target people in the organization will make good use of it. In 99% of instances, nothing happens.

- The IT department at your organization decides a new piece of collaboration technology would be a good idea.

- The IT department goes out and purchases what they think is needed, and gets it installed, configured, and ready to go.

- The CIO sends out a one-time email to everyone in the organization, saying "The new kit is available; go for it."

What's going to happen? In 99% of instances, a big fat nothing. There has been no communication or expectation setting about where the new tool should be used, nor how much, nor what it's designed to replace. No stories have been told about the benefits people and teams will receive by using the new tool—neither exemplar stories from within your organization, nor real-to-life scenarios that have been developed to communicate context and prospect. And there is no cultivation of a movement among the staff to reinforce the validity and potential of the new tool. The CIO's email is going to fall flat. End of story!

What are the costs of this?

1. Waste of money, time, and effort from IT in discovering, learning and deploying the new tool. In a large organization, this could range from hundreds of thousands to millions of dollars wasted. In light of today's economic realities, few organizations have the freedom to do this.

2. Further erosion of the trust and partnership between the IT department and the rest of the business. In too many organizations, IT is already seen as the "business prevention department." Failure in collaboration technology initiatives represent further strikes against this trust and partnership.

Low Adoption is Costly

One way to understand the cost of not doing any intentional work around user adoption is to include it in your financial models! Do a sensitivity analysis on the impact of less than perfect user adoption. In a recent blog post, Jason Whitehead wrote:

> ... most business cases assume 100% user adoption and ignore the impact low levels of adoption have on return on investment (ROI). As you know, benefits are only realized if your people actually use the system consistently and effectively. Unless you currently have full and effective adoption of your existing systems, it is naïve to think that you will achieve 100% adoption of your new systems.
>
> **Most business cases assume 100% user adoption and ignore the impact low levels of adoption have on return on investment (ROI).**
>
> To account for less than perfect user adoption, you need to examine how different adoption levels affect your business case. If you find that the projected ROI no longer makes sense you can either scrap the project or determine what additional resources and effort is required to increase adoption to the point that it will deliver an acceptable ROI.[11]

What's the benefit of doing this sensitivity analysis? You will gain a very clear picture about the importance of user adoption in a language that senior executives can understand. This will be of great benefit to you in advocating for the kind of intentional user adoption work proposed in this book.[12]

Looking at the cost of low adoption from another angle, consider an organization of 1,200 employees embarking on the collaboration journey. The technology costs $200 per employee, and the decision is to license it for everyone immediately, and then run a pilot program for 6 months with 400 staff. These 400 staff receive training and encouragement to use the new approach (at $300 each). Twelve months later, only 200 people are using the technology, and then only in a half-hearted way. Of the $360,000 out-of-pocket expenditure, $260,000 has been wasted.

Figure 1-1. Poor Adoption Equals Wasted Expenditure and a Lost Opportunity

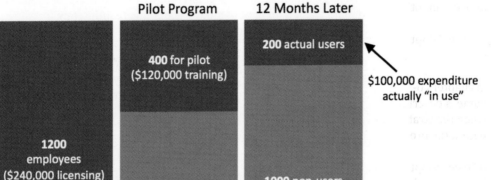

The failure to adopt new collaboration technology and ways of working results in wasted expenditure, missed opportunities, and a low chance of achieving the initial vision that drove the investment in the first place. User adoption is critical to success.

There is a third way that adoption is costly too: it creates a littered landscape of poorly-adopted tools. One team uses Yammer. Another team uses SharePoint, plus a bit of Basecamp for working with external parties. A third team uses LotusLive. A fourth uses another tool. This situation has many negative implications, such as confusion among staff about what tool to use, high ongoing licensing fees payable to vendors, high internal support costs due to the burden of supporting so many tools, difficulties in delivering training, and severe challenges when on-boarding a new employee. There is no "way we do things around here," but rather an incoherent collection of tools used by specific teams for specific purposes. Complexity reigns.

User Adoption Strategies—The What

In the first half of this chapter, I set the background on the user adoption challenge and its importance. In order to be clear on what we are talking about with user adoption strategies, this section defines three ways this book uses the phrase and its derivatives.

The collective phrase "User Adoption Strategies" refers to a grouping of individual strategies that an organization can use to encourage people to start using a new collaboration technology. In this sense it's the global term to refer to all available strategies for user adoption.

A "User Adoption Strategy" is a single self-contained way of encouraging people to start using a new collaboration technology—for example, the Real-to-Life Scenarios strategy (page 117), is a "user adoption strategy." When I profile a particular user adoption strategy in chapters 6-9, the strategy includes a name, a description, and instructions about when the strategy can best be applied within the process of user adoption work.

A "User Adoption Approach" refers to the intentional plan developed by a specific organization to encourage the process of user adoption by a specific group or set of groups. Either one user adoption strategy or multiple user adoption strategies will be embraced within the User Adoption Approach. The approach should be contained in a document of some form, although the document is intended to convey a shared agreement and commitment from a group of people within the organization about the user adoption approach.

> A "User Adoption Strategy" is a single self-contained way of encouraging people to start using a new collaboration technology —for example, the Real-to-Life Scenarios strategy.

Second Wave People

The term "second wave" is used throughout this book, and "second wave people" are the intended audience for your user adoption work. They are your target market. Let's examine what second wave people are like.

"Second wave people" or "second wavers" represent the largest body of people in a group, community or organization.[13] They are generally the ones who have to use the new collaboration technology as it's given, rather than having any direct input into what it is and how it could be used. They are very different from "first wave people"—the early adopters of anything new, the advocates, the champions, the enthusiasts. First wavers are more at peace with change, permissive of chaos, unfazed by ambiguity, and actually derive enjoyment from figuring something out. As I said, they are very different from second wave people!

Here are the differences between first and second wave people, differences which form the fabric within which the advice in this book is given. Think of these differences as "ideal-type hallmarks." Not all of them will apply to every individual in the two waves, but if you see more than two in a given person, then it's likely they are a second waver.

- *What-why reversal.* A first wave person is attracted to the "what" of the new collaboration technology, but may struggle to articulate the "why"—the future oriented picture—to other people. They may "get it" implicitly, but struggle to put it into words. A second wave person gets the "why" (if it's conveyed in terms of their work), but will need help with the "what."

- *Different reference groups.* A first wave person sees their use of the tool within a self-created reference group, usually outside of their organization. A second wave person sees their own work, and the use of tools contextualized within an internal reference group.

- *Different rewards.* Getting to use new tools is reward enough for first wavers, but second wavers have to understand where and how the new tools will improve their current work.

> Getting to use new tools is reward enough for first wavers, but second wavers have to understand where and how the new tools will improve their current work.

- *Speed of adoption.* First wavers will quickly embrace new tools, and will learn how to do so through trial-and-error. Second wavers need greater external help and handholding to successfully make the transition from current tools and approaches to work.

- *Nature of involvement.* First wavers have a high degree of involvement in defining what could be done, what should be done, and how to do it. Second wavers are generally expected to follow along and do what they're told.

- *Dealing with the old.* First wavers will be quick to call the old stuff "dead" and will want to move away from it as quickly as possible. Second wavers want to embrace new things within the context of what they already know and have.

- *It is their job vs. It could be used for their job.* First wave people often have an organizational responsibility to try out new things, and see what could be useful to the way work gets done. It's part of their job to explore the new. For second wavers, they actually have a "real job" to do—that's how they describe it—and the specific technology to enable interaction and collaboration is, at best, tolerated.

Note that second wavers won't wear a badge proclaiming their membership in the Second Wave Adopter Club. Recognizing them requires paying attention—looking out for the types of indicators I have listed above. Note, too, that although the book is focused on people in the second wave, the advice will also help people in the third and subsequent waves.

People sometimes ask how first wave people can influence or "preach to" the second wavers. The most effective way is to "live the message." Once you have people in your organizations who are using the new tools as part of their day-to-day work, other people will see that. If the new tools and approaches are relevant to their work as well, they will be "brought into the fold." Clearly this means the new system has to work, it has to show benefit compared to current ways of working, and it needs to become absorbed into the working approach of the organization. People who are not in the early waves don't want to invest time and effort learning a new system that lacks the capability to deliver on its promises.

> Having people in the IT department actively using the new system doesn't solve the user adoption problem—in fact, it is more likely to cause the user adoption problem.

The difference between first and second wave people is a key reason why deployments of collaboration technology driven by the IT department usually fail. Having people in the IT department actively using the new system doesn't solve the user adoption problem. In fact, if it's just the IT department that is actively using the new system, it is more likely to cause the user adoption problem. IT people are "abnormally profiled" in comparison to the rest of the organization, and there can be quite a level of antagonism between IT and other groups. For user adoption to become less of a problem, you have to get beyond the IT department through engagement with business teams and groups. For more on business engagement, see Chapter 6 in my book *Collaboration Roadmap: You've Got the Technology—Now What?*

"Users" or "Staff Members"

A quick note on the use of the word "user" in this book. It's been said that drug addicts and people who use computer software are the only two groups in society who go by the label "users." While I don't have a particular love for the use of the word "user," other alternatives sound worse. We could talk about "staff members." But then we'd have "Staff Member Adoption Strategies"—quite a mouthful. We could talk more generally about "people," but then we'd have "People Adoption Strategies." That doesn't work for the same reason. Let's be clear though that the focus is on people who work inside the organization —the employees, the staff members, the managers, and the executives. In short, "user adoption" is the best phrase we have.

Summary

This introductory chapter has laid the foundation for this book. We've talked through why an intentional focus on user adoption is important, and have considered the evidence that user adoption challenges are not limited to any one particular technology. It's a broad-based problem. User adoption doesn't happen by default, regardless of the technology involved.

> User adoption is a broad-based problem. It doesn't happen by default, regardless of the technology involved.

This chapter also looked at three other issues. First, it addressed the cost of not taking the user adoption challenge seriously, and proposed one way of quantifying the financial impact of less than perfect user adoption. Second, it defined key terms that will be used throughout this book, such as "user adoption strategies," "user adoption strategy," and "user adoption approach." Third, it provided insight into the difference between first wave and second wave people, the latter being the key focus of this book.

In Chapter 2 we turn our attention to the organizational context in which our work with user adoption takes place.

[1] Scott is the Managing Partner and CEO at Jornata, a business and technology services provider in the United States. This quote is based on a presentation he gave at the SharePoint Conference in Las Vegas in October 2009. See www.jornata.com.

[2] One of Lee's recent presentations is called *8 Things You Must Do To Drive SharePoint 2007 and 2010 User Adoption*, available to view at www.slideshare.net/leereed/driving-sharepoint-user-adoption. You will meet Lee later in this book; he writes a sidebar in Chapter 7.

[3] Kim's post can be read at the Mindsharp Blogs web site, sharepoint.mindsharpblogs.com/Kim/archive/2009/12/08/How-to-Increase-SharePoint-End-User-Adoption-.aspx. Kim talks about pain points, overcoming the pain points, and where to get help.

[4] Clare's white paper, *SharePoint: Barriers to End User Adoption—and How to Overcome Them*, can be downloaded (no registration required) at blog.pentalogic.net/SharePoint-End-user-adoption.pdf

[5] For example, see the Global360 white paper, *How are Businesses Using Microsoft SharePoint in the Enterprise: Market Survey Update for 2011*, available at www.global360.com/download/sharepoint-survey. Another report is from Azaleos—*SharePoint Census 2011: State of the Market*—available at www.azaleos.com/whitepapers/signup/SharePoint-Census-2011--State-of-the-Market.

[6] Socialtext's white paper on user adoption is available for download at www.socialtext.com/products/wp_implementation.php. Registration is required. The paper proposes six steps to drive social software adoption, including (1) encourage a range of use cases, (2) recruit energetic champions, and (4) focus on repeated activities.

[7] NewsGator's white paper on user adoption is available for download at www.newsgator.com/webinars/2009/roadmapsocialcomp.aspx. Registration is required. Like Socialtext's white paper, NewsGator's proposes six key steps within an adoption roadmap, including (1) identify business problems and goals, (2) define use cases to help solve business problems, and (5) identify obstacles to participation.

[8] The UC View article on user adoption for Lotus Connections can be accessed via www.michaelsampson.net/ucview.html. You have to be a subscriber to access the article on UC View.

[9] With Business Objects no longer being a standalone vendor, the white paper isn't available directly anymore. If you want to track down the white paper, search for *Achieving User Adoption: How to Unlock the Full Value of a Business Intelligence Implementation*.

[10] See *User Adoption in the #1 Challenge for Business Intelligence Too*, at currents.michaelsampson.net/2010/11/uas-bi.html.

[11] You'll meet Jason Whitehead again later in this book; he writes a sidebar entitled *Re-Thinking WIIFM?*, starting on page 73. Until then, read Jason's blog post on financial modeling of less than perfect user adoption at trituns.wordpress.com/2010/01/04/the-business-case-user-adoption/.

[12] If I take off my "user adoption within the enterprise" hat and think back to earlier in my career working for a large telecommunications company in New Zealand, this type of sensitivity modeling was central to my work. Part of my role was to forecast the potential impact of introducing new services to market. The driving question was always about return on investment, and one of the key factors was our assumptions about how quickly potential end users in New Zealand would adopt the new service.

[13] I thought I came up with the "second wave" phrase and idea, but just a few weeks before going to press I discovered two other people using it. After picking myself up off the floor, I decided to continue with the theme in this book. However, for the record, Nancy White used the phase in November 2006 (see www.fullcirc.com/,log/2006/11/second-wave-adoption.htm), and the team at Headshift used it a couple of times in 2009 (see www.headshift.com/blog/2009/05/secondwave-adopters-are-coming.php from May 2009 as one example). I like the elegant simplicity conveyed in the phrase, so I will join with the great people who have already used it.

Chapter 2.
The Context for User Adoption Strategies

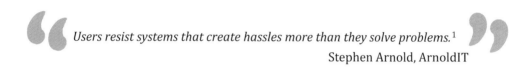

Users resist systems that create hassles more than they solve problems.[1]

Stephen Arnold, ArnoldIT

Adoption by users of a new collaboration technology isn't an isolated event. It doesn't just happen all of a sudden, with nothing beforehand and nothing afterwards. It is part of a process, and the effectiveness of the user adoption approach is dependent on the nature of this wider process. In this chapter, we look at the context for user adoption strategies, and learn how to make our specific work with user adoption as effective as possible.

In this chapter, we will:

- Think about why we are doing this.

- Look at two process models that provide a good context for user adoption strategies for collaboration technology.

- Review one (all-too-frequently-used) model that provides a poor context for user adoption strategies.

Ugly or Beautiful

User adoption isn't the first thing done when approaching new collaboration technology, but neither should it be an isolated event tacked on the end. An organization can't take an ugly piece of collaboration technology, do a beautiful job of user adoption, and expect success. The two don't work together. Likewise, you can't be beautiful at the upfront things, and expect overall success if you take an ugly approach to user adoption. Again, the two don't work together. But effective user adoption is essential to the overall approach to new collaboration technology.

> **An organization can't take an ugly piece of collaboration technology, do a beautiful job of user adoption, and expect success. The two don't work together.**

For example, it's unlikely you woke up this morning and said, "We need to focus on user adoption!" just because you felt like it. On the contrary, if you did wake up and say that—and congratulations if you did—you were thinking about user adoption within a particular setting, as part of a staged process, and with a specific result in mind.

Figure 2-1. The Context of User Adoption

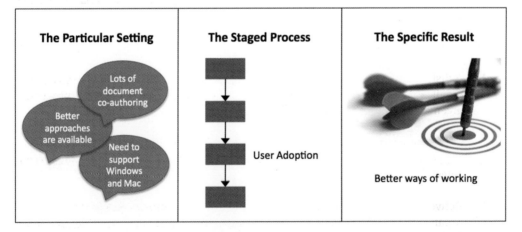

User adoption isn't a random or disassociated event in relation to new collaboration technology and approaches at work. It happens within a particular setting, as part of a staged process, and with a specific result in mind.

The context of user adoption has three elements:

- The **particular setting** is when a new tool has been tested and evaluated, and found by some people within the organization to offer something of value to other people and groups within the organization. That is, there is some evidence from direct experience within the organization that by using different collaboration technologies, something better is possible.

- The **staged process** is when user adoption work happens after the infrastructure is built out, business engagement has been done (to discover needs, opportunities, and requirements), and the focus switches from having great technology available to using great technology to improve the business.

- The **specific result** is improving the way individuals and groups work together, as a consequence of adopting a new way of working. The specific result is not the use of the technology as such—it's what happens as a consequence of the technology being used.

Let's look further at each of these three elements.

Element 1. The Particular Setting

In most organizations, the responsibility for choosing new collaboration technology to support work is a task for the IT department—or depending on where you work, the "IT group" or "IT organization." Members of the IT department should have specific training to help them identify appropriate technology to support collaborative work, as well as an appreciation of the integration pathways needed between any new system and the existing suite of systems.

For example:

- A distributed research team that works on documents together is currently using email and attachments. There are better ways of carrying out this work process, given the availability of newer technologies.

- IT knows any new technology considered for this work process must be able to support Windows and Mac desktops, because members on the research team can select the desktop they prefer.

- Active Directory is the authoritative source of people information for the organization, and any new system must integrate with it to support identity and login.

The great hope with such a context is that "the business" isn't ignored. Phrases such as "Business-IT alignment" and "Business-IT partnership" were designed to evoke the idea of both groups working together—IT bringing a deep appreciation of specific technologies and how they could be used within business groups, combined with the business contributing a deep appreciation of their opportunities and threats, along with dreams for how to seize or mitigate these, even if they didn't know the specific way of doing so.

How your organization approaches this matter is really important. In its 2008 report on Web 2.0 technologies in business organizations, McKinsey & Company found that the approach taken to introducing new technology is correlated with both satisfaction and dissatisfaction (see Figure 2-2).[2] Note that McKinsey uses the term "adoption" to convey the initial presentation or introduction of the technology to the enterprise, rather than talking about "user adoption" as we do in this book. What's startling is that in every case, satisfaction is higher and dissatisfaction is lower if the business had some involvement early in the process of technology introduction compared to an IT-dominated approach. That is option 2, "The IT department finds and tests new technologies and then brings them to the business units" receives the lowest level of satisfaction

> McKinsey: Compared to an isolated IT approach, satisfaction is higher and dissatisfaction is lower if the business has some involvement early in the process of introducing new technology.

and the highest level of dissatisfaction. In each of the other six options, business units have varying levels of greater involvement earlier in the process, resulting in a higher level of satisfaction and a lower level of dissatisfaction.

Figure 2-2. McKinsey on How Companies Adopt Web 2.0 Tools

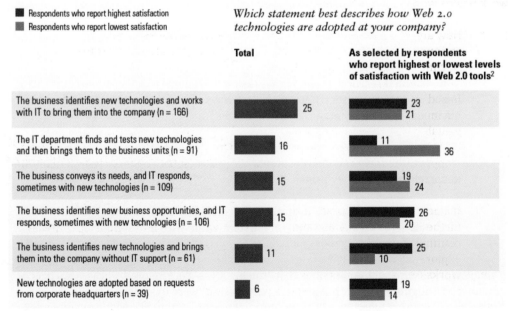

McKinsey found that business involvement and leadership in the process of introducing Web 2.0 technologies at work resulted in higher satisfaction and lower dissatisfaction with the tools. Involvement and engagement during selection translated to higher satisfaction.

Element 2. The Staged Process

There is a staged process in which user adoption strategy work takes place. It's not the first thing you do, nor the last. For example, you are not going to head out to a random desk at the office tomorrow, find a user sitting there, and invite them to a two-hour training course on the new collaboration technology. First you must:

1. Complete the due diligence work to assess the capabilities of the new technology.

2. Decide to push ahead with further investment.

3. Write the business case to secure senior management support.

4. Build out the underlying infrastructure.

5. ... and so on.

Yes, there is a role for early user involvement, but only for specific users within the staged process.

Broadly speaking, here are the activities that happen before the user adoption strategy work begins with second wave people:

- New and existing vendors are constantly being monitored for new announcements that may provide value to the organization. This is the "technology scanning" role of the IT department.

- Based on what the IT department understands about how different parts of the business work, potentially valuable new technologies are highlighted for further investigation within the IT department.

> Based on what the IT department understands about how different parts of the business work, potentially valuable new technologies are highlighted for further investigation.

- If a new technology passes the further investigation stage and continues to show business merit, exploratory discussions or workshops are set up with specific business groups to evaluate potential fit.

- If a fit can be demonstrated and a leader on the business side is willing to take an active role in championing the use of the technology within their department or group, then a deeper round of business and IT engagement starts. This would usually include the creation of a pilot infrastructure, the design of a pilot program to test the applicability of the collaboration technology within the department or group, and the development of a business case to outline joint expectations.

Now, a warning. Don't read the above and conclude that a focus on user adoption can wait until the last moment. Although you won't start working with second wave people until the tail end of the implementation process on user adoption as such, you have to start planning your user adoption approach long before reaching the end of the process. How to encourage user adoption is a constant theme that underpins the entire process, even though the work happens at a particular time.

> Warning: focusing on user adoption can't wait until the last moment. How to encourage user adoption is a constant theme that underpins the entire process.

Also keep in mind that work on adoption happens when business users are helped to transition from the way they work now to a new way of working. Once the new way has become the new "now way," adoption efforts have served their purpose and are no longer required.

Figure 2-3. Adoption and "The Way We Work New"

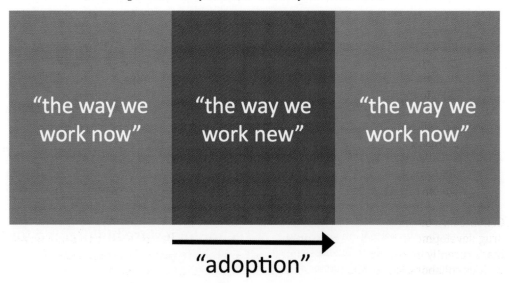

Adoption of new technology and approaches to work takes place when transitioning from working in one way to working in a different way. Once the new way has become the new "now way," adoption efforts have succeeded.

Element 3. The Specific Result

The final element of context is the specific result that happens as a consequence of using new collaboration technology. In the workshops I run on collaboration strategy, I call this "the global why." Why is the use of this tool beneficial to the organization—surely it's not being implemented just because it's new?

For example, it could be that:

- Running a team project in SharePoint is much better than using email and the file server. Document attachments are reduced, making it much clearer who has the latest edition. There is no more document chaos, because there is ever only one current edition of the document. Growth in storage requirements for email is one of the most pressing concerns for many IT organizations, and by implementing SharePoint—or one of the alternative collaboration workspace offerings—they are anticipating a leveling off of this growth. Actually, when I run through the document co-authoring scenario during a SharePoint Collaboration and Governance masterclass,[3] which compares using email and SharePoint to support document co-authoring, the attendees discover that storage savings of at least 80% are possible by shifting the co-authoring process to SharePoint. In addition, hands-on time for co-writing the document is cut by half, if not more.

- Feedback on new ideas is gathered more quickly through Yammer than in email blasts. Someone is able to ask a question and target it to a specific set of people in the organization, and engage in rapid dialogue about pros and cons. The organization is able to quickly gauge the pulse of the staff through Yammer, and then form subgroups to attack new market segments and opportunities.

- Visibility into key business processes is currently terrible! No one knows the status of their requests, no one knows who to call to get an answer, and it's just one big black hole! Implementing collaborative workflow capabilities in Lotus Notes provides an opportunity to resolve these issues, and for everyone to see the current status of their requests within the wider context of other requests.

Genentech, a biotech company, describes one of its desired results as reducing the cost of drug development. Bringing a new drug to market used to take 10 years and $1 billion; but that's recently increased to 14 years and $1.5 billion. Genentech is focusing its use of various collaboration technologies on reducing this timeframe and cost.[4]

It could also be that "the global why" is driven by less appealing prospects. Perhaps the organization is about to become subject to new industry or governmental regulations about information capture and archiving, and current approaches just aren't cutting it. Or the firm has just been acquired, and its existing technology is being thrown out in favor of the acquirer's technology platform.

Three Context Models

Now that we have investigated the context for user adoption strategies, let's take a look at three models for approaching collaboration technology in the organization. I recommend two of the models—the Collaboration Roadmap model, and the Scenario-Led Planning model. I do not recommend the third model, but have included it to describe the all-to-frequent default approach taken by organizations.

Model 1. Business Collaboration Roadmap

In my strategy roadmap book—*Collaboration Roadmap: You've Got the Technology—Now What?*—I outline a seven-stage roadmap for approaching collaboration technologies in the organization.[5]

The seven stages are:

1. *Really Understand the Technology*. Examine new technology and the opportunities it affords for improving the way work is done. The IT department will usually lead this process, but it should be done in collaboration with business groups.

2. *Outline the Vision*. What is the vision that drives our interest in and work with collaboration and collaboration technology in our organization? The vision isn't about using new technology—it's about improvement in processes, organizational effectiveness, and innovation, among others.

3. *Accept Technology is a Small Factor in Success*. While technology provides an opportunity for working in different ways, it's only 10% of the success equation. Other disciplines—including governance, engagement, and user adoption—carry much more weight.

4. *Determine Your Governance Approach*. Many collaboration technologies are broad-based and can be used in many different ways—it's the set of governance decisions about how and where it will be used that makes the difference. The governance strategy lays out initial shared expectations about the method of use, as well as a process for revision.

5. *Make Every Effort to Engage the Business*. A joint exploration into the possibilities for how a specific collaboration technology can improve the performance of a particular business group or department, using one or more engagement strategies, e.g. workshops, one-to-one meetings, and proof-of-concept examples.

6. *Apply Intentional Effort to Adoption*. The process of encouraging user adoption for the new collaboration technology, using one or more user adoption strategies, e.g. exemplar stories, real-to-life scenarios, and over-the-shoulder watching.

7. *Pursue Increasing Value.* After achieving initial success with new collaboration technology and approaches to work, pursue value in other areas.

Figure 2-4. The Seven Stages of Collaboration Roadmap

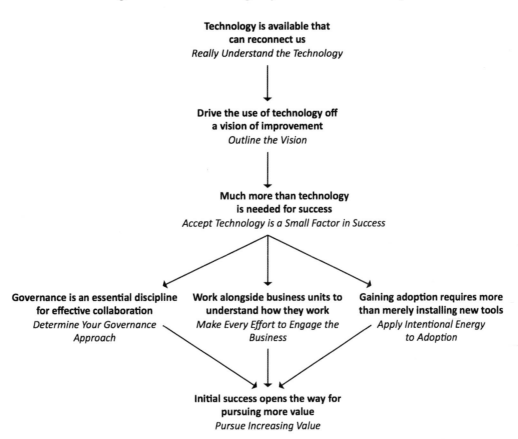

Creating a business roadmap for collaboration technology involves seven stages, including understanding the technology, developing a governance approach, engaging with the business about areas for improvement, and user adoption strategies.

In other words, the user adoption strategies stage happens near the end of the process, but this stage is intensely impacted by what comes before. It's impossible to involve everyone in choosing and evaluating new tools. Most people in the organization aren't that interested, let alone have the time to do so, but a representative sampling of staff should be involved as part of their work.

While the user adoption strategies stage happens near the end of the process, it is intensely impacted by what comes before.

Model 2. Scenario-Led Planning

The second model—Scenario-Led Planning—doesn't even mention user adoption strategies, but nonetheless lays out an approach that is very user adoption strategy friendly.[6]

It is a huge responsibility to be charged with articulating and implementing a collaboration strategy for an organization. Fundamentally, it requires structuring the way people interact with others, and comes with great power for good or bad. Therefore, before taking action consider these four key points:

1. Identify the key user groups in the business, and create scenarios of how they could work better through new and improved collaboration technologies.

2. Understand the facts of the tools from the vendors, but define your own architecture.

3. Know what the exit strategy is for working with any vendor.

4. Consider what is involved in migrating away from the current environment.

Consideration 1. Collaboration Scenarios

Collaboration scenario planning happens when key user groups in the business are interviewed to understand what they do, and then the analysis is combined with an understanding of new tools available for doing the work in a different way. This allows for some estimation of the benefits of working in the new way, as well as the costs of changed work practices to the people involved.

Our work practices combine habitual ways of working with tools and technologies that have been around for ages. One of the most common patterns of collaborative work is for a Microsoft Word document or Microsoft PowerPoint slide deck to be emailed around for comment. With the new technology available today, both for deployment inside the organization and as hosted services on the Web, this pattern can be exchanged for something different. Documents can now be drafted in Google Docs, and colleagues can be invited to read, review and comment on the document without it ever being emailed about. There are benefits to the latter approach that do not exist with the former.

> Collaboration scenario planning happens when key user groups in the business are interviewed to understand what they do, and then the analysis is combined with an understanding of new tools available for doing the work in a different way.

One of the key mindsets in choosing a collaborative tool is to find something flexible enough to deal with a wide range of end-user scenarios. By creating a new platform of commonality in tool availability and usage, things that work in one department can then be carried over and used in other departments. Put another way, skills picked up in one setting will apply to other settings. If the technology is too tightly focused on one or two use cases, then people will have to learn to adopt a multitude of tools, which is not going to happen. It also makes the movement and correlation of data between systems difficult, which leads to a more complex environment.

Consideration 2. Facts and Architecture

"He that defines the terms, rules the conversation." Vendors define their own architecture for collaboration and attempt to impose their view of the world on others. In so doing, they hope everyone will see the world from their perspective, and will thus become intellectually aligned with their products and services.

There is another way: Define the terms yourself. Create a reference architecture for collaboration centered in the needs and requirements of the people and teams in your organization. By all means learn from vendors about what they offer, but do not take the vision of one vendor as objective truth—it's just their point of view. To help start on this process consider using the Seven Pillars, a vendor-neutral framework I developed in 2005, that describes seven core requirements for collaborative teams.[7] In my strategy book, *Collaboration Roadmap*, two additional frameworks are presented—for collaborative groups and collaborative organizations.[8]

Once the architecture is defined, seek to understand the facts about the capabilities of the tools offered by different vendors. How do the products work? What can they actually do? What can't they do? Then put this set of facts against the reference architecture to see how well a given vendor meets the needs of your people, and study the mitigations needed to cover the gaps.

Consideration 3. Exit Strategy

When choosing a vendor and a product, know what the exit strategy and cost are likely to be. Be sure to select a vendor who meets your risk profile for systems that support core business activities. Just as email has become a mission-critical system, so too will the collaboration platform become a mission-critical system. This is not the place to skimp and save every penny, nor the time to align with a vendor who has insufficient strength to last for the long haul.

> The chosen collaboration platform will become mission-critical, so when selecting a vendor and a product, know what the exit strategy and cost are likely to be.

Another question is the availability of local support, not just at the corporate office, but in other places around the world where you do business. Where does your organization work today? Can the vendor or its business partners provide support in those locales?

Consideration 4. Current Environment

The final key consideration is to model what is involved in migrating away from the current collaboration environment. Very few organizations have a green fields opportunity, due to current and embedded tools. Transition and migration costs for IT investments are sizable, plus there is the need to re-train staff and administrators, or find new ones. More than one collaboration platform review has been cancelled because the costs of migration far outweighed the perceived benefits. Also consider which current systems can be turned off as a result of your work. The aim should be to create a streamlined place of working.

Finally, be wary of assuming that you must shift to a new platform in order to rationalize your current information architecture. Some organizations which have shifted from IBM Lotus Notes and Domino to Microsoft Exchange and SharePoint, for example, have said how wonderful it has been to reduce duplication of information, to re-architect certain applications so that the information is better shared across the organization, and more. Yes, those are great outcomes—but you do not have to shift platforms to do it. It is possible to improve what you already have and reap the same benefits, although making a switch can give you more clout to get certain changes underway.

Reflections

Scenario-Led Planning doesn't even talk about user adoption strategies as such, but it lays a great foundation for moving to a user adoption focus. People outside of the IT department have been involved. The people inside the IT department evaluating the technology have done so from a business-oriented approach. Starting with scenarios and enhancing the execution of those scenarios gives the IT people a much clearer picture of how to support and enhance work, rather than starting with the cool features and functions of some new piece of kit.

Model 3. Build It and Throw It Out There

I said at the beginning of this chapter we would look at one approach that provides a bad context for working with user adoption strategies. This is called the "Build It and Throw It Out There" approach to new collaboration technology implementation. Unfortunately, it's often the current default approach when dealing with collaboration technologies.

When the "Build It and Throw It Out There" (or "BITIOT" for short, although that looks too close to "IDIOT" to be used more than once) approach is taken, these are the hallmarks:

- The IT department discovers a new collaboration technology and starts to explore all its cool features and functions. Technologists love features and functions!

- After the IT department has played around with it for a while, the decision is made within IT that it's time for the rest of the business to start using it.

- A new implementation of the collaboration technology is spun up within the server room, and a memo is sent out to heads of departments saying, "This is the new tool you will be using from now on." Perhaps a training course is run one Tuesday at 2pm, but that's the extent of it. There is no attempt at engagement. There is no realization that user adoption is a process, not a one-time event.

> The "Build It and Throw It Out There" approach does technology "to" a team, group, or organization, rather than "with" them.

The "Build It and Throw It Out There" approach is quite different in ethos and intent from the previous two approaches—it does technology "to" a team, group, or organization, rather than "with" them. It's not the approach I recommend. Actually, it's the one I want to get rid of.

What's Your Context?

Now it's your turn. Reflect on the context in which you are doing your work with user adoption strategies. The two approaches I have advocated in this chapter—the Business Collaboration Roadmap, and Scenario-Led Planning—are ideal context approaches through which I have sought to make the following points:

- User adoption strategies may come at the end of the technology implementation process, but they should not be an afterthought. Someone has to think about this long and hard to get it right.

- The ultimate users of the new tool should be involved throughout the process, not just have the thing dumped on them at the end.

- People must feel respected for who they are and the work they are currently doing.

- People must feel as though they have been heard.

"Build It and Throw It Out There" is a very different approach, and one I am reluctant to consider as being valid. If you are struggling with adoption of the system you have created and implemented on your own, with no involvement from anyone else, could it be your own fault? A failure at user adoption may signal a key factor has been overlooked.

Switching to a different tool that is "thrown out there" will not solve the problem. The root cause must be correctly identified and a new approach developed which involves people much earlier in the process.

Summary

This chapter has built on the foundation of chapter 1 by expanding our view of where user adoption strategy work fits into current organizational practice. User adoption isn't something that happens in a vacuum. It happens within a particular setting, as part of a staged process, and with a specific result in mind. In terms of the specific result, recall that the result isn't the adoption of the technology as such, but rather what happens as a result of the technology being adopted.

Three context models for user adoption were presented. Two are recommended models—Collaboration Roadmap, and Scenario-Led Planning. The current default (and very bad) approach to doing user adoption —"Build It and Throw It Out There"— was also presented, not in the hope of encouraging you to follow it, but rather with the desire to point out its fundamental flaws.

> The specific result isn't the adoption of the technology, but rather what happens as a result of the technology being adopted.

In the next chapter, we turn our attention to the topic of change. Given that we're asking people to change the way they work, we need some understanding of what that will mean.

[1] Stephen is an expert on search and content processing. This quote is from Stephen's October 2009 blog post on SharePoint and user adoption, at arnoldit.com/wordpress/2009/10/11/sharepoint-and-user-adoption/. The article questions whether the user adoption problem for SharePoint specifically points to more fundamental and core issues that Microsoft has to resolve—around interaction design, for example.

[2] McKinsey & Company, *Building the Web 2.0 enterprise: McKinsey global survey results*, 2008. See www.mckinsey.com/clientservice/bto/pointofview/pdf/building_the_Web_enterprise.pdf.

[3] The SharePoint Collaboration and Governance masterclass is based on my book, *SharePoint Roadmap for Collaboration*. The public masterclass is a one-day success pitch for organizations working with SharePoint—it teaches them how to think through the business, technology and people aspects. Learn more at www.michaelsampson.net/sharepointroadmap-masterclass.html.

[4] Thomas Claburn, *Genentech Fights Social 'Noise' By Setting Goals*, The BrainYard, November 2011. See www.informationweek.com/thebrainyard/news/231903082/genentech-fights-social-noise-by-setting-goals.

[5] For more on *Collaboration Roadmap*, see www.michaelsampson.net/collaborationroadmap.html. Two other publications advocate a similar approach, albeit an earlier version: *SharePoint Roadmap for Collaboration* (www.michaelsampson.net/sharepointroadmap.html), and *Lotus Roadmap: Enhancing Business Collaboration with Lotus Software* (www.michaelsampson.net/2010/01/lotus-roadmap.html).

[6] This model originally appeared in *Messaging News* magazine in February 2008, and is reproduced here with permission from the publisher—thanks Jeff. See www.messagingnews.com/story/investing-collaboration-tools.

[7] The 7 Pillars framework, more fully entitled *The 7 Pillars of IT-Enabled Team Productivity* is available for free download. It's 50 pages long, and each of the seven pillars talks through the current practice, examines the productivity impacts of current practice, outlines an ideal future, talks about the productivity benefits of the ideal, and reviews some products from 2005 that went some way towards meeting each pillar. See www.michaelsampson.net/get7.html to get your free copy.

[8] See Chapter 2 in *Collaboration Roadmap: You've Got the Technology—Now What?* for the three frameworks (teams, groups, and organizations), as well as an expanded discussion on the collaboration scenarios approach. www.michaelsampson.net/collaborationroadmap.html.

Chapter 3.
What We Know About Change

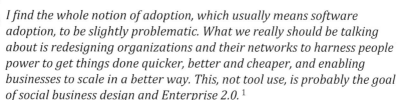 *I find the whole notion of adoption, which usually means software adoption, to be slightly problematic. What we really should be talking about is redesigning organizations and their networks to harness people power to get things done quicker, better and cheaper, and enabling businesses to scale in a better way. This, not tool use, is probably the goal of social business design and Enterprise 2.0.* [1]

Lee Bryant, Headshift

The concept of "user adoption" is intimately linked with "user de-adoption," which is an inelegant way of saying that in acquiring something "new," something currently used has to go or become less important. This brings us to the topic of change, a matter that has already consumed much paper for books, articles, and PhD dissertations. This chapter presents a bird's eye view of current thinking on change, and is intended to set a baseline for our subsequent discussions on the user adoption challenge.

In this chapter, we will:

- Review roadblocks to change for people, groups, and organizations.

- Explore five models of change, which propose different ways of thinking about the change challenge.

- Consider the change levers for user adoption, pulling together our analysis of the roadblocks and the models.

This crash course on change will look at what we know about how people respond to change, contemplate how we can navigate this area, and come up with some very practical principles to guide our user adoption work.

Roadblocks to Change

One of the first realities we come up against when exploring the subject of change is the matter of resistance—and it's not just a recent factor to do with new collaboration technology; it's an enduring issue across many types of change. People don't want to change. Group norms fight against change. Organizations neuter change efforts. Therefore, let's start by talking about the roadblocks we will face on our journey. Discussed in these next three sections is one way of looking at the constituent parts of resistance to change. Note, however, that there are interplays between the roadblocks at each level, and interdependencies between roadblocks across the levels.

> **People don't want to change. Group norms fight against change. Organizations neuter change efforts.**

Roadblocks from Individuals

There are numerous reasons why individuals resist change. Here's eight of them:

1. Fear of the unknown.

2. Comfort with the status quo.

3. Pushback on being forced to change.

4. No sense of the future possible benefit.

5. Being a stakeholder in the status quo.

6. Fear of transparency about their work.

7. Being overwhelmed with possibilities.

8. Loss of faith in IT's ability to deliver.

Let's consider each in turn.

Individual Factor 1. Fear of the Unknown

Fear is probably the largest de-motivator to change. Fear of what other people will think, or not think. Fear of what will happen, or not happen. Fear is a debilitating emotional response, and while it may not stand up to logical analysis or scrutiny, it has a big influence.

One particular type of fear is that of the unknown—what might or might not happen. In relation to ways of working and new collaboration technologies, people and groups have existing patterns of working together, and when a new way is proposed, they do not know exactly how it will pan out. Suppose the proposed future state is worse than the current state? None of us can be 100% certain about what will happen, and this can hold people back from taking the leap. Sometimes talking through the change and its possible ramifications helps reduce the level of fear, because people in the group are able to differentiate between likely and unlikely outcomes, and in light of input from colleagues and peers, come to a more reasoned position.

> Suppose the proposed future state is worse than the current state. None of us can be 100% certain about what will happen, and this can hold people back.

Individual Factor 2. Comfort with the Status Quo

Comfort with the status quo is a second common resistance factor. It's human nature to develop habitual ways of working, and indeed, habits are essential for efficiency in life and work. If habits are strong enough, many of the actions required to complete work tasks can be done almost mindlessly, thus freeing up thought capability for the more taxing parts of the work. For example, being able to touch type on a QWERTY keyboard means a writer can focus on crafting wonderful text, not which button to press next. Even though there may be better ways of typing, the certainty of the status quo is more appealing than the uncertainty of the future.

Individual Factor 3. Pushback on Being Forced to Change

A third common resistance factor surfaces when people have no input into an upcoming change. They are forced into it. I didn't make up the saying *People resist being changed, but like changing*,[2] but I say it quite a lot in presentations. The saying contains a subtle riddle, and signals a contradiction. Let's consider the first part now, and come back the second part later in this chapter.

The phrase *People resist being changed* signifies a dislike or internal pushback about having change legislated on you. You have no control. You have no say. You are told what to do differently with no input or option to discuss. Even if the idea is great, is better than what you've got today, and has benefits for you, whatever—even if all of this is true— people still resist it.

Individual Factor 4. No Sense of the Possible Future Benefit

A fourth common resistance factor is having no sense of the possible future benefits. When change is forced on people—if the change itself is the focus rather than the future benefit—people will resist. This can be for a number of reasons, such as:

- The change and the associated benefits haven't been explained in language that's meaningful to the individual.

- The individual assigns low credibility to the person waxing lyrical about the promised future state. They just don't believe them.

- There are outward signs of compliance, but the change is merely a projected image. There is no reality to the change; it's just for show.

Thankfully cartoonists can capture the funny side of these dynamics.

Figure 3-1. User Adoption is Key

User adoption involves helping people make the transition from one way of working to another way of working. Geek and Poke presents an insightful view of the challenges along the way. Copyright Oliver Widder. Used with permission.[3]

Individual Factor 5. Being a Key Stakeholder in the Status Quo

The fifth common resistance factor is being a key stakeholder in the present way of doing things. An individual may have introduced or implemented what has become the current status quo, and as a result feels a high degree of commitment to what currently happens. They may resist any changes that suggest they were wrong in their previous change efforts, or that the changes they introduced were not beneficial to the organization.

Individual Factor 6. Fear of Transparency About Their Work

Collaboration highlights work-in-progress—as Martin White likes to say, *there is no work and there is no progress.*[4] Working with others in regular group meetings, and even using technology tools to support tracking of task allocations between meetings, quickly gives a sense of what is not happening. Specific people aren't completing their assigned tasks, and this has a negative effect on group performance. Work-in-progress is highlighted, and what's seen is all bad!

> Specific people aren't completing their assigned tasks, and this has a negative effect on group performance.

If people are currently able to hide their lack of progress through carefully crafted excuses, the introduction new collaboration technology will be seen as a threat—and will be met with resistance. Sometimes the people who complain the loudest are the ones with the most to hide by keeping on working in the current way.

Individual Factor 7. Being Overwhelmed with Possibilities

Many IT departments are terrified of underwhelming people with new systems, especially when lots of time and money has been spent on selecting and implementing new technology. The IT department wants to show the multitude of new things that can be achieved through the new system. However, this approach overwhelms people with possibilities they have no need for, and instead of a focused conversation about what the individual needs, the conversation is fragmented. Because the IT analyst is not talking at a level understood by the individual, the changes are resisted.

Individual Factor 8. Loss of Faith in IT's Ability to Deliver

The final resistance factor is caused by individuals losing faith in the IT department's ability to deliver new systems that make work life better. If the IT department has a poor delivery history, is known for systems that fail, takes too long to deliver new systems (years go by between initial discussions and system delivery), or treats people poorly during the requirements capture "nightmare," people will resist what's coming. Past actions have undermined the trust that should exist between the IT department and the business, and unless this lack of trust is addressed, people won't try to change.

Roadblocks from Groups

Changing the behavior of a group is even more difficult than changing individual behavior. Consider the following four factors:

1. Group habits are often set firmly in place.

2. Change may be irrevocable.

3. Work practice and technology are inseparable.

4. An imbalance exists between energy and action.

Group Factor 1. Group Habits Are Often Set Firmly in Place

Groups develop habitual patterns of behavior, and the re-contouring of these group habits is difficult. Members of the group develop expectations about how other group members will do things, as well as developing mechanisms to cope with what other people do. These developments take place over time, and unstitching how the group works then putting it back together in a different way is really hard.

For example:

- Janice will send out the meeting agenda by email only minutes before the event, but everyone on the group has already had a little conversation over coffee about what will be discussed.

- Fredrik asks for feedback on his document with too little time for people to do a full review, so the reviewers compare their notes before going back to Fredrik.

- Bob is always grumpy about deadlines being shifted, so he gets a "special" edition with false deadlines.

> Breaking groups habits and developing new ways of working can be painful and take time and re-negotiation.

Breaking these habits and developing new ways of working can be painful and take time and re-negotiation. Janice has to be told to be more prompt with the meeting agenda. Fredrik has to be warned that his document will not be reviewed if he doesn't give everyone sufficient time. Bob has to grow up and live with shifting deadlines.

Group Factor 2. Change May Be Irrevocable

Loss of the status quo and an inability to go back to the old approach is the second group factor leading to change resistance. When groups develop patterns of working together, they get very efficient at the various steps. Efficiency is a great success measure—for example, getting a new product to market 30% faster than the competition can confer huge financial benefits on the organization. When a change of approach to work is advocated, it means becoming inefficient at work for a while, until the new way is learnt and internalized. Once the transition is made, the status quo is lost, and if the new status quo actually isn't any better, it may be impossible for the group to go back.

Group Factor 3. Work Practice and Technology Are Inseparable

Group technology becomes an invisible part of the way groups get their work done. Group members don't see their work practices as being separated from the technology underpinning it—both are one-and-the-same. Consensus is reached by having a meeting—but the meeting isn't seen as a "technology," it's just a "meeting." Document co-authoring takes place over email, but that isn't "technology," it's just "email." When the technology and tooling underpinning work practices are pulled away, it's like separating skin and flesh. It tears, and it hurts.

> When the technology and tooling underpinning work practices are pulled away, it's like separating skin and flesh. It tears, and it hurts.

Group Factor 4. Too Much Energy, Not Enough Action

Some people appear very keen to embrace new approaches in their group, and keep asking for more—or more precisely, for "just one more thing." But this request for something additional in the pursuit of apparent usefulness is used as an excuse for not taking action with what is currently available. It's used as a roadblock for change—the system isn't perfect—and until it is perfect it won't be used.

Roadblocks from the Organization

Roadblocks can also be thrown up at the organizational level. When these happen, they are outside of the control of any one individual or group, but act to further dampen change initiatives. Resistance factors at the organizational level are:

- *A History of Success.* When the organization is achieving significant success, those advocating change face a difficult challenge. Why should the organization change the way it works when it is already successful? Change is risky and threatening.[5]

- *Culture.* The culture of an organization will help or hinder the willingness to change. A culture of marketplace entitlement will prevent an organization from seeing it has to earn the right to sell to a customer. A culture of nasty criticism will prevent people from suggesting new and slightly crazy ideas. We will talk more about culture before this chapter is over.

- *Politics*. When different individuals fight among themselves over whose view of the past, present or future will be correct, "politics" rears its ugly head. Who do the other people in the organization follow, and how can they force others to embrace their view too? When politics gets ugly, the willingness to collaborate disintegrates because people are too focused on winning whatever the cost.

- *Inconsistency*. If leaders are unwilling or unable to state a single future direction, but instead vacillate between different future possibilities—this week one idea, next week a different idea, the week after yet another idea—change is resisted. Of course, no one is really sure what they are resisting because it keeps changing. But the lack of clarity over vision will erect a roadblock to change.

- *Systems*. Organizational systems are habitual ways of doing things at the organizational level, and are often encoded using technology and process. If systems are brittle, change will be feared and avoided.

- *Time*. It takes time to change, as we will discuss shortly in this chapter. If people are kept busy 24/7, with no opportunity to think or experiment with new ideas, change will be resisted. People have no capability to embrace change because they are too busy.

Other roadblocks to change at the organizational level include informal reward structures, formal compensation plans, and historical baggage.

Summarizing the Roadblocks to Change

How do we summarize all these roadblocks? While there will never be one authoritative summary statement that everyone agrees with, here's my attempt: *People resist change when it doesn't make sense*. When they can't see the benefit, it doesn't make sense. When the future benefit is only marginally more appealing than the status quo, it doesn't make sense. When organizational factors fight against the change, it doesn't make sense.

Marc Elsmar penned these words about change and the reasons why change is resisted:

> *If you really want to change, are there reasons not to? We may feel these are "safeguards" which protect us, or we might assume these to be "cast in iron" requirements or procedures. But often when they are investigated, they are found to be movable, and thus "changeable." We simply need to recognize that they are really only an excuse not to change.*[6]

Yes, there are roadblocks to change, but change is possible! So before we throw our hands up in despair and cry "It's no use; I'll give up while I'm still ahead," let's shift our attention away from the roadblocks and contemplate five models that address introducing and enabling change for individuals, groups, and organizations.

Five Models of Change

I started this chapter by noting that much has been written on the topic of change. This section offers a sampling of models of change.

Model 1. Stages of Change

Academics have studied change processes for decades. One academic model developed in the late 1970s and early 1980s is called *Stages of Change*.[7] It has its origins in research looking at how smokers give up smoking. The researchers, James Prochaska and Carlo DiClemente, proposed a model with five stages of change:

1. *Pre-contemplation*. In the first stage, or "pre-change" stage, people are happy with where they are. They are not interested in changing. They will defend their current choices to other people, and with great passion if required.

2. *Contemplation*. Without committing to making a change, people start to consider what it would be like to change, and whether change is even possible. The key emotion in stage 2 is ambivalence.

3. *Preparation*. An internal decision is made to change, and some small steps are explored about putting the internal decision into practice. People will search out strategies for change, and resources to help them make the desired change.

> In the "pre-change" stage, people are happy with where they are. They are not interested in changing, and will defend their current choices to other people.

4. *Action*. People start to take active steps to bring about the change they have decided internally they want to see. They need willpower to keep going with the various actions—not buying cigarettes for example—and are likely to seek out the support and help of other people.

5. *Maintenance*. The change has been made, and a new status quo is in place. In the final stage, the focus is on retaining the new status quo, and not slipping back into past habits.

Figure 3-2. Stages of Change Model

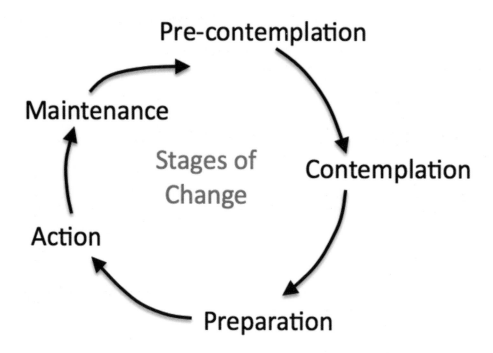

Prochaska and DiClemente found that smokers went through a five-stage process when giving up smoking habits. The model has been applied more widely to other areas.

What they said, in essence, is that change doesn't just "happen"—it's less an event than a process. There are five stages in their view of change, and each takes time.

Kurt Lewin, a psychologist, also saw change as a process, albeit one with three stages rather than five. His three stages are:

- *Unfreezing.* The initial part of the process, where roadblocks to change are overcome, and the existing way of doing things is dismantled.

- *Change and Transition.* The introduction of the new approach, which results in a time of uncertainty, confusion, and transition. Efficiency drops as people learn a new way of doing their work.

- *Freezing.* The change is becoming the new way of doing things, and people are becoming increasingly comfortable with the new approach.

Model 2. Diffusion of Ideas

A second model of change is called *Diffusion of Ideas*. The essential idea is that people are more likely to adopt a new behavior when someone they respect or admire endorses the behavior. The opinion leader makes the change safe, and as a result the change becomes a new social norm in a particular community.

Figure 3-3. Diffusion of Ideas

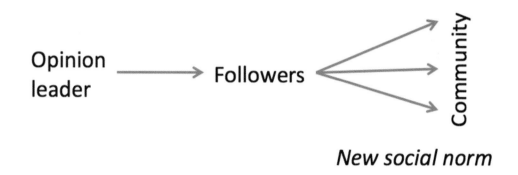

Change flows through people in a social context. People who are quick to embrace a new way of doing things have an impact on others who admire or respect them.

In order for the opinion leader to be effective in introducing change to the community, the following concepts need to be true:

- The leader has to demonstrate the change. There must be a very clear difference between current practice and the demonstrated change in order for it to be recognized as something different.

- The leader has to be willing to be viewed as being different, and not part of the crowd. If they don't get any followers, they will face ridicule.

- The leader has to welcome new followers into their idea, and then make the idea about the collective, not about them. They have to give up sole claim to the idea once more people risk their reputations on the idea.

- The first and early followers are critical to the spread of the idea to the rest of the community. If they are unable to embrace the idea and emulate the example set by the leader, the idea will die before it can impact the community. The leader needs to make the change something others can embrace.

I see good crossover between this model and Stages of Change. The Diffusion of Ideas model highlights the role influential or significant others have in the process of change for an individual. This can become part of the context used within the Stages of Change model to assist with pre-contemplation (I see someone else I admire doing something) and contemplation (I would like to do what they are doing).

Model 3. The Change Journey

The Change Journey model embraces the word "journey" rather than "stages" or "process" in its title.[8] One of the presuppositions of the Change Journey is that change is not a linear process, but rather a place of exploration, experimentation, and redefinition along the way. People embarking on the change will have some sense of what's coming up, some initial goal to work towards, but much of the journey will be about responding to the unexpected.

> Change is not a linear process, but rather a place of exploration, experimentation, and redefinition along the way.

There are four distinct aspects in the Change Journey model:

1. *Preparation.* The initial part of the journey requires getting ready for the upcoming change—some things will be known, and some things will be unknown. People going on the journey need to explore and understand the various options for getting where they think they need to go, as well as deciding who to travel with.

2. *Starting the change journey.* Getting started on the change journey itself is based on joint planning and agreement about where to head. The first steps are taken to start shifting the individual or group towards its desired goal.

3. *Living the change journey.* As the journey progresses, there will be challenges, new opportunities, even new people along the way. Deciding how to embrace these changes, and whether to make small or major adjustments is a critical part of the change journey.

4. *Creating skills for working in constant change.* The final aspect of the change journey is in developing skills to cope admirably with change as it occurs. People need to be ready for new changes, and developing responsiveness to change quickly is a critical individual and group skill.

Key lessons from the Change Journey model include the importance of conversation and group agreements about where to go, as well as the importance of developing skills and competencies to deal with change as it happens.

Model 4. Culture and Work Practice

I said earlier we would come back to culture before this chapter was finished. I have a strong view about culture and work practice for collaboration technologies. As with the word "collaboration," "culture" can be thrown about in conversation as a way of muddying the waters. Or to put other people off, as in, "It's all about culture, you know" (and therefore unknowable, and therefore let's not even try).

> The word "culture" can be thrown about in conversation as a way of muddying the waters, or to stop the conversation.

I dislike it when the word "culture" is used as a conversation stopper, and thus my aim in this section is to transform the word "culture" into a conversation stimulant. Let's start by seeing if culture can be isolated from work practice.

Culture and Work Practice

If the implementation of new technology requires a "change in culture," then my view is that the words, nuances and ways people express themselves to other people also need to change. For example, if you get someone to change from reacting with "That's stupid" to "Help me understand your perspective," you have changed the culture of their interaction.

Work practice is simply the way people carry out the tasks and activities of their role. If I communicate and collaborate with other people via email—holding conversations about a project, working on documents together, reminding others about commitments and expectations—then the work practice involves the use of email. If work practice changes, then people choose to use different tools to carry out their work, with associated pros, cons, and implications for other people.

I'm not attempting to argue that a change in work practice is by definition simple. It may be—if everyone in the group or team recognizes the problems and feels the pain of how they practice work now. But it may not be—if the people on the team or group think everything is going well, do not have the mental time or space to think about doing things differently, or don't believe the benefit of the change is sufficient to offset the costs and short-term reduction in efficiencies.

Work Practice Is Only One Part of Culture

It turns out that work practice is only one part of culture. Other more important parts include shared attitudes, values, and goals.[9] While work practice encompasses the way work is done within a particular social setting, these three additional aspects address the group's view on particular topics (shared attitudes), what it collectively views as being valuable (shared values), and why the social setting exists (the shared goal being pursued).

Therefore, one way to explore the degree of "cultural" impact of new collaboration technology is to assess which aspects of culture are affected. For example, take an intact group or team, and explore with them their current culture. What attitudes do they share? What do they value? What goal is the group or team working towards? What practices do they follow to get their work done? It may be that the introduction of new collaboration technology only changes work practice. The work practice may change from using email for working together, to using an online team workspace.

> One way to explore the degree of "cultural" impact of new collaboration technology is to assess which aspects of culture are affected.

Conversely, the introduction of new collaboration technology can impact on the other three aspects of the cultural matrix, and this is where things get complicated. Let's look at how attitudes, values, and goals may be changed as a result of introducing new collaboration technology.

- *Changing Attitudes.* The group's attitude to openness is an important cultural factor. If a group has the shared attitude of private working, then people do their own work towards the group's overall goal, with periodic reporting points. People are largely left to their own devices. A technology like Yammer demands greater openness to work—so if this is introduced into a group with the shared attitude of private working, it is going to require a change of attitude to one of greater openness.

- *Changing Values.* The value the group places on individual feedback versus group consensus will have an impact on potential change requirements. If a group currently demands that people's comments in a document are traceable back to individuals—either for idea ownership or as part of wider records management mandates—the group will be less inclined to embrace wiki technology where individual contributions melt away in light of wider group consensus over the document form and structure. Fully embraced, wiki technology leads to a suppression of individual identity in favor of the group. This is a significant transformation of a group's value, and if the technology is directive in this sense, it requires a much more significant change than just a change of work practice.

- *Changing Goals.* A group's goal can be changed as a result of introducing new collaboration technology. Perhaps the goal was to inform the rest of the organization what was happening with the development of a new product, and this was enacted through a monthly email newsletter. By introducing a blog, this work practice becomes a monthly blog post. Then when people start commenting and requesting additional feedback, a weekly blog post is introduced. Then people from other parts of the organization start giving ideas for improving the product, and thus the goal changes from informing a group of people to acting as a steward for new ideas. It's a very different outcome from what was expected.

An Example: Document Co-Authoring

Consider the example of working on a document—the document co-authoring scenario. The traditional approach involves a lead author working on the document until they are fairly happy with it, and then distributing it for feedback and reaction. This might happen by email, or by uploading it into a collaboration space, using Central Desktop, Basecamp, Huddle, or Lotus Quickr. Other people look at the document, and give their feedback. The lead author then takes the comments they want to take, and incorporates them into the "new master" edition of the document. This is a change of work practice only.

The fun starts when a more extensive change is proposed, such as obliterating the current approach to document co-authoring and replacing it with a radical alternative. Take the example of a wiki being introduced. Now it is completely possible for a wiki to be introduced without changing the fundamental work practice—the lead author still writes the document, albeit in the wiki rather than Word, and then notifies the other people on the team that the document is ready for their review. Reviewers open the wiki page, read through the current status, and leave comments at the bottom of the wiki page; they don't change the text directly. In this case, the technology has changed, and the work practice has changed, but that's about all.

In order for wiki technology to live up to its promise of open, freeform document creation by a loose federation of contributors, a more fundamental change is required. Instead of having a lead author, there is now a group of people working on the document, pretty much all at the same time. Instead of one person claiming "ownership" of the document, it's "owned" by a collection of collaborators. This is a major revision to the work practice of the group, and means there are now things to be wrestled with. For example, you know you have a not-just-work-practice issue when you hear comments like:

- *"But it's my document!"*

- *"I'm not ready to show you what I've written yet!"*

- *"But it's just a draft!"*

- *"Why are you changing my words?"*

In this scenario, the change in work practice is minor in comparison to the changes required in attitudes, values and goals! The shared attitude has to be revised to say other people have good ideas, and they are permitted to see—and change—your in-progress thinking. This is based on the belief that earlier feedback and involvement from others will lead to a better outcome for the whole group.

Shared values have to change too—the value that we place on less-than-perfect ideas, the value of one person's work in relation to the contributions of others, and the greater value attributed to openness and transparency versus private work. While one person in the group may quickly buy into a new set of values, it's only if the value statements are shared and enacted together that the new approach makes any sense.

Finally, there is a goal change too. The lead author used to see the goal as demonstrating their brilliance at writing a great document, and getting a round of "well-done" comments from others on the team. Now the goal is for the team to write a better and more rounded document, working together throughout the process.

Figure 3-4. Analyzing Document Co-Authoring for Culture Changes

Activity	Develop a Document with other People
Goal	Write the RFP response that wins us new business
Values	Ask when you need help
Attitudes	Author does the heavy lifting Reviewers critique and challenge
Work Practice	Lead author, with feedback from other people, distributed by email

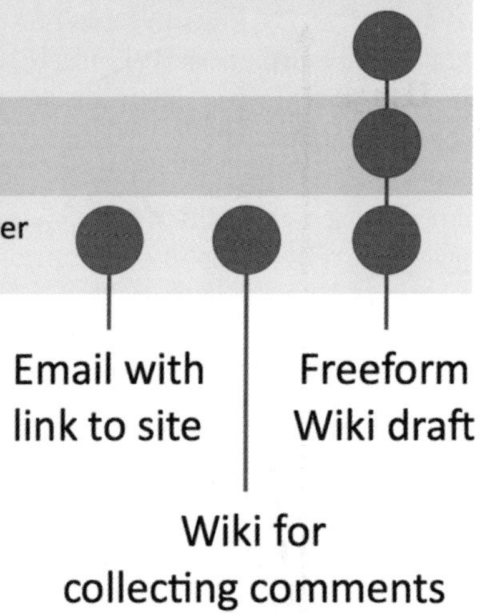

Email with link to site

Freeform Wiki draft

Wiki for collecting comments

New technology for document co-authoring can be introduced in different ways. These different ways cross one or more dimensions of culture. The more dimensions the change crosses, the more difficult it is to introduce the change.

In summary, this model is about recognizing the different levels in "culture" across which change can be introduced. The more levels the change crosses, the greater the degree of change is required. If it's just a revision of work practice—swapping one tool for another—the change is much easier than if it involves attitudes, values, and goals. If the higher levels of culture must be modified in order for the new technology to make its promised difference, then a proportionately greater amount of time and space must be provided for the change to be explored, discussed, and negotiated.

Model 5. Sticks and Carrots

No discussion of change is complete without reference to "sticks" and "carrots." Both are used as motivators for change—a stick is something that hurts you if you don't change (less pay, getting fired, being relegated to the "out-crowd"), and a carrot is something you get if you do change (higher pay, a promotion, a bonus, being part of the "in-crowd"). Both motivators have a different profile of effectiveness.

At Salesforce's annual customer conference a few years ago, John McGuigan from Fiberlink Communications presented a case study on the adoption of Salesforce at his firm, and compared the short-term and long-term effectiveness of different motivational routes to user adoption.[10]

Figure 3-5. Path to Sustained Adoption

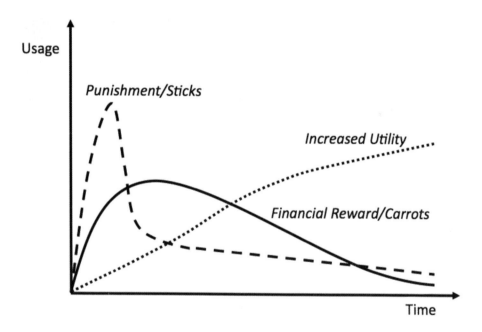

The threat of punishment is the highest motivator for short-term change, followed by the promise of financial reward, but both deliver only short-term gains. For long-term change, increased utility is the highest motivator.

As you can see from the graph, while punishment ("sticks") was the fast route to quick adoption, it quickly fizzled out. Financial reward ("carrots") offered a less rapid route to user adoption, and while it was sustained for a longer time compared with punishment, it too fizzled out. The most effective strategy over the long term was to orient the user adoption approach around increasing utility—such as making the work easier to do, and making Salesforce a critical part of day-to-day work flow.

Summarizing the Models of Change

Much more could be said about change, the cultivation of change, the management of change, the introduction of change, and the effectiveness of change, but what we have covered is enough for now. Note these summary statements:

- *Change is a process, not an event.* Change doesn't just magically happen in an instant; there is a process to be worked through. Different models propose different stages in the process.

- *Change takes time.* Individuals have to re-wire the way they work, and re-factor the habits they have internalized about how work gets done. This is even more so for groups, when group habits have to be re-wired in the new way.

- *Change is social.* The right people can have a large impact on the introduction of change into social settings. Early opinion leaders who model the desired change, and win early converts, can fundamentally rewire the way groups and communities work together.

- *Change is made real by what people do.* Change starts as an idea—an imagined future state in someone's mind. It becomes increasingly real through a process of discussion, exploration, experimentation, learning, and mid-course corrections. While the concept of the ideal future state may appear quickly, its realization in a group takes time.

A Roadmap to Change

We have covered a lot of material in this crash course on change, and it's time to round out our discussion. Here are seven critical concepts we can take from this chapter into our user adoption work:

1. Involve people in the change.

2. Deploy the right levers for change.

3. Make it about organizational improvement.

4. Use repetition to make the proposed change real.

5. Encourage change rather than drive change.

6. Give people time and space for change.

7. Prove that the change works.

Concept 1. Involve People in the Change

Earlier in this chapter we evaluated the first half of the saying, *People resist being changed, but like changing.* Given what the first half says, how can the second half hold any validity?

Since the phrase hinges on the word "but," there is an active comparison between the first and second halves of the phrase. What's true in the first half is not true in the second half, so the conditions that bring about the pushback on change in the first half are not the same conditions that bring about change in the second half. This means that people like changing, when the following is true:

- Change is not legislated on them. They are the legislature, or an active participant in it.

- They have control over the change—whether that's partial or total control. They have time to think about it, and are involved in the process.

- They have a say in what's happening—they can express their opinion, argue their view, make their voice heard.

Consider the different change response you get when a new and larger flat screen TV is released to market. If Robert waits until Daniel, his neighbor, has purchased one, the conversation may go something like this:

> Daniel. *Robert, I've just purchased the new 65" TV. It's awesome. You've got to get one.*

> Robert. *Well, that's fine for you, but my 42" TV is more than adequate. I don't see any reason for anything bigger. It's a waste of money.*

Robert interprets Daniel's comment as forcing change, and pushes back. As an alternative, if Daniel and Robert go to the TV shop together, look at the new 65" TV together, and discuss the pros and cons of updating their current 42" TVs together, Robert has an involvement in the proposed change and is much more likely to celebrate Daniel's purchase, if not buy one for himself at the same time.

Involve people in the process of what's going on. Hold the engagement meetings and issue an invitation for people to attend. Keep them updated with what's coming.

In summary, as much as possible, involve people in the process of what's going on. Hold the engagement meetings and issue an invitation for people to attend. Keep them updated with what's coming. Let them feel a degree of involvement and control over the process. Be collaborative in your style and approach, not dictatorial.

Concept 2. Deploy the Right Levers for Change

There are numerous motivators that can lead people to change—be they a small change like buying a new 3D television, through to a big change in career or educational aspirations. Deploy the right motivators for change in your work.

Common motivators are:

- *Pain.* The desire to avoid actual or perceived pain is a motivator for change. The more real and immediate the pain, the greater willingness people have to change and do things differently. Pain can sometimes be attributed to missing out on something other people have. Some people like to be first—they are first movers in getting the new model car, the new large screen TV, the new iPad from Apple—they gain an internal benefit from being first and knowing that. Fear of missing this pride of place can be a motivator for doing extreme things, like waiting in line for many hours to get one of the latest Apple iPhones!

- *Actual Social Pressure.* Verbal (or even non-verbal) pressure from other people that you are not measuring up or are missing out on something, can be a motivator to change. When everyone else in the management group starts turning up to management meetings with a printout of their performance chart for the week, and these are compared and discussed during the meeting, even the slowest adopter of new technology is going to get quickly onboard. This motivator is about making change popular.

> The belief that "everyone else is doing it" is a huge motivator for people to act in a certain way. People want to be part of great movements, and don't wish to be an outlier.

- *Perceived Deviance from the Norm.* Robert Caldini, author of *Influence: The Psychology of Persuasion,* an influential book on persuasion and change, said that the belief that "everyone else is doing it" is a huge motivator for people to act in a certain way. They want to be part of great movements, and don't wish to be an outlier. Whether everyone else is actually doing it or not is largely irrelevant; if someone believes everyone else is, they will be motivated to change.

- *Better Defaults.* Change can be very nuanced. Default choices can have a big impact on what people do. For example, organizations that send out monthly newsletters by email find that subscriber numbers are vastly different if the default is "no" versus "yes." Only 5% of their customers will actively sign up if the default is "no," whereas on the other hand, only 5% of their customers will opt out if the default is "yes." It's subtle, but makes a huge difference.

- *Getting Pleasure*. The desire for pleasure is also a motivator of change, even though the prospect of pleasure is a lower motivator than the threat of loss or pain. Pain is a much greater motivator, but the prospect of pleasure or benefit can work in some situations.

- *Linkage to a Higher Goal*. The final motivator or lever for change is linking the current change to a higher goal. It's not about switching from email to a team workspace, it's about getting to market 30% faster. It's not about changing the way groups work together, it's about beating a competitor who is making inroads into key customer accounts. Providing a wider perspective on the change secures buy-in and commitment.

I have personal experience with pain as a motivator for change. In 2007, I developed repetitive strain injury (RSI) in my wrists as a consequence of typing so much. So I studied the options of how to eliminate the pain—stopping typing wasn't an option (writing and typing is essential in my work). I had previously read that the QWERTY keyboard layout is not as efficient as Dvorak. As a result, a QWERTY typist is more likely to get wrist pain than a Dvorak typist. So I decided to change—to drop my typing habits of 17 years with QWERTY. I was pretty good at typing too; I never had to look at the keyboard, I could type relatively fast (60 words a minute or so), and I had trained my fingers to type without even thinking about it.

Then I switched to Dvorak, where the only two keys that remain the same are "A" and "M." Everything else is different! My typing speed dropped from 60 to five words a minute. My head hurt at the end of the day—I felt physical pain! But I stuck with it, and although it took me a lot longer than I was expecting—nine months rather than the one month the books had promised—the Dvorak approach really worked. My wrists are fine—the RSI has gone. It now feels easy to type. Dvorak is much more efficient. The avoidance of the pain of RSI was the motivator I needed to make such a massive change.

Concept 3. Make the Change About Organizational Improvement

Change calls into question the value of the current approach to work. By default, when change is proposed, the people performing the current approach will think it is because they have failed. This is all the more so when the people who designed the current approach are still around and have invested in making it work.

For this reason change needs to be framed as organizational improvement, and in particular, how the proposed approach builds on and extends the current approach. That is, the current approach provides an essential foundation on which the new approach can be built, and the current approach and the new approach are

> Change needs to be framed as organizational improvement, and in particular, how the proposed approach builds on and extends the current approach.

merely two steps on the same journey. In the same vein, there will be various factors making the next step important—for example, the market is changing, customer expectations are changing, key partners are changing, or the business strategy is changing. Be clear in your conversations about what factor is leading the need for change, and celebrate what went before.

Concept 4. Use Repetition to Make the Proposed Change Real

Did one of your schoolteachers ever say, "*Repetition is the mother of knowledge?*"[11] Mine sure did! Math facts. Historical facts. Bible verses. People's birth dates. In all cases the more you repeated something, the more likely you would "get it"—remember it for the exam, and then retain it for later use.

The same concept applies in change. Repetition is the "mother of change," the way of bringing about a different set of habits. It's about re-grooving the way we do things. In a 2009 blog post, Harvard Professor Rosabeth Moss Kanter wrote:[12]

> *In my experience, people don't "get" the important messages leaders try to send the first time around. This isn't intentional, but there's too much noise and too many distractions. And leaders with a lot of ideas find that people wait to see which ones take priority, which ones will be acted on, and which ones the leader really cares about.*
>
> *I also find that people don't automatically read all of their emails or download attachments. They read the subject line to see if they should. If the subject line is blank, there's a risk that the message will be missed. (I now try to stuff the gist of the message in the subject line.)*
>
> *Furthermore, even if people hear something once, they don't necessarily remember that they did. Busy people with multiple projects might forget that something has already been discussed and raise it again at a meeting. Leaders cannot assume that just because it has been said, it has been heard.*
>
> *So use the principle of redundancy. If the message is very important, send it through multiple media, in various forms, and do it a few times. It seems annoying, I know, but the delete key is so easy to use. I never mind a polite follow up (after a little time has passed), especially if it is easy to respond.*
>
> *As for speeches, make those headlines dramatic, repeat them several times, and keep the theme going in the next few speeches.*

Use the principle of redundancy. If the message is very important, send it through multiple media, in various forms, and do it a few times.

I don't think redundancy is waste; I think it provides focus. If you want everyone to be on the same page, put the page in front of them conveniently and often.

Repetition makes the idea real. It reinforces that other people are actually serious about the idea and the change; it's not just a flight of fancy. It helps re-pattern the way people think so they start to follow the idea, with small or large steps.

Concept 5. Encourage Change, Don't Drive It

The mindset of the person introducing a change and advocating for it is really important. One common mindset is that of "driving"—you have probably heard the phrase "driving change," or in our context, "driving user adoption." I really dislike the phrase "driving user adoption."

If you take a "driving" approach, it will come through in the way you engage with people, the way you talk to them—in fact, the whole demeanor of your approach and ethos. The "driving" idea always makes me think of a slave driver, whipping the slaves to make them work harder and faster. I don't know about you, but that's not an image that I want to bring to life in the organizations I work with.

The alternative word, and the one I always use, is "encouraging," as in "encouraging user adoption." It's a totally different mindset, and results in a different way of engaging with people, talking with them, and helping them through a process of change. It takes into account the core ethos that people have to be involved in the process. While the word is softer, I don't think it signifies any of the following:

> "Encouraging user adoption" is a totally different mindset, and results in a different way of engaging with people, talking with them, and helping them through a process of change.

- That you are wishy-washy, and don't know what you want.

- That you are willing to leave it up to chance.

- That you are a pushover and will back down quickly if challenged.

David Gurteen, a knowledge management consultant, speaker and facilitator, recently wrote an article that speaks to the difference between driving and encouraging change. He said: [13]

> *In a recent interview at the KM India conference, I was asked for my views on "Incentivizing Knowledge Management." Well I explained the reasons for not doing it but did not suggest an alternative approach. So here it is.*

If traditional incentives can have a negative impact, what's the workaround?

First stop using them; they don't work and do great harm. The problem with traditional incentives, rewards and talk of motivating people, engaging and empowering them etc. is that this approaches the situation from a mindset of "doing things to people." It says, "They are lazy people; we know best and we will find ways of manipulating them to do what we would like them to do." People see through this; they resist; they become cynical and it actually makes matters worse!

Here is my answer: "Stop doing things to people and start to work with them!" Rather than "Hello I am here to help you!," take the attitude "Hello, let's talk and see how we can better work together."

It's that simple!

But there is secondary issue here. Asking—"How do we incentivize people?"—makes the big assumption that they need to be incentivized. Yes, they may not be doing what you would like them to be doing but how do you know that the reason is lack of motivation? You don't. If there are problems then you will only find them out by sitting down and talking with them!

Work with people, not at them. Explore how work can be done better by getting alongside the people doing the work. Jointly explore the benefits that are possible by working in new and different ways.

> Work with people, not at them. Explore how work can be done better by getting alongside the people doing the work. Jointly explore the benefits that are possible by working in new and different ways.

Finally, contemplate the difference in approach taken by a gangster and a coach. The gangster turns up uninvited, tells people what to do, and outlines serious ramifications for non-compliance—broken fingers perhaps, although probably something worse!

A coach is very different. The coach is invited to come, plans for improvements are collaboratively developed, and those plans are implemented in a collegial environment. Feedback, discussion and mid-course corrections are a natural part of working with a coach. An idea for improvement part way through the process isn't taken as an affront, but the stimulation to work more effectively to a mutually desired outcome.

In short, gangsters drive; coaches encourage.

Concept 6. Give People Time and Space for Change

If we accept that changing something is a process, not an event, then it follows that people need time and space to make the required changes. In an organizational setting, having this time and space available without fear of reprisal is essential. For example,

- *People need time to consider the impact of the change.* They are doing the work, and a new work practice and collaboration technology will re-contour how they do it. Time is required to examine and explore how it will change. We should expect people to want to understand how something is likely to change before leaping ahead with no forethought.

> People need time to consider the impact of the change. They are doing the work, and a new work practice will re-contour how they do it. Time is required to examine and explore how it will change.

- *People need time to see what works best.* The people doing the work have the best understanding of what's involved getting the work done. If an external party advocates a change in technology, the people doing the work need the opportunity to explore the impact of the change. Does it really make a difference? They will be best placed to make that judgment.

- *Groups need time to discuss potential changes.* In re-contouring the way a group works, discussion about work practice will take time. Re-thinking the way work is carried out today, and re-evaluating how it could best be done with new technology requires a significant investment of time and effort.

Lack of time has a negative impact on user adoption too. One respondent to a recent survey on user adoption wrote:

> Sadly our user adoption strategy has NOT worked. Folks are just too crazy-busy. I work for a very small non-profit organization with a barebones staff, although we will soon hire several new key people. Existing staff members completely balked at switching out of Google Apps, in which they have a heavy history of investment using the calendar, documents, and email for managing their virtual collaboration. It just did not "take"; there was no buy-in.

While other user adoption issues are contained in the comment above, lack of time and space to make the change—due to being "crazy-busy" or "schedule-slammed"—is clearly a contributing factor.

Concept 7. Prove That the Change Works

Finally, prove that the change works. Deliver on what's promised. Work with people to help them achieve the proposed benefits—stick around until the job is done. Being able to talk about the teams and groups in your organization that have already successfully made the transition to the new approach and technology is very powerful; much more so than painting a picture of what work life could be like.

Summary

Changing the way people work is essential for user adoption strategies—some change in approach and technology will be required. The change itself may be large or minor, but it's a change nonetheless, and if approached in the wrong way, can have dire consequences for user adoption.

> The change itself may be large or minor, but it's a change nonetheless, and if approached in the wrong way, can have dire consequences for user adoption.

In exploring the topic of change in this chapter, we have laid a foundation for our subsequent discussions on user adoption. We started by looking at the major roadblocks to change, at the individual, group, and organizational levels. We then considered five models of change, and extracted some key lessons from each. We concluded by outlining seven critical concepts to make change work in line with user adoption.

In the next chapter we turn our attention to new ways of working, and look specifically at various collaboration technologies that may be introduced into an organization. Our user adoption work happens within the context of change, and these new technologies are part of that context.

Sidebar: Re-Thinking WIIFM?—by Jason Whitehead

Employee motivation for adopting new technology is critical for IT success. The prevailing attitude is that employees will have "no choice" but to use the system. The reality is that employees have many choices in how, when, and the degree to which they adopt new systems. For example, employees choose if they are going to follow business rules, if they will keep information outside of the system, if they will enter data right away or wait days or even weeks before sharing it, and if they will enter complete and accurate data.

For years many pundits have said the best way to motivate user adoption is to "sell" people on what they get for using the new system. They argue that you need to constantly tell each person, "What's In It For Me?" (WIIFM). So, after many years of organizations beating the WIIFM drum, we find most IT systems still suffer from low or ineffective user adoption. Is it time to re-think WIIFM?

What's Wrong with WIIFM?

I strongly suspect the people who first came up with WIIFM were management consultants, not psychologists. The WIIFM message, while logical on the surface, doesn't hold much appeal upon closer inspection.

Back in the 1960s Yale psychologist Victor Vroom developed the Expectancy Theory that deals with employee motivation and behavior. In essence, Expectancy Theory states that individuals are motivated to take action IF:

- There is a positive correlation between efforts and performance.

- Favorable performance will result in a desirable reward.

- The reward will satisfy an important need.

- The desire to satisfy the need is strong enough to make the effort worthwhile.

Expectancy Theory means employees need to believe that by adopting the new system they will gain a reward that is significant and meaningful to them. The problem is that the WIIFM message—as it is typically applied—rarely meets these criteria. Here's why:

- The reward for adopting the system needs to be meaningful and desirable for each individual employee. Many IT projects do not actually take the time to learn what is a meaningful and desirable reward for the individual employee.

- The rewards we desire change over time and vary from person to person. What motivates a young employee at the start of their career may be very different from what motivates an older person close to retirement. Also, different life phases and priorities—like planning a wedding, caring for a sick relative, getting divorced, and spending time with children—all influence what rewards are meaningful to the individual at any given time.

- Many organizations, especially those with a poor track record of implementing systems, lack the credibility for employees to believe that the system will deliver the anticipated benefits and/or that the employee will receive the promised rewards for adopting the system.

- While WIIFM messaging promotes the benefits of adopting the new system, it often ignores the costs/effort involved. Many times it just "isn't worth it" to the employees to go through the pain of adopting the new technology.

A Better Approach

Instead of trying to sell employees on WIIFM, help them focus on the need to shift their behavior. The psychological theory of Cognitive Dissonance shows us that when people hold conflicting views on a subject they are motivated to change (or justify) their attitudes, beliefs, or behavior. This means we need to help people realize that the business needs, environment, performance requirements, and management expectations have changed and the behaviors that made them successful before need to shift. We can do this by:

- Setting expectations that it is no longer business as usual. Explicitly state what has changed and what are the new expectations for employee performance. For example, you might stress things like changes in the economy require that we become more competitive by doing E. Or that new government regulations require we do X, Y, and Z. Or that in order to be eco-friendly and good corporate citizens we need everyone to do A, B and C.

- Instead of focusing on one-way, passive communications, focus on engaging employees in two-way discussions. Ask them questions so they are forced to think about what has changed and how they need to adjust their behavior to be successful in the new reality.

- Explicitly state that how you perform your job (the work practice) is just as important as how well you perform (the work outcome). Communicate it is no longer sufficient to be a great individual performer if the way you utilize systems and processes prevents others from excelling in their jobs.

IT professionals have relied on the WIIFM message for years with little success in motivating user adoption. Is it time to re-think WIIFM? You bet it is.

About Jason Whitehead

Jason Whitehead is the Founder and President of Tri Tuns, LLC., an IT and organizational effectiveness consulting firm in the United States. See www.trituns.com.

---

[1] Lee Bryant from Headshift in London included this quote in his *Behavioural transition strategies for E2.0* blog post in August 2009. See www.headshift.com/blog/2009/08/behavioural-transition-strateg.php. Note that Headshift is now part of the DACHIS Group, a global advisory practice focused on bringing social technology to the enterprise.

[2] The actual quote is "*People don't resist change. They resist being changed!*" by Peter Senge, so even my version goes beyond what Peter says. See www.leadershipnow.com/changequotes.html.

[3] Oliver Widder shares his view of current events on Geek And Poke, a blog filled with cartoons. His cartoon on user adoption is from 2007—see geekandpoke.typepad.com/geekandpoke/2007/11/user-adoption-i.html. Subscribe to Oliver's blog for regular updates.

[4] I don't know if Martin is the originator of the quote as such, but I heard it first from him at a conference in Europe in 2010. So I treat it as "Martin's quote." For more on Martin White, his books, and his consulting work around intranets, see www.intranetfocus.com.

[5] For more on protecting success, see Melba Kurman's February 2011 article, *Why People Resist Change*, at Innovation Excellence. www.innovationexcellence.com/blog/2011/02/19/why-people-resist-change/.

[6] This quote is from Slide 5 of Marc Elsmar's presentation *Discovering Change*. See elsmar.com/Discovering_Change/sld001.htm.

[7] Among other resources, this discussion on the Stages of Change model is drawn from www.addictionalternatives.com/philosophy/stagemodel.htm.

[8] For more on the Change Journey, see www.changejourney.org.

[9] Wikipedians have written much on the topic of culture. See en.wikipedia.org/wiki/Culture.

[10] The session was called *The Cardinal Rules of User Adoption* (see www.salesforce.com/dreamforce/DF09/pdfs/ADMN017_Williams.pdf). John McGuigan of Fiberlink Communications presented their approach to user adoption, and included this excellent chart about the short-term and long-run effectiveness of different philosophies of user adoption for the Salesforce customer relationship management system. Please note that I have re-mastered John's chart for this book.

[11] Or more accurately, they'd say, "*Repetition is the mother of knowledge. Repetition is the mother of knowledge. Repetition is the mother of knowledge. Repetition is the mother of knowledge.*" Right?

[12] See blogs.harvardbusiness.org/kanter/2009/02/the-secret-to-getting-your-mes.html.

[13] David Gurteen, the "king of knowledge cafes," is based in London and is a frequent traveler for conferences, workshops and knowledge cafes. His website offers a wealth of material on knowledge management, learning, creativity, innovation, and related topics. See www.gurteen.com.

Chapter 4.
New Ways of Working

Business data and business processes are unifying forces within the enterprise. By putting your new collaboration tools in the context of a business process or objective business measure, you can drive adoption across the entire spectrum of employees. [1]

Joe Schueller, Cisco Systems

There are hundreds of products that fall under the phrase of "collaboration technology." Since we are focusing on user adoption of new collaboration technology and approaches for greater business benefit, it is helpful to have an understanding of the types of technologies that are available, and that set the context for our work. In this chapter, I will discuss common collaborative scenarios—the fundamental building blocks of technology-supported collaboration—and highlight new technologies for approaching each scenario.

In this chapter, we will:

- Learn about collaborative scenarios people do regularly.

- Consider current ways of approaching each collaborative scenario, and the problems that result.

- Look into new collaboration technology that can support existing scenarios in new ways, and the associated benefits.

Collaboration Scenarios

Various approaches can be taken when talking about the technology that is used to support collaboration. For example:

- You can differentiate by product groupings—such real-time interaction (presence and availability, instant messaging, and web conferencing), calendaring (enterprise, web-based, and mobile), team workspaces, and social collaboration (activity streams, rating, and commenting). Such a lens creates a differentiation based on accepted industry product areas.

- You can differentiate by intent—for teams that would be creating a shared place for joint access, location independence, and real-time joint editing and review, among others.[2] This approach looks across different product groups to highlight the specific needs of a team, group, or organization from the technology.

> Collaboration Scenarios starts with a collaborative activity people carry out as a regular part of their work, not the technology.

- You can differentiate by Collaboration Scenario—an approach that starts with the different collaborative activities people carry out as a regular part of their work, and then links those activities with particular types of technology. The technology is only considered in the context of the scenario.[3]

This chapter takes the third approach.

Common Collaboration Scenarios

Among the many Collaboration Scenarios, common ones include:

- *Managing a Team Project*. When teams work together on a project—an initiative with a particular outcome, set membership, and definite end signal.

- *Sharing Team and Organizational Updates*. How different parts of the organization are kept up-to-date with current happenings and future plans.

- *Finding Expertise*. When people need to locate others who have expertise or special knowledge in a particular topic or field.

- *Collaboratively Authoring Documents*. When two or more people work on a document together—planning, drafting, writing, editing, and the final polishing.

- *Collaborative Idea Management*. When many people have ideas on what could or should happen, and how those ideas are brought together for analysis.

- *Making Group Decisions*. When many people are involved in forming decision options, evaluating the options, and making a decision.

- *Managing Meetings*. When people meet to discuss ideas, make decisions, explore possibilities, and otherwise communicate "in the now." The scenario includes the pre-meeting planning activities, as well as the post-meeting follow-up.

- *Sharing Learning and Best Practices*. When many people are doing similar work, and innovations in the work approach made by one person could benefit other people doing the same work.

- *Holding Discussions*. When teams or groups discuss ideas, challenges, problems, and opportunities, with a view to exploring the boundaries of what's known.

- *Individual Coherence*. A special Collaboration Scenario that considers the impact of introducing new collaboration technology on an individual—how they track and coordinate everything they have to do.

Examining Collaboration Scenarios

In this chapter, we are going to focus on six of these scenarios:

1. Managing a Team Project.

2. Sharing Team and Organizational Updates.

3. Finding Expertise.

4. Collaboratively Authoring Documents.

5. Collaborative Idea Management.

6. Making Group Decisions.

The chapter concludes with a brief look at three other scenarios: holding meetings, requesting feedback, and sharing best practices.

Managing a Team Project

Email is the most commonly used collaboration technology today. It's the most common tool people use to collaborate on team projects—discussing issues, checking up on timeframes, swapping documents. But email is not ideally suited to managing team projects, for a variety of reasons:

- *Document Chaos*. When co-authoring a document, no one is sure if they are working on the most recent edition, and someone has to bring together all the suggested changes to create a new master copy. It's messy, error-prone, and takes far too long.

- *Versioning Chaos*. When Jim is looking for a particular document or spreadsheet, how does he know whether the copy on his desktop, in the file folder, or one of multiple copies in his email inbox is the most current version? Basically he doesn't. It's a wild guess.

- *Communication Chaos*. Using email for conversations leads to chaos. Although modern email clients offer the ability to show related messages in a thread, threading is not sufficient to give a proper and natural ordering of email messages when many people are conversing on an issue over a multi-day or multi-week timeframe. Messages will be sent and received out of order. Some team members will respond to earlier messages in the thread, not the latest one. They're not trying to be malicious (in most cases)—they're trying to contribute—but since their contributions are handled via email and not a more appropriate tool, they contribute to conversation confusion.[4]

What can be done? Many organizations are experimenting with collaboration sites for team projects—Microsoft SharePoint, Lotus Quickr, and Central Desktop (see Figure 4-1), among others.

> Many organizations are experimenting with collaboration sites for team projects. It introduces changes to the way work is done.

A change of collaboration technology introduces changes to the way work is done:

- People switch to the collaboration site, and stop using email for the communication, collaboration and coordination work of the team project. The big idea with a collaboration site is that all of the documents, conversations, meetings, and tasks related to the project are brought together in a single application, instead of being separated across several different applications.

- Documents are stored in the team site, and not emailed around. All work on a document, spreadsheet or presentation is done out of the collaboration site; people don't work any more with local copies. That means a document is opened directly from the collaboration site, and after the changes have been made, it is saved directly back into the collaboration site.

- Communication and discussion happens in a discussion area within the collaboration site, rather than in email. This can be quite a big change for people, because discussions no longer come through to their BlackBerries and iPhones. Although the discussion can be much easier to follow, there is a single version of the truth, and no one has to keep their own copy of the discussion.

- The coordination around the team project happens within the collaboration site. Tasks are created and assigned to people. Meetings are scheduled, and held. Project time lines are shared, and updated.

- People can be easily added to and removed from the collaboration site, to accommodate changing project membership. New project team members can quickly review what's been happening in the project, and examine the current status of its different aspects.

Figure 4-1. Central Desktop for Managing Team Projects

Central Desktop's cloud-based collaboration platform, SocialBridge, connects people and information in the cloud, making it possible to manage projects, share files, combine knowledge, inspire ideas, and more. See www.centraldesktop.com for more.

Sharing Team and Organizational Updates

Keeping everyone on the same page, whether it be in a team, a department or across the entire organization, is a major communications job. The act of getting the message out is just one small part of the overall process; ensuring that people understand the message, and can then change to work in a different way are much bigger aspects.

The most common approach to sharing updates across a group of people is email blasts.

- A project leader sends out a weekly project status update email to all team members, with the message in the body of the email along with an attachment for them to read (probably a new version of the dreaded project plan). The project leader knows that she'll have to deal with at least one person in the coming days who is working off the wrong project plan.

- A departmental manager writes a fortnightly email to everyone in his department, explaining senior management's current top priorities, and outlining where he'll be in the coming weeks. In inviting comments and feedback, he knows that a few people will ask the same question, but he's become used to copying-and-pasting from previous emails so as to save time.

In keeping with our focus on changing work practice, each of these areas can be revamped given new collaboration technologies. For example, a blog could be used in both instances to facilitate the same process of communicating, but in a different way:

> The project leader would post her weekly update on the team's blog, and everyone on the team would know where to find the current edition of the project plan.

- The project leader would post her weekly update on the team's blog, and everyone on the team would know where to find the current edition of the project plan. In that respect, the project plan changes from being a "file" that has to be downloaded and reviewed, and becomes a web page in the team's collaboration site that is always up-to-date with the latest information. There is no more searching or calling around to find the current plan.

- The departmental manager changes his work practice and now writes a regular blog on his departmental intranet site. Rather than merely restating what management have been talking about, he is able to link to the blog posts from his seniors, in order to give his people access to the source message. He is then able to add his interpretation of the message for his people. Through the comment function on the blog, people within the department are able to ask questions and provide their feedback directly, without having to send private emails. Everyone in the department is able to see the questions that have already been asked, as well as the responses that have been given. They can seek further clarification on particular topics if something remains unclear, or put their energy into asking a different question.

Figure 4-2. Sharing Team and Organizational Updates via a Blog

Blogs provide a way of sharing updates within a team or group. People can request that updates are pushed to them (via a subscription), and are able to leave comments for the original author and other blog readers to see.

A law firm used a blog to replace its monthly inside newsletter. One benefit they quickly discovered was the faster "time-to-market" for newsletter articles, which no longer sat around for weeks on end before being released. A second benefit was that management developed a more natural and informal "voice" for staff communications.

Finding Expertise

How do you find experts within your organization? For many it's a hit and miss endeavor. You know someone, who knows someone, who knows someone, and eventually you get linked up to ask the question. But sometimes it takes too long, and the customer on the other end of the phone isn't getting the answer they want. Or it does sort-of work. You get through to someone who is apparently the expert, but they can't understand what you are trying to say. Unfortunately this work practice is all too common in organizations today, leading to lost opportunities, disappointed customers, and much wasted time.

With new collaboration technologies, locating experts can be done in a different way—through a different work practice.

> You know someone, who knows someone, who knows someone, and eventually you get linked up to ask the question. But it takes too long.

- People have a profile within the collaboration technology, where they describe what they see as their areas of expertise—such as strategic analysis, financial projections, facilitating group discussions, or automotive industry analysis . Other people are able to browse through the profiles and expertise areas, to see who has expertise and experience in a particular area.

- When looking at a profile, there are links to the person's current work projects, some recent blog posts, and some items they have posted in discussion forums. Before you make contact, you are able to read the source material and evaluate for yourself their expertise.

- Once you have found the person you want to speak with, embedded presence information tells you if they are currently online and available for interaction. If they are not available, through a link to their electronic calendar, you can see where they are and when they expect to be back.

- Newer expertise profile systems also highlight areas in which the other person has a common interest to you, and lists people that both of you know. The point of this is to convey their trustworthiness, put the person in a wider social context, and to suggest some topics to talk about when making contact with the other person for the first time.

There has been a lot of recent vendor activity around expertise profiles. For example, IBM includes these capabilities in IBM Connections.

Figure 4-3. Discovering and Evaluating Experts via Profiles

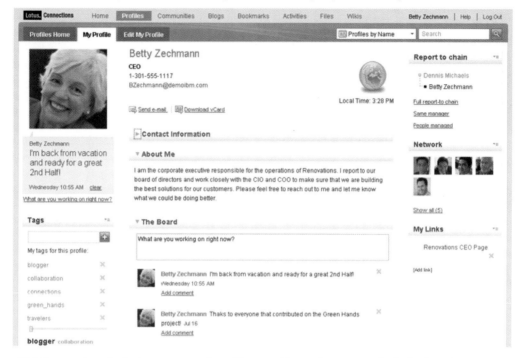

IBM Connections includes a personal profile page for each person, which displays key information about their work and areas of contribution. Contact information is also displayed, to speed time-to-contact. See www.ibm.com/lotus/connections.

The profile part of IBM Connections started life as an internal system at IBM to help people find experts—it was called BluePages. One of the enduring challenges with expertise profiles is that asking people to manually keep their profile up-to-date doesn't work, and secondly, the experts in the organization may not want to be found because of the extra requests for assistance they'll receive. IBM found that having ways for experts to share their knowledge through non-real-time means made the adoption challenge much easier:

> *Once we gave Contributors the choice about how to share their knowledge and experience, we found that they were more likely to contribute using these social options, since they realized that the result would be fewer emails, IMs and phone calls asking for their basic expertise. Once Seekers find an expert via Profiles, they are able to consume some of their knowledge and expertise without disrupting them. The nature of the remaining email/IM/phone requests from Seekers were about their deeper experience, their knowledge that will always remain tacit. In effect, Contributors sharing their more 'basic' expertise online enabled Seekers to accelerate whatever collaboration they further required from Contributors.[5]*

Collaboratively Authoring Documents

Preparing a document—a snapshot in time as to the current thinking of a team or group—is a frequent process for information workers. The standard work practice today revolves around a lead author drafting the document on their computer, attaching it to an email message, and sending it out to other people to review. Once the other people have marked up the document with their comments, the lead author gets numerous copies back which they have to reconcile and collate into a new authoritative "master" copy.

Thanks to new collaboration technologies, there are different ways of collaboratively authoring documents.

- Using a wiki like Socialtext or Atlassian Confluence, the lead author can start writing using an online web-based document. When they are ready for others to add their input and feedback, they send a link to the wiki page. The other authors have the ability to change the text directly (with roll-back capabilities in a wiki, the lead author can roll-back to an earlier version if required), or leave comments on the bottom of the page.

- With a tool like PleaseReview, the document can be uploaded to a central server and all the reviewers can be invited to see the document. All edits and changes are carefully maintained on the PleaseReview server, and reviewers are able to see everyone else's changes, thus leading to a reduction in the duplication of the same comment. Finally, because everyone is working directly within the master copy, albeit in a controlled way, the integration of multiple copies into a new master goes away for good. See Figure 4-4.

  > With a tool like PleaseReview, the document can be uploaded to a central server and all of the reviewers can be invited to see the document.

- At a more basic level, rather than the document being sent out by email, the lead author can store the document in a Microsoft SharePoint team site, and when they are ready for input and review from others, can start a "Collect Feedback" workflow process. This prompts reviewers for feedback, and all in-line edits and out-of-line comments are saved into a single copy stored in SharePoint. The lead author no longer has to correlate multiple copies, and reviewers can see the comments and input of others.

In essence, there are many new and different ways of collaboratively authoring documents—and the three examples above are by no means exhaustive.[6] It's a different work practice from what most people are used to.

Figure 4-4. Document Co-Authoring with PleaseReview

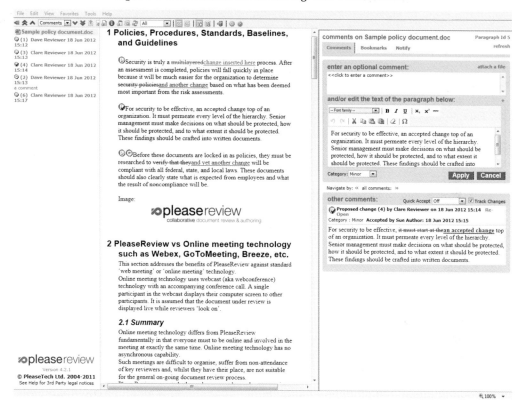

PleaseReview from PleaseTech is a collaborative document authoring and reviewing service. It enables many people to work on the same document simultaneously. See www.pleasetech.com/pleasereview.aspx.

Changing the way teams work on documents can have significant advantages. When I discuss the collaborative authoring scenario in a workshop, we invariably get a saving of at least 50% in process time across the target collaborative team. This is a result of eliminating the need to merge comments into the master document, make comments that other people have already stated, and giving quicker access to each team member to review and comment on the document. PleaseTech, the vendor of PleaseReview above, say that their clients are seeing savings of up to 65%.

Teams can get a document prepared 50% faster by eliminating the need to merge comments, make comments that other people have already stated, and removing wait time.

Collaborative Idea Management

Creating, collecting and ranking ideas for process improvements, new products and services, and many other areas of business and organizational life are great ways to make continual innovation a part of the fabric of how work gets done.[7] To do so, you need some way of collecting the ideas in the first place. This can be done by email, where people send their ideas to a particular address (newideas@mycompany.com for example), but then the ideas are hidden, not available for everyone to see, and generally get forgotten. This leads to cynicism among employees because they never hear back about their ideas, and the organization misses out on a potential treasure trove of insights and motivation for improving operations, technology, and customer service.

New collaboration technology provides a much better approach to idea management. Ideas are submitted in an open forum, allowing for everyone inside the organization to see what is being proposed. Any employee can contribute their perspective on an idea, providing a way for managers to gauge the motivation and feeling behind specific ideas.

Here's how this different approach works:

- A space for new ideas is created, most likely with sub-spaces for different groupings of ideas (an idea space for a product, one for a particular client, another for a certain process, and so on). This needs to be set up so people can see related ideas together, without having to wade through ideas that are irrelevant to them.

- People are invited to visit the idea space, and type in their ideas. The idea space displays an up-to-date list of all the ideas which have been contributed.

- Other people are able to browse through the ideas in the idea space, and read what others have written. They have some options for contributing: they can add a new idea themselves, they can comment on someone else's idea ("I think this is great, and would really help Sales move more of these," for example), and they can vote. Ideas with greater numbers of votes move to the top of the list, while those ideas with fewer votes move to the bottom.

> When it's time to make decisions about where to invest in new products, how to serve clients better, and how to improve processes, the underlying contributions have been made.

- When it's time to make decisions about where to invest in new products, how to serve clients better, and how to improve processes, the underlying contributions have been made, and the person responsible has a goldmine of thinking to help guide their decisions.

- People can search for ideas on particular topics, related to particular products and services, or with particular keywords in the title or description. In very active collaborative idea management systems, this helps people quickly find ideas that are relevant to their work.

Collaborative idea management is supported by collaboration technology from Elguji Software, NewsGator in Social Sites, and Kindling, among others.[8]

Figure 4-5. Idea Management with IdeaJam

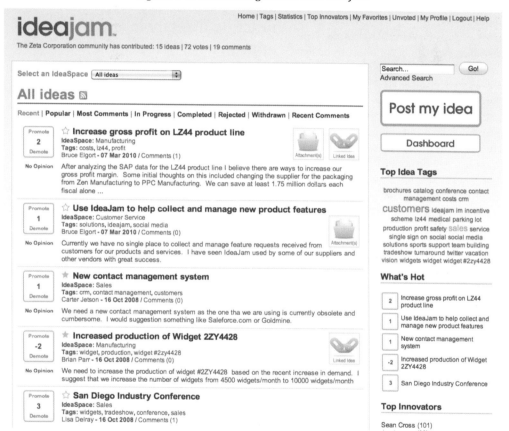

IdeaJam from Elguji Software enables everyone within a group, team or organization to see what ideas have been proposed, to give more details (via comments), and to vote for ideas. See www.elguji.com.

Making Group Decisions

A final example of changing work practice is how decisions are made in a group. Today a common work practice is that the group meets once a month and reviews the various ideas and requests they have received. Some decisions are made, and the meeting disbands. This approach leads to "decision crawl," as it takes too long for decisions to be made.

There is a different work practice in how groups can make decisions. This involves creating a collaboration site where all inputs for the decision can be located, combined with a new work practice which sees the different members of the decision group visiting the collaboration site on a regular basis to read and review the requests or ideas. When someone has a point of view to share, they type their reaction directly into the appropriate place in the collaboration site. When everyone has had sufficient time to review the materials, everyone is asked to vote for the requests they think are best. Most decisions get made outside of a traditional meeting as such, leaving any actual meeting time to debating particularly difficult issues.

> When someone has a point of view to share, they type their reaction directly into the appropriate place in the collaboration site. When everyone has had sufficient time to review the materials, everyone is asked to vote for the requests they think are best.

Collaborative decision making can be undertaken using a range of collaboration technology:

- A SAP StreamWork site could be set up for a particular decision. Depending on the nature of the decision needed, various tools—an Agenda, a Pro/Con table, a SWOT analysis, a Quick Poll, and others—can be added to the site to provide structure and focus for the team members. See Figure 4-6.

- A Microsoft SharePoint site could be set up with a Custom List, where each item is a decision request. Members of the decision group can review each decision request, and discuss and vote on the various matters. This approach to decision making is quite popular among some large organizations using SharePoint.

- GroupSystems ThinkTank is another collaborative decision-making tool. ThinkTank offers a variety of decision-making tools—for structuring ideas, for commenting on ideas, and for voting on ideas, among others. ThinkTank is also available as a hosted service, called ThinkSpace.

Figure 4-6. Collaborative Decision Making with SAP StreamWork

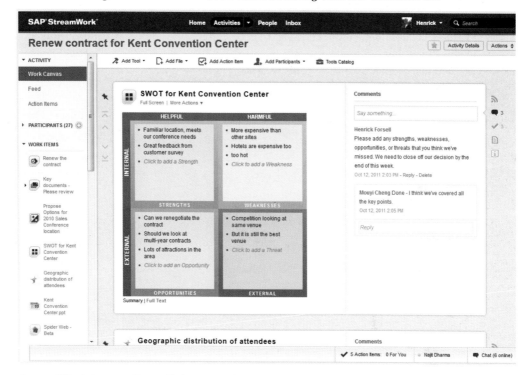

StreamWork is an online collaborative decision-making service from SAP, which enables people from one or more organizations to work together on decisions. See www.sapstreamwork.com.

These tools can also be used by people during face-to-face or virtual meetings. They provide a way of structuring and visualizing the decision being discussed. Direct Relief International uses SAP StreamWork in this way: [9]

> *"We were looking for a solution that could help us drive projects forward," said Ross Comstock, IT director at Direct Relief. "It helps us quickly get a group of people together and focused on working through a problem, even if they're in different countries. For that purpose, SharePoint was too general. SAP StreamWork was much simpler, with a lot of tools built into it to drive decision-making. When I have a meeting with stakeholders, I can pop into SAP StreamWork and illustrate where we are on a project. It offers a simple way to tell a story, and it helps our communication with stakeholders."*

Other Collaboration Scenarios

There are other collaboration scenarios not covered above, but that doesn't make them any less valid. For example, change of work practice can be explored for:

- *Holding meetings.* Travel is frequently used as a way of bringing people together for meetings, or the meeting is held by phone (one-to-one, or a conference call). New technology can be used to replace or enhance both types of meetings—video conferencing and TelePresence instead of travel, and screen sharing as a complement to phone-based interactions and meetings.

- *Requesting feedback.* Asking other people what they think about a particular work item—a report for a client, a quotation from a potential supplier, a blog post for the outside blog—is a common collaborative scenario. Email is frequently used today as the means of sharing the work item and seeking feedback. In the future, there is an opportunity to use new tools which offer better support for this scenario, such as workflow routing systems, screen sharing, and quick surveys.

- *Sharing best practices.* Being consistent in service delivery is essential to winning the reputation of being great at what you do. It can be hard enough for one person to deliver to the same consistent standard day-after-day, but it's even harder where many people do similar jobs for different clients or segments of the market. How do good ideas get debated and brought into common practice? Today's approach is usually based on email distribution lists and the odd face-to-face meeting. New technology can support sharing best practices using group-editable web pages in a wiki, with ties to the group's core methodology.

Summary

Technology is important when it comes to supporting collaboration between people. The technology creates opportunities for new ways of working, but demands an alignment between what the group needs to get done, and the nuances of the work practices. We have looked at a number of common collaboration scenarios in this chapter, and explored how current scenarios can be carried out in new and better ways with new collaboration technology.

We have covered a lot of ground up to this point, all aimed at setting the context and getting our thinking in line for the user adoption challenge ahead. Chapter 5 marks a significant shift in focus. The Four Stages Model of User Adoption is introduced, followed by extended discussion on each stage in chapters 6-9.

[1] See Joe's article, *Culture is an OUTPUT, not an INPUT*, on Cisco Communities from July 2010, at communities.cisco.com/community/technology/collaboration/enterprisesocialsoftware/blog/2010/07/13/culture-is-an-output-not-an-input. I do need to have a talk to Joe about his use of the phrase "driving adoption" though.

[2] These three are the first of the 7 Pillars in my 2005 report, *7 Pillars of IT-Enabled Team Productivity*, available for free download at www.michaelsampson.net/get7.html.

[3] For more on using the Collaboration Scenarios approaches, see Chapter 2 in *Collaboration Roadmap*, at www.michaelsampson.net/collaborationroadmap.html.

[4] I wrote a much longer article in January 2007 about this topic. See *Unresolved Issues with Email: Confusion in Conversation Flow*, at currents.michaelsampson.net/2007/01/unresolved-issu.html.

[5] Gia Lyons, *SharePoint My Sites: It ain't just about profiles, people*, December 2007. See www.giatalks.com/2007/12/sharepoint-my-sites-it-aint-just-about-profiles-people/.

[6] For more on the Document Co-Authoring collaborative scenario, see my blog posts at currents.michaelsampson.net/document-co-authoring/. The topic is also analyzed in more depth in Chapter 2 of *Collaboration Roadmap*.

[7] Brainstorming is another collaborative scenario, and there's an art to doing brainstorming virtually. For more on this topic, and the use of IdeaJam to support such virtual space brainstorming, see my May 2008 blog post at currents.michaelsampson.net/2008/05/brainstorming-i.html.

[8] Find out more about each of these Idea Management offerings at the respective web sites. For Elguji Software, see www.elguji.com. For NewsGator Social Sites, see the Idea Stream at www.newsgator.com/products/social-sites-for-sharepoint-2010/idea-stream.aspx, and for Kindling, go to www.kindlingapp.com.

[9] See *SAP StreamWork for Direct Relief International: To Focus and Accelerate Projects*, at currents.michaelsampson.net/2012/02/directrelief.html.

Chapter 5.
The Four Stages Model of User Adoption

 Adoption cannot be mandated. End users have to want to use the product, and will do so when they see a net benefit to them and their work.[1]

Michael Idinopulos, Socialtext

When I talk to groups, they quickly learn three things about me. First, I use a Mac for most of my work. Second, I have lots of children (see page 304). Third, I like frameworks as a way of explaining the world and giving a simple method for understanding something complex. This chapter is a frameworks chapter, and in it I outline the Four Stages Model of User Adoption.

In this chapter, we will:

- Learn why talking about the features and benefits of a new product aren't enough for user adoption by second wave people.

- Be introduced to the Four Stages Model of User Adoption.

- Discover what's coming up in the next four chapters, which look at each stage of the model in turn.

- Find out how the Global Survey on User Adoption Strategies informs the ranking of use and effectiveness of different user adoption strategies.

Does Talking About Features Work?

A collaboration software vendor who offers an add-on product for Microsoft SharePoint recently ran a seminar focused on moving people from collaborating using email to collaborating using SharePoint. In its advertising for the seminar, it outlined the following agenda topics:

1. The benefits of shifting from email to SharePoint.

2. What features are missing by default in SharePoint.

3. How to add missing features to SharePoint by using an add-on solution.

4. Options for improving the features in SharePoint.

5. Best practices when using the product features of SharePoint.

In examining the above list, I see the following underlying user adoption ethos: speak briefly about the benefits of shifting from the old technology to the new technology, and then describe how the add-on product improves on the default experience of the new technology.

What's the problem with this? Simply extolling the benefits of product features as a user adoption strategy isn't enough—it lacks the power to change behavior and won't lead to people actually adopting the new technology. Result: it will fail.

> Simply extolling the benefits of product features as a user adoption strategy isn't enough—it lacks the power to change behavior and won't lead to people actually adopting the new technology.

Something much greater is needed, and this chapter presents the framework that will guide our discussion about the "much greater" things.

Four Stages of User Adoption

One of the key conclusions coming out of Chapter 3 was that "change is a process, not an event." In other words, change doesn't regularly happen with a single "big bang" event; there are a series of distinct events that make up the overall process.

When we apply this thinking to the challenge of user adoption for new collaboration technology with second wave people, there are four distinct events—although the phrase "stage" is preferred in this book.

The four stages in the model are:

1. Winning Attention.

2. Cultivating Basic Concepts.

3. Enlivening Applicability.

4. Making it Real.

Figure 5-1. The Four Stages Model of User Adoption

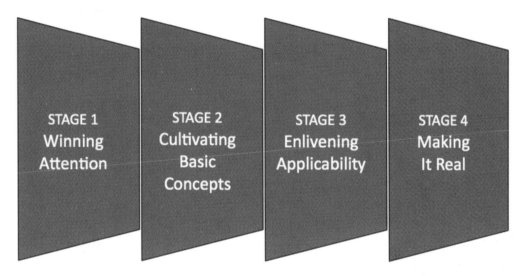

The Four Stages Model of User Adoption provides a framework for approaching second wave people with new collaboration technology.

Quick Overview of the Four Stages

Let's take a quick look at each of the four stages. Note that developing a User Adoption Approach around Yammer is used as an example in this section.

In Stage 1, you have to win the attention of second wave people. By their very nature, second wave people have little interest in product features and benefits stated within the context of product features. Something else is necessary, and in this first stage, there are various strategies that can be used effectively to win attention. For example, if Yammer is being explored as a new collaboration technology for a firm, providing a "Real-

> Second wave people have little interest in product features and benefits stated within the context of product features.

to-Life Scenario" about how Yammer could help particular groups become more effective and efficient is a common way to win attention.

In Stage 2, having won their attention, you have to communicate the basic concepts of the new technology. This means second wave people need to understand a few core concepts about the new technology in order to have a reasonable discussion about how it could be applied to their work (in Stage 3). For example, understanding the basic idea of a hashtag in Yammer is essential to understanding how Yammer could be applied within a work group for project tracking, or in a community of interest for sharing and discussing current topics.

> Understanding the basic idea of a hashtag in Yammer is essential to understanding how Yammer could be applied within a work group for project tracking.

In Stage 3, the focus shifts from explaining the basic concepts to bringing the applicability of the new approach to life. During this stage, the applicability of the new technology is explored within the context of a particular group or team, and there are various strategies which can be used to do so. Continuing the Yammer example, a "Facilitated Group Re-imagining" session could be set up with a group to explore how they currently keep other people up-to-date with what they're working on, combined with an ideation session about how Yammer could enable them to do so in a different way (and the benefits which could accrue).

The final stage, Stage 4, is about making the new collaboration technology real and relevant to people and groups. The previous three stages have discussed what could be, and stage 4 is where it actually has to happen. For a group that decides to use Yammer, this is the stage where alternative ways of keeping other people up-to-date are physically removed ("Zero Other Options") or socially frowned on ("Stop Doing, Start Doing Patterns").

Deep Dive on the Four Stages

The next four chapters talk through each of these stages in turn, and provide a range of strategies for meeting the objective of each stage. For example, in Stage 1 you can use the strategy of "Exemplar Stories" to win the attention of second wave people. Chapter 6 on "Winning Attention" talks all about Exemplar Stories—what they are, how to apply them, and how effective they are.

In each chapter, the presentation of a user adoption strategy follows a similar format. The particular intent is to go beyond merely naming each strategy, and to comment in much more detail about where and how it can best be used, and for what types of collaboration technologies it would work best. For each strategy, the following is included:

- The name and description of the strategy.

- Instructions on how to implement the strategy.

- Thoughts on when to use it within the lifecycle of your user adoption approach.

- Analysis of why the strategy works to encourage user adoption—drawing on our discussion on change and motivation in Chapter 3.

- Survey data on what other people and organizations are doing with user adoption strategies, based on my recent global survey on user adoption. See the next section for more on this survey.

One of the strategies—the Bulk Loading Party—even comes with a five page case study! Landcare Research in New Zealand used a Bulk Loading Party with one of its groups, and the positive effects that resulted are explored.

Is the Process Linear?

Figure 5-1 depicts four stages, starting on the left-hand side of the page and progressing to the right-hand side of the page. I have also used the word "stage" in naming and describing the model. Does this mean the process is linear—that Stage 1 must be fully completed before moving to Stage 2, which in turn must be fully completed before moving to Stage 3? In a word, No.

The intent is this: take a linear approach to planning your user adoption work, but a circular or repetitive approach to the implementation of your plan. That is, make a general plan about how you will approach the user adoption challenge, and then implement it in small ways with different groups, capturing what you are learning in each stage to inform and improve the way you implement the stage the next time. For example:

> Make a general plan about how you will approach the user adoption challenge, and then implement it in small ways with different groups, capturing what you are learning in each stage to inform and improve the way you implement the stage the next time.

- You develop a couple of Real-to-Life Scenarios (for Stage 1, Winning Attention), and make these available to people within your organization through the intranet, a road show, and various channels of communication.

- A few people show quick interest in learning more, and so you schedule a Web-based training session with them and their group. The basic concepts of the new collaboration technology are explored (per Stage 2, Cultivating Basic Concepts).

- One group wants to apply what they have learnt in their work, and various strategies from Stage 3 (Enlivening Applicability) are put in place. For example, a Facilitated Group Re-imagining session is held to explore current and new ways of working.

- Finally, after the group develops a new picture of how it is going to work, a Bulk Loading Party is staged to get everyone into the new way of doing things, and then current ways of working are de-emphasized (Zero Other Options).

- What you have learnt through the process of working with this particular group is linked back to the Stage 1 activities. In particular, a new Exemplar Story is created, which will form the basis for future "Winning Attention" endeavors.

In summary, Figure 5-1 could show the model as a non-linear process, but while the depiction would be more true-to-life, it would be much more confusing about what you should actually do.

Don't Do Them All

Before we jump to a brief discussion of the user adoption survey, a vital comment needs to be made. There are over 20 strategies discussed in the next four chapters. Don't do them all. The purpose of discussing each strategy isn't to be directive and say that you should do it, but rather to be informative about what you could do within the context of each stage. Remember, it's the stage that matters, not the particular strategies. The strategies are just possible ways of implementing the intent of the stage. Equally, you may have a different idea for a strategy to use in each stage. Go for it! If you know how to implement the strategy, and have experience with its effectiveness, then run with what you know.

> There are over 20 strategies discussed in the next four chapters. Don't do them all.

The Global User Adoption Strategy Survey

It is easy to write about a strategy for user adoption, and how it could be used, but there is much greater value for you if the write up of a strategy includes use and effectiveness data from a wide group of people around the world. The first part gives an idea of how a strategy could be used in practice. The second part reports on actual usage and perceived effectiveness from real people who are putting a particular user adoption strategy into practice. Both aspects are necessary, and both are presented in the next four chapters.

Two Surveys

To provide the required insight on actual usage and perceived effectiveness, I commissioned two global surveys on user adoption. The first survey in early 2010 gave initial data for the first edition of this book. The second survey—running from late 2011 to early 2012—repeated the first survey, but with some changes in how the key questions were ranked by the respondents. These changes were introduced to strengthen the results in the second survey, and to allow a deeper analysis of the data.

Both surveys collected user adoption data across multiple collaboration products and services: Microsoft SharePoint, IBM Connections, Socialtext, Google, and Central Desktop, among others. The first question to the survey allowed multiple answers, so respondents could indicate if there were multiple collaboration technologies being used at their organization.

The surveys received a high number of responses:

- *Survey 2010.* Over 400 respondents completed the survey, with high representation from organizations with less than 100 employees. This was due to the large number of respondents who were using the Central Desktop service. In terms of collaboration tools, respondents were basically equally split between Central Desktop (a hosted collaboration service) and Microsoft SharePoint (usually an in-house collaboration service).

- *Survey 2012.* Over 180 respondents completed the survey. The highest representation was from organizations with over 10,000 employees. The most common collaboration tools in use by respondents were Microsoft SharePoint and IBM Connections, both of which are enterprise-focused collaboration tools. Compared to the respondents from Survey 2010, almost three times as many respondents to Survey 2012 had a written user adoption document or plan to guide their work.

Figures 5-2 and 5-3 provide a graphical snapshot of both surveys, covering respondent information, size of organization, and products used, among others. Figures 5-4 and 5-5 present summary findings on the use and effectiveness of the strategies from the surveys.

Figure 5-2. Snapshot of the 2010 Survey Respondents

Number of Respondents

Size of Organization

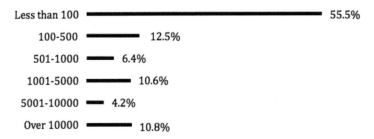

Less than 100 — 55.5%
100-500 — 12.5%
501-1000 — 6.4%
1001-5000 — 10.6%
5001-10000 — 4.2%
Over 10000 — 10.8%

Product of Focus (multiple answers permitted)

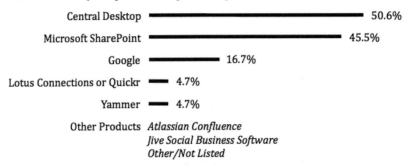

Central Desktop — 50.6%
Microsoft SharePoint — 45.5%
Google — 16.7%
Lotus Connections or Quickr — 4.7%
Yammer — 4.7%
Other Products — *Atlassian Confluence*
Jive Social Business Software
Other/Not Listed

Written User Adoption Document or Plan

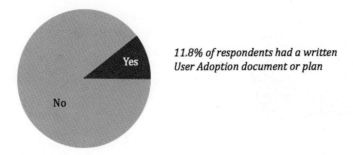

11.8% of respondents had a written User Adoption document or plan

The survey of 2010 gained over 400 responses, with high representation from small firms, and widespread use of both Central Desktop and Microsoft SharePoint.

Figure 5-3. Snapshot of the 2012 Survey Respondents

Number of Respondents

Size of Organization

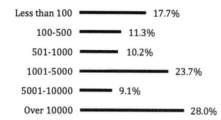

Less than 100	17.7%
100-500	11.3%
501-1000	10.2%
1001-5000	23.7%
5001-10000	9.1%
Over 10000	28.0%

Product of Focus (multiple answers permitted)

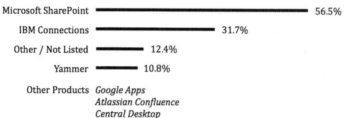

Microsoft SharePoint	56.5%
IBM Connections	31.7%
Other / Not Listed	12.4%
Yammer	10.8%
Other Products	*Google Apps* *Atlassian Confluence* *Central Desktop*

Length of User Adoption Work

10%	17%	20%	24%	17%	12%
Not started	*0-6 months*	*6-12 months*	*1-2 years*	*2-4 years*	*>4 years*

Written User Adoption Document or Plan

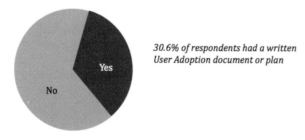

30.6% of respondents had a written User Adoption document or plan

The survey of 2012 gained over 180 responses, with high representation from larger firms, and widespread use of both Microsoft SharePoint and IBM Connections.

Figure 5-4. Summary Findings from Survey 2010

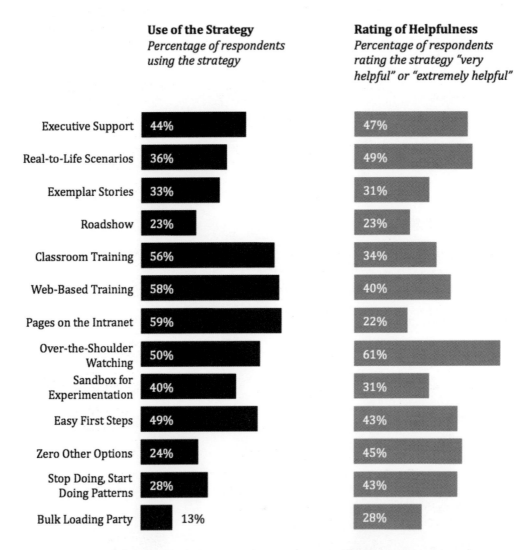

Use of the Strategy
Percentage of respondents using the strategy

Rating of Helpfulness
Percentage of respondents rating the strategy "very helpful" or "extremely helpful"

Strategy	Use	Helpfulness
Executive Support	44%	47%
Real-to-Life Scenarios	36%	49%
Exemplar Stories	33%	31%
Roadshow	23%	23%
Classroom Training	56%	34%
Web-Based Training	58%	40%
Pages on the Intranet	59%	22%
Over-the-Shoulder Watching	50%	61%
Sandbox for Experimentation	40%	31%
Easy First Steps	49%	43%
Zero Other Options	24%	45%
Stop Doing, Start Doing Patterns	28%	43%
Bulk Loading Party	13%	28%

Respondents were asked to rank their use of particular user adoption strategies, and assess the helpfulness of the strategies they were using. Summary findings for the 13 strategies are shown above.

Figure 5-5. Summary Findings from Survey 2012

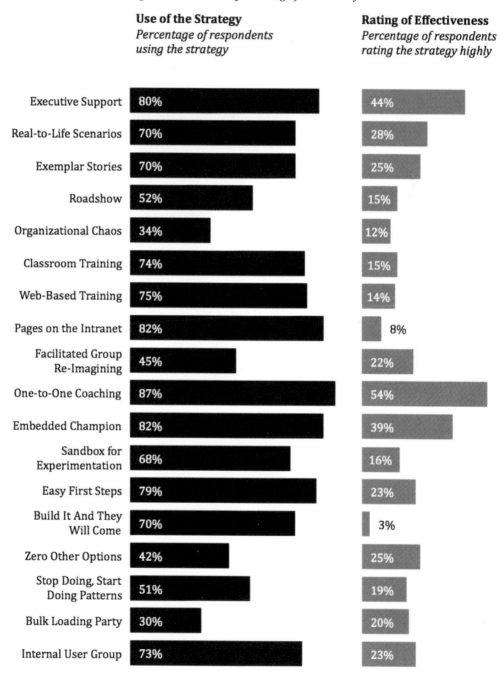

Use of the Strategy
Percentage of respondents using the strategy

Rating of Effectiveness
Percentage of respondents rating the strategy highly

Strategy	Use of the Strategy	Rating of Effectiveness
Executive Support	80%	44%
Real-to-Life Scenarios	70%	28%
Exemplar Stories	70%	25%
Roadshow	52%	15%
Organizational Chaos	34%	12%
Classroom Training	74%	15%
Web-Based Training	75%	14%
Pages on the Intranet	82%	8%
Facilitated Group Re-Imagining	45%	22%
One-to-One Coaching	87%	54%
Embedded Champion	82%	39%
Sandbox for Experimentation	68%	16%
Easy First Steps	79%	23%
Build It And They Will Come	70%	3%
Zero Other Options	42%	25%
Stop Doing, Start Doing Patterns	51%	19%
Bulk Loading Party	30%	20%
Internal User Group	73%	23%

Respondents were asked to rank their use of particular user adoption strategies, and assess the effectiveness of the strategies they were using. Summary findings are shown above.

Based on the data collected through the two surveys, for most strategies in the next four chapters, you will find related survey data on the use and effectiveness of the strategy. There will also be direct quotes (with slight edits to correct grammatical errors, or to make the quote read more easily) from respondents about their use of each strategy.

> Based on the two surveys, for most strategies in the next four chapters, you will find related survey data on the use and effectiveness of each strategy.

For Survey 2010, two product-specific user adoption reports were developed —one for Central Desktop,[2] and one for Microsoft SharePoint[3]—and if you are using either of these two products, I encourage you to look at the specific strategies being used and the effectiveness being reported by the survey respondents. The survey data from both surveys reported in this book is not broken down by product, but rather reported at the level of the strategy. That's the key difference between this book and those two reports—the book doesn't break strategy use down by product, but the reports do. No product-specific reports had been developed based on Survey 2012 at the time of publishing this book.

Summary

This chapter introduced the Four Stages Model of User Adoption, a new framework for approaching the user adoption challenge. A brief discussion about the four stages was provided in this chapter, with Yammer being used as an example of how it could be applied. The next four chapters—6 through 9—take each stage in turn, and analyze various strategies that can be used within the context of each stage.

The chapter also provided insight into the survey data that will be reported for many of the strategies in Chapters 6-9. In brief, the data is from two global surveys that ran in 2010 and 2012, gathering data on the use and effectiveness of various user adoption strategies. The surveys were not focused on one particular technology, but rather gathered data from many people and many organizations using a range of technologies.

[1] Michael is the Vice-President, Professional Services and Customer Success at Socialtext (www.socialtext.com). This quote is drawn from the Socialtext white paper *Six Steps to Drive Social Software Adoption*, available at www.socialtext.com/products/wp_implementation.php.

[2] For more information, see *User Adoption Strategies: The Central Desktop Approach* at www.michaelsampson.net/2010/03/useradoption-centraldesktop.html. The report presents data on the use of particular strategies by over 200 organizations using the Central Desktop online collaboration service, as well as the strategies they found most effective. Note that this report is based on the survey from 2010.

[3] For more information, see the *SharePoint Governance for Collaboration: User Adoption Strategies* report, at www.michaelsampson.net/2010/03/useradoption-sharepoint.html. This report looks at the use and effectiveness of user adoption strategies from over 180 organizations using SharePoint. Note that this report is based on the survey from 2010.

Chapter 6.
Winning Attention

Social marketing is the adaptation of commercial marketing technologies to programs designed to influence the voluntary behavior of target audiences to improve their personal welfare and that of society of which they are a part. [1]

Alan Andreasen, Georgetown University

There are many possible factors that make a person interested in something—the internal warm-and-fuzzy feeling from being first, the desire for promised benefits, the need to be seen as "getting it," or the wish to keep up with the crowd. For any of these factors to be triggered, though, something has to first grab their attention, cutting through the noise and busyness of their lives. Welcome to Stage 1 of the Four Stages Model of User Adoption: Winning Attention.

In this chapter, we will:

- Learn about the need to win people's attention.

- Discover five strategies that can be used to win attention.

- Find out more about each strategy, and how to apply it within our work.

- Compare the relative effectiveness of each strategy, based on results from a recent user adoption strategies survey.

What's Going On Here Then?

Winning attention. It's a pithy phrase, but contains a deep nugget. "Winning" signifies that there are other competitive factors at play. In the case of second wave people, these include being busy and having little time to stop and think about better ways of doing things, having an established way of doing things, and giving little credence to the claims of first wave technologists. The second word—"attention"—signifies being especially alert to a particular person or idea, and ready for action, should that be required.

The goal of Stage 1 is to win someone's attention to a new way of working. For this we need practical strategies that will enable our message to rise above the noise and clutter of day-to-day life.

The major goal of Stage 1 is to win someone's attention to a new way of working. For this we need practical strategies that will enable our message to rise above the noise and clutter of day-to-day life, and be noticed by second wave people. Without their attention, we won't get their intention.

Strategies to Win Attention

Five practical strategies for winning the attention of second wave people, in the context of collaboration technologies and approaches to work, are discussed in this chapter.

1. Executive support and sponsorship that focus on the use and role of the new technology and approach in their work.

2. Real-to-life scenarios that portray how the new technology and approach could be used.

3. Exemplar stories giving specific instances of where the new technology and approach are currently delivering value and benefit within the organization.

4. A roadshow to carve out a specific slice of time to focus on the possibilities of the new technology and approach.

5. Organizational chaos where the normal rules of business are ineffective and thus suspended, and people are more willing to consider new rules.

Survey Snapshot

Figure 6-1. Snapshot of Survey Results for Stage 1

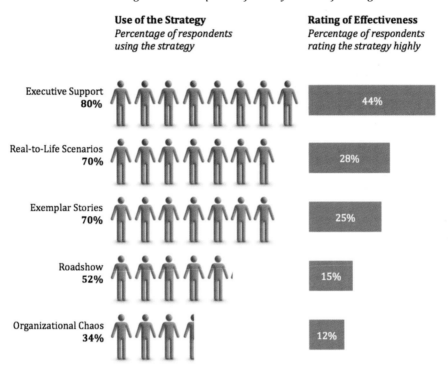

Use of the Strategy
Percentage of respondents using the strategy

Rating of Effectiveness
Percentage of respondents rating the strategy highly

- Executive Support **80%** — 44%
- Real-to-Life Scenarios **70%** — 28%
- Exemplar Stories **70%** — 25%
- Roadshow **52%** — 15%
- Organizational Chaos **34%** — 12%

Highest Use by Size of Organization
Most commonly used strategies by size of organization (number of employees)

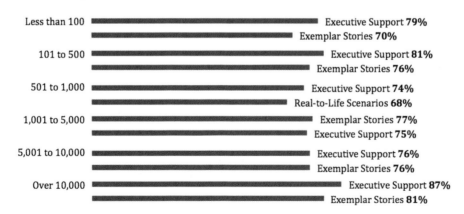

- Less than 100 — Executive Support **79%** / Exemplar Stories **70%**
- 101 to 500 — Executive Support **81%** / Exemplar Stories **76%**
- 501 to 1,000 — Executive Support **74%** / Real-to-Life Scenarios **68%**
- 1,001 to 5,000 — Exemplar Stories **77%** / Executive Support **75%**
- 5,001 to 10,000 — Executive Support **76%** / Exemplar Stories **76%**
- Over 10,000 — Executive Support **87%** / Exemplar Stories **81%**

Executive support, real-to-life scenarios, and exemplar stories were the highest used strategies in Stage 1. Executive support ranked highest for effectiveness.

Strategy 1.1 Executive Support

Executive support is the first "winning attention" strategy. The use of this strategy is not limited to encouraging user adoption with collaboration technology, but is advocated widely as a critical success factor for successful IT projects. Thus it should not be a surprise that it can be highly effective at encouraging user adoption.

Description

Having executive support means the changes in work practice you are advocating within your organization have strong middle or senior management support. Executives are willing to get involved and "cover your back" from the naysayers and detractors who will inevitably come forward. They will remove organizational roadblocks that are thrown up.

Executive support for winning attention can take two forms:

- *Talk*. Executives talk about the benefits that can be accrued through the use of the new collaboration technology.

- *Action*. Executives themselves use the new collaboration technology as part of their work.

> Executives play a key role in allocating resources—people, time, and budget—to the overall program of work. This will normally have happened before the user adoption work begins.

While our focus in this section is on Executive Support as a strategy for winning attention, it's important to remember executives play a key role in allocating resources—people, time, and budget—to the overall program of work. This will normally have happened before the user adoption work begins, but being able to point to sign-off on the program is just as important as pointing to active personal usage by executives.

How to Use It

Using the executive support strategy involves three core steps:

1. Convince senior executives that improvements in performance are possible and attainable as a consequence of changing work practices. If executives have already signed off on the initiative and allocated resources to make it happen, this step is essentially won.

2. Get senior executives to speak about the new way of doing things, the new way of working. This should be done in internal town hall meetings, on the internal CEO blog, in conversations with others, and so on.

3. Get senior executives to start using the new approach—assuming it's relevant to their work—and to be seen to be actively doing so.

> There are pre-conditions to using the executive support strategy. You can't just bowl up to an executive and ask them to start doing stuff publicly and within their own work practice without laying any groundwork.

There are pre-conditions to using the executive support strategy—make no mistake about that! You can't just bowl up to an executive and ask them to start doing stuff publicly and within their own work practice without laying any groundwork. In other words, you need to be credible in their eyes (by having a history of delivering good outcomes for the organization), have a credible message (what you are saying is logical and believable, and you can back it up with facts and reasoning), and show a credible link between what you are advocating and the changes and improvements they are trying to bring about in the organization (they can see the value and benefit in line with their wider objectives). In summary, executives invest in people they trust.

Therefore be very clear that gaining executive support takes time. It's much less about a conversion experience as a result of a one-time three-minute conversation in the hallway, and much more about relationship building and proving yourself over months or even years. If you don't have it, find someone who does.

When to Use It

Use the executive support strategy as part of the upfront Winning Attention stage. When a second wave person hears an executive talking about the new technology, or receives an invitation from an executive to take part in a conversation on a blog, they will reach out for greater understanding.

It's important to note that executive support provides only the environmental context setting for people, and doesn't address the specific requirements of individual users. Knowing that the use of the new technology is "supported by" and "actively used by" the executives, is insufficient to drive change by itself. Executive support is a critical factor, but only as a starter.

You can't use the Executive Support strategy to overcome resistance you have created by being rude and obstinate during the earlier parts of the collaboration journey. If you have not listened to the feedback from business people, nor been proactive in seeking out the real needs of the organization, don't think that executive support will save you. It smacks of forcing people to change, and the most common result is that your work and approach will be undermined. Executive support can be a beautiful complement to a well-executed collaboration journey, but it can't fix an ugly one.

Why It Works

Why does executive support work?

- A "significant other" is seen to be actively using the tool, thus giving organizational sanction and credibility to its use. It's not just "those guys down in IT" (or wherever); it's being championed by executives. Strong executive support can be effective in removing organizational roadblocks.

- It sends a significant social and contextual message that "This is important!" If the lead advocate for the new work practice through a new collaboration technology has secured executive support, and the executives are raving about it, and using it actively, then people pay attention.

> If it's good enough for the executive team to use the new collaboration technology to support their meetings and discussions, then it's good enough for others as well.

- For people who want to move up in the organization, using the tool becomes part of their journey. If it's good enough for the executive team to use the new collaboration technology to support their meetings and discussions, then it's good enough for others as well.

- It sends the signal that executives have already learned to use the tool, and by implication, other people will be able to learn to use the tool also.

A warning: Executives can say the wrong thing, and screw up your best plans. Perhaps they cast the new way of working using a ridiculous metaphor—"It's the new ant farm" for example—and this turns people off and sets back your plans. If this happens, go back, talk to them some more, and give them a better metaphor to use in the future. In the ideal situation, though, you should ensure they have a great metaphor ready to go so you aren't relegated to life as an ant.

Data from Survey 2012

Figure 6-2. Data from Survey 2012 for the Executive Support Strategy

Use of the Executive Support Strategy
Percentage of respondents using the strategy sometimes or frequently

Effectiveness of the Executive Support Strategy
Effectiveness rating by respondents using the strategy sometimes or frequently

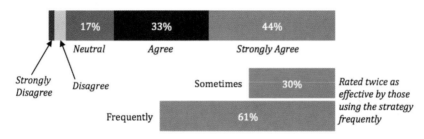

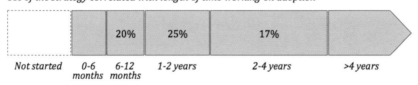

Highest Use in the Adoption Lifecycle
Use of the strategy correlated with length of time working on adoption

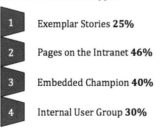

Complementary Strategies
Other adoption strategies most commonly used with Executive Support

1 Exemplar Stories **25%**

2 Pages on the Intranet **46%**

3 Embedded Champion **40%**

4 Internal User Group **30%**

Comparison with Survey 2010

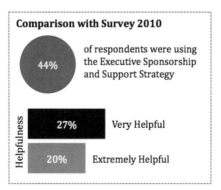

44% of respondents were using the Executive Sponsorship and Support Strategy

Helpfulness
27% Very Helpful
20% Extremely Helpful

The Executive Support strategy is commonly used, and ranked highly for effectiveness. Only a few respondents said it was not effective.

Examples and Case Studies

Here are some examples of how organizations have used the executive support strategy:

- Susan Hanley, a SharePoint consultant and author, recently wrote: *One of the more successful SharePoint solutions I've observed was in an organization where a key executive stopped responding to any e-mail message with an attached document. He politely replied to each sender that he would read the message when the message included a link to the document they wanted him to review rather than an attachment. He truly "owned" the solution and took accountability for effecting change by modeling the behaviors he wanted every employee to follow.* [2]

- An international organization purchased IBM Connections and IBM Quickr. The IT staff at one office worked with the executive team to enable them to gain access to upcoming board meeting papers stored in a Quickr space from their iPads, thereby eliminating the need to print and distribute bulky reports once a week. The executives loved the new approach, and encouraged their PAs and other heads of departments to do the same.

> The IT staff worked with the executive team to enable them to gain access to upcoming board meeting papers stored in a Quickr space from their iPads, thereby eliminating the need to print and distribute bulky reports once a week. The executives loved the new approach, and encouraged their PAs and other heads of departments to do the same.

- During the early investigations into opportunities for using SharePoint, it was discovered that the IT Steering Group was not functioning as a high-performing team. One reason: they were relying on email and attachments for sharing all their information, and there was nothing to bring the group together. This meant that issues were taking months to be resolved. The SharePoint administrator created a Meeting Site for the steering group, and invited the members to join. One new capability in the Meeting Site was the ability to assign tasks to specific executives, and this was adopted by the group. The result was that group members had a clearer picture of what they were responsible for, and they starting coming to meetings much better prepared to make decisions about current issues. Other people in the organization also noticed the improved performance.

- A small organization with employees spread across many remote locations embraced Central Desktop. Management mandated that Central Desktop had to be used for tracking projects, and this mandate flowed through to actual usage.

Strategy 1.2 Real-to-Life Scenarios

Real-to-life scenarios provide a narrative picture of how using a particular technology can improve the way work gets done. Let's explore the use of real-to-life scenarios for new collaboration technology, and how this strategy can be used for winning people's attention.

Description

The real-to-life scenario strategy paints a picture of what could be if a person or group of people started using a new collaboration technology as part of their work. The intent is that as people hear the scenario, they can compare and contrast what is being talked about with the experience they have today with current tools and approaches. If the scenario is sufficiently compelling, they will want to learn more about how to get involved. The strategy is designed to evoke an "I want that" desire on the behalf of people who hear or read the scenario.

Real-to-life scenarios in the work context could be on:

- A day in the life of customer services.

- A project being carried out by a research team.

- Discovering experts in unlikely places.

A scenario can be used to emphasize the benefits of the new way of working, especially if the new way of working eliminates time-consuming steps without reducing the effectiveness of the process. Think back to our discussion in Chapter 4 about Document Co-authoring, or Making Group Decisions. In both cases, new technology and approaches to these processes can make a significant difference.

> A scenario can be used to emphasize the benefits of the new way of working, especially if the new way of working eliminates time-consuming steps without reducing the effectiveness of the process.

How to Use It

There are three steps involved in making use of the real-to-life scenario strategy at your work.

1. Think about the main business activities undertaken at your work. Depending on the nature of your organization, you'll come up with a short list (not very diverse, fairly focused organization) or a very long list (highly diverse firm, broad focus). You need to develop the real-to-life scenario in the context of the work of your organization in order for it to hold power.

2. Select one activity from the list. Ideally, it should be an important activity frequently carried out within your organization, and where you know some of the people who are involved in doing that activity.

3. Write a story—or if you think that term is best left for what you read to your kids at night, write an "end-to-end narrative scenario"—about how the business activity can be enhanced through the application of new collaboration technology.

Before considering two specific scenarios, recall our discussion from Chapter 2 about the two context models for user adoption work. In the first, Business Engagement came before User Adoption Strategies. In the second, the development of Scenarios was the first step in the model. What this means is that you should already have some reference points from earlier work that propose specific scenarios about how work can be improved. Make use of this work. It links your current work with the foundational ideas of the overall process, and it also streamlines the effort you will need to expend in identifying and elaborating on scenarios.

> You should already have some reference points from earlier work that propose specific scenarios about how work can be improved. Make use of this work.

Let's look at two specific scenarios.

Scenario 1. Team Project Collaboration

My first book, *Seamless Teamwork: Using Microsoft SharePoint Technologies to Collaborate, Innovate, and Drive Business in New Ways* (Microsoft Press, 2008) has two roles. First, as an easy-to-read manual for business users and business teams that explains how SharePoint can improve work practice. Second, as an example of a real-to-life scenario, in this case an end-to-end team project. For more on *Seamless Teamwork*, see michaelsampson.net/seamlessteamwork.html.

The book is organized around the idea of someone—in this case Roger—getting a new project to lead at work, and then examines how SharePoint supports the execution of that project. The reason for choosing this approach is that many people can identify with some or all of the aspects of what Roger and his team have to work through. And by identifying with them, they start to see themselves in the book.

Here are the highlights of *Seamless Teamwork*:

Roger works for Fourth Coffee as a project manager, and he comes into work one day to find he's been given a new high profile project to manage, Project Delta. However, he is directed to use SharePoint for managing the project, something he hasn't done before.

Chapter 1 includes an exploration of why using SharePoint for managing a team project is better than using email.

Roger needs to find a set of qualified people from within Fourth Coffee and other partnering firms, to work with him on the project. He uses the My Site capabilities of SharePoint to find the internal people, based on their previous experiences, their work context, and their organizational affiliations. This is covered in Chapter 2.

After finding a team, Roger needs to create a place in SharePoint for the team to work. But it needs to work for more than just the direct inner team members, as there are two other groups in the organization who will need support from SharePoint to make the project work. Chapter 3 addresses the design of these three SharePoint sites, and in the process, introduces the reader to topics such as sites, lists and libraries, and Web parts.

With the team ready to work, and the team's work place set up, Roger has to bring the two together. Chapter 4 talks about what Roger does, covering off technical considerations like email or RSS alerts to keep team members in the loop on current status, and human factor considerations such as how the team blog can be used to overcome the risk of silence in virtual teams.

Fourth Coffee has a standard process for projects like Project Delta, and chapters 5 to 9 describe Roger's enactment of the project process within SharePoint.

- Chapter 5 outlines the team's need for a shared vision for Project Delta, and how the team's wiki and other capabilities can be used for discovering and documenting this.

- Chapter 6 addresses brainstorming using SharePoint, as a way of thinking broadly about the range of options for meeting the performance outcome from Chapter 5.

- Chapter 7 deals with taking the options identified in Chapter 6 and exploring each one. The use of the Idea Analysis briefing Content Type is addressed, covering the benefits of content types as a way of making a standardized document template available throughout the firm.

- Chapter 8 works through the decision making process for Project Delta, where the team needs to take the leading ideas it has documented as a result of Chapter 7, and decide which one is the best. A SharePoint survey as a way of evaluating the starting positions of team members is addressed, along with the use of out-of-the-box SharePoint workflows to collect feedback on a document from other people.

- Chapter 9 addresses the need for correctly closing out Project Delta, both at a human level through a team celebration, and then also the technical tidy-up required in SharePoint and other places. For example, each team member's My Site should be updated with details about Project Delta. They should all write a blog post in their My Site blog about their role in Project Delta. And if they have linked SharePoint with Outlook, Groove or Colligo Contributor, those links need to be removed.

Chapter 10 wraps up the book with some backwards glances and future ponderings. The backwards glances recap the main tenets of *Seamless Teamwork*. The ponderings outline some ideas on using SharePoint for other purposes.

Scenario 2. Collaborative Document Creation

A research firm is composed of cross-disciplinary researchers, who work together on specific projects. Their main work activity is writing proposals and research reports—in other words, collaborative document creation. The current way this happens is through Microsoft Word, a file server, and email. To use a real-to-life scenario means to create an end-to-end narrative story about how a new collaborative document creation technology could be used to enhance the way these groups work together:

- All new proposals and research reports are created in a project-specific collaboration space. People involved are invited to be members of the space.

- Researchers use a wiki page to create the overall structure of the document, and then link to specific sub-documents in the Document Library for each part. The wiki page gives the overall context to the document, and notes the current status of each sub-document.

- There is one lead author per document, as well as a supporting cast. Using email notifications, changes to the relevant documents are broadcast to interested parties. When someone is working on the document, it's shown as being checked out, to prevent others from working on it at the same time.

> The scenario becomes a communications bridge between the IT department offering particular technology capabilities and the research groups needing to get their work done in better ways.

- When it's time to formally review the different parts of the document, a workflow process is used to request feedback from multiple people. There is only ever one copy of the document in existence.

With the scenario developed, it can now be tested with a specific research group. This means the scenario becomes a communications bridge between the IT department offering particular technology capabilities and the research groups needing to get their work done more effectively.

When to Use It

Use the real-to-life scenarios strategy at the beginning of your user adoption approach. In addition to communicating the big idea to the people you are engaging with, it also sends the signal that you have thought through their work and understood what could be done. It can be used instead of Exemplar Stories (because you don't have specific experience within your organization), or in addition to Exemplar Stories (because you want to push the boundaries on what has currently been done). Exemplar Stories are the focus of the next section.

When you find a group of people who love the scenario and want to embrace it, you will need to:

- Provide specific training on the basic concepts of the technology, so they can translate the narrative scenario into something they can actually do. This is Stage 2 of the Four Stages Model of User Adoption, and is discussed in Chapter 7.

- Have some way of gathering stories or measures about how the real-to-life scenario played out for the team involved. Maybe it significantly reduced the stress of being involved in multiple projects—a great story. Perhaps it reduced project completion time by 30%—a key measure. Or it shrunk the document review cycle by 50%—another key measure. Gather what you learn, so you can use these "real and from-my-organization" illustrations in future Real-to-Life Scenarios or new Exemplar Stories.

Why It Works

The real-to-life scenario strategy works because:

> A real-to-life scenario shows the possibilities of the new technology and work practice embedded within their work reality. It's not just a feature/function checklist with no context. It's about them, and their work.

- *It's personal.* If you've got the right scenario—and by that I mean something people do on a regular basis—they can see themselves inside the story.

- *It's practical.* It shows the possibilities of the new technology and work practice embedded within their work reality. It's not just a feature/function checklist with no context. It's about them, and their work.

- *It's "promptive."* Yes, I made that word up, but it provides them with something to think about. They remember the story, they recall the concepts, and it may lead them to wanting to know more.

Data from Survey 2012

Figure 6-3. Data from Survey 2012 for the Real-to-Life Scenarios Strategy

Use of the Real-to-Life Scenarios Strategy
Percentage of respondents using the strategy sometimes or frequently

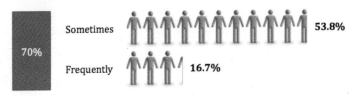

70%

Sometimes 53.8%

Frequently 16.7%

Effectiveness of the Real-to-Life Scenarios Strategy
Effectiveness rating by respondents using the strategy sometimes or frequently

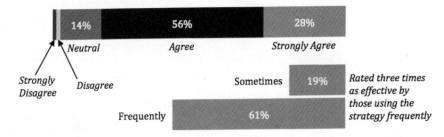

14%   56%   28%

Neutral   Agree   Strongly Agree

Strongly   Disagree
Disagree

Sometimes 19%

Frequently 61%

Rated three times as effective by those using the strategy frequently

Highest Use in the Adoption Lifecycle
Use of the strategy correlated with length of time working on adoption

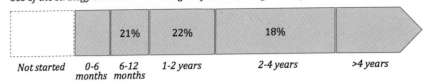

21%   22%   18%

Not started   0-6 months   6-12 months   1-2 years   2-4 years   >4 years

Complementary Strategies
Other adoption strategies most commonly used with Real-to-Life Scenarios

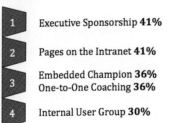

1   Executive Sponsorship **41%**

2   Pages on the Intranet **41%**

3   Embedded Champion **36%**
     One-to-One Coaching **36%**

4   Internal User Group **30%**

Comparison with Survey 2010

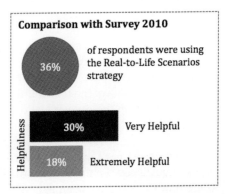

36% of respondents were using the Real-to-Life Scenarios strategy

Helpfulness

30%   Very Helpful

18%   Extremely Helpful

Over half of all respondents used the Real-to-Life Scenarios strategy sometimes. Those using the strategy frequently strongly agreed that the strategy was effective for user adoption.

Examples and Case Studies

DNV, a global risk management firm, used a real-to-life scenario to highlight the benefits of sharing and communities. The scenario was presented in a light-hearted animated video and was released for internal use. It's also available on YouTube—see the footnote.

Figure 6-4. A Real-to-Life Scenario

Hexagon Wrench has mastered the art of working alone, but when he is unable to finish a new design project, he discovers that there are other people in his firm who can help. As he gains their assistance, he begins to make small steps toward helping others as well.[3]

In a similar vein, but using real people rather than animated ones, Microsoft takes the same approach with its *That's Why I Use SharePoint* resource site.[4] The site offers ten videos that take a before-and-after approach to explore the value of SharePoint. It's lighthearted, but poignant. The scenarios include:

- Take a Number, about sharing what you know through a blog.

- Team Player, about coordinating input from many people.

- The Elusive Chris Smith, about people search.

After watching each of the videos, there is a link to an explanation about how to make the scenario work in SharePoint. Thus the site paints a scenario of what could happen, and also gives specific advice about how to set up SharePoint to enable the scenario. What Microsoft has done in general can be applied more specifically within organizations.

Strategy 1.3 Exemplar Stories

Exemplar stories are a commonly used user adoption strategy, designed to show how a particular aspect of a collaboration technology is being used by a real group or in a real situation in the organization. Good exemplar stories are aligned with the vision and strategy for new collaboration technology and approaches in the organization—they provide an exhibit of the vision and strategy in action. Exemplar stories are different from a real-to-life scenario that discusses what could happen, while an exemplar story relates what is actually happening or has happened.

Description

Everyone can relate to a story—a word picture of something actually happening. An exemplar story is a case study about a particular group within your organization, and how they are using a new collaboration technology well, and the benefits they are getting from it.

> An exemplar story is a case study about a particular group within your organization, and how they are using a new collaboration technology well, and the benefits they are getting from it.

Exemplar stories are much more powerful if they are drawn from within your organization, rather than from outside. This is because the social and cultural sifting has already happened in order for the exemplar story to work. On the social side, the exemplar story has happened with people who work within the same organization, which means that anyone else who hears it has the opportunity to actually go and talk to them. And on the cultural side, the story shows it's actually been proven that the new technology can work within your organization, thus eliminating potential roadblocks.

How to Use It

During your engagement work across the organization, there will be some people who grasp the new technology and run with it. They see a clear need, and want the benefits the new technology offers. Stay in touch with these groups so you can figure out how to improve what is being offered, as well as capturing what is being learnt. In your situation, it could be:

- A group in marketing that is using the new collaborative document co-authoring service to work with outside marketing professionals. As a result, they have cut the co-authoring cycle times by 40%.

- A group in product development have switched from tracking projects on a whiteboard to using Lotus Quickr, and are now able to see current status at any time, from any place. Everyone feels much more in control of their work, and tasks are completed 30% faster.

- The executive team has stopped using printed reports for their fortnightly meetings, and instead all members of the executive team have been given Apple iPads. Executives can read the documents in advance of the meeting—they are posted into the Executive team's wiki site in Atlassian Confluence—and then during the meeting mark-ups and revisions to the documents are shared in real-time with everyone.

Once you have identified the target group, capture the story. Write it up. Do a video interview with the people involved. Put it on your intranet. Include it in your internal newsletters from corporate communications. Hold a brown bag lunch and get the person to come and speak about what they are doing and what happened. Let the audience ask questions so they can understand for themselves what happened and the benefits that resulted. Use the story—and its method of communication—to spark people's interest in further engagement, social interaction and influence, and understanding.

When to Use It

Exemplar stories are a great way to win people's attention, in advance of them starting to use the new collaborative technology, as well as after they have started using it by demonstrating additional options and opportunities. The pre-condition for using exemplar stories within your organization is that you already have a few people or groups using the particular collaboration technology, and you are able to interact with them to capture what they have been doing. You also need trusting relationships to get the truth about what's happening.

Why It Works

Exemplar stories work because they convey the business value that a known or knowable person or group

An exemplar story has high social validity—it's something real that happened to people and groups within the current organization. It's not a story from "out there."

has achieved as a result of using a particular collaboration technology. The story has high social validity, because it is something real that happened to real people and groups within the current organization. It's not a story from "out there" that "probably won't translate into our environment." If people want to check it out and see for themselves whether it really happened, they have the opportunity.

A factor of why the strategy works is risk reduction. People are presented with real people from their own organization talking about something that has really happened. It is from inside, and it has been done already. It's not just an idea that might work. It has worked, and there are real people who will attest to it working.

Data from Survey 2012

Figure 6-5. Data from Survey 2012 for the Exemplar Stories Strategy

Use of the Exemplar Stories Strategy
Percentage of respondents using the strategy sometimes or frequently

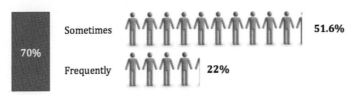

Effectiveness of the Exemplar Stories Strategy
Effectiveness rating by respondents using the strategy sometimes or frequently

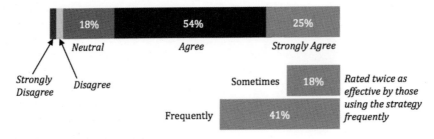

Highest Use in the Adoption Lifecycle
Use of the strategy correlated with length of time working on adoption

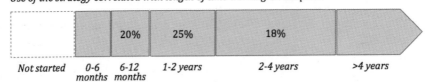

Complementary Strategies
Other adoption strategies most commonly used with Exemplar Stories

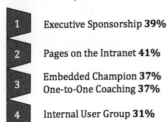

1. Executive Sponsorship **39%**
2. Pages on the Intranet **41%**
3. Embedded Champion **37%**
   One-to-One Coaching **37%**
4. Internal User Group **31%**

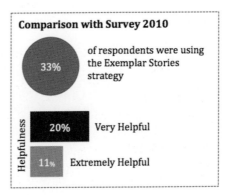

Comparison with Survey 2010

33% of respondents were using the Exemplar Stories strategy

Helpfulness

20% Very Helpful

11% Extremely Helpful

Exemplar Stories is a commonly used strategy for user adoption. Respondents rank the strategy highly for its effectiveness.

Examples and Case Studies

Here are three examples of the Exemplar Stories strategy in use at different organizations:

- An insurance firm with offices around the world used Exemplar Stories as a strategy for spreading learning and winning the attention of people and teams not currently using the new collaboration technology (SharePoint 2010). These were discussed at a monthly internal web conference, with a representative from a business team presenting on their specific use of the technology. For example, one business team discussed how they were using a SharePoint site to capture risks and issues during their regular project meetings. As a consequence, their monthly reporting was much simpler because the core data and subsequent follow on actions had already been captured in the system.

- Lowe's, a major home improvement chain in the United States, implemented IBM Connections in 2010 to support an enterprise collaboration strategy. Here's one of its exemplar stories: *During beta tests, an enterprising Paint Department employee decided to try something new to demonstrate the ease of cleaning a Teflon paint tray. She poured latex paint into it, let it dry, and then peeled the paint out whole. She left both the paint "mold" and the paint tray on the paint counter. Customers were amazed and delighted. Suddenly, she was sold out of the paint trays and shoppers were clamoring for more. The employee turned to all her traditional channels to get additional inventory. She accessed the company's enterprise inventory system, however, like most major retailers, the business process tightly controls the amount of additional inventory employees can request. After exhausting other traditional sources, the employee then turned to the Connections platform and asked "out loud" if anyone knew how she could get more inventory. Funny thing happened. Although everyone felt her pain on the inventory shortage, they started replicating her paint mold/tray demo in their stores. And guess what? Suddenly other stores were selling out of the paint trays too. As interest in the thread and the display idea grew in popularity, sales skyrocketed. When applied on an enterprise level, the unique display idea represented more than a million dollars in additional revenue of the SHUR-LINE Teflon 9" Metal Tray.*[5]

- At a large multinational retailer of technology and entertainment products, Sarah Haase—the Collaboration Manager—has seen the power of exemplar stories to help people put into words what they want. Sarah describes it this way: *The majority of my requests come as: "I need a SharePoint site because I have a new project" or "I saw someone else's SharePoint site that you created, and I want a site that looks like that." From those requests, I have to work with the team to distill down to what they actually need. I offer up ideas and examples of things we could implement to really make a difference in how they do work on a day-to-day basis. We discuss, come to a consensus and then I build out the SharePoint solution.*[6]

Strategy 1.4 Roadshow

Picture the scene: a 40-ft articulated truck, painted up with your corporate logo, kitted out with the best that collaboration technology has to offer (including hands-on testing computers in the trailer), free drinks and snacks for attendees, you get to drive, and you have three months to tour the country and visit all the offices in your organization. Your mission is to show off the latest and greatest capabilities coming in the next generation of collaboration technology. At each stop, you are inundated with fans from each office, desperate to get inside and catch a glimpse of the future, eager to sign up for the new gear, and hugely delighted that you have come to give personal attention. Ah, the life of the roadshow!

While such a scene might work for large organizations during an advertising blitz for a new product, getting senior management sign-off for a collaboration technology roadshow —40-ft articulated truck and all— probably isn't going to happen. So what is a "roadshow" in our context?

> A roadshow involves creating a small collection of presentations that convey the promise and potential of new collaboration technology to improve work.

Description

A roadshow involves creating a small collection of presentations that convey the promise and potential of new collaboration technology to improve work, and then setting up a series of onsite meetings with people at various locations to present the ideas and engage in conversation and discovery with them. You (and ideally a few others) travel to different offices within your organization, make the presentations, demonstrate the potential, and gauge the level of interest from attendees— based on their questions, discussions during morning or afternoon tea, and follow-up email or phone calls. Those who show high interest become key contacts for pilot programs and early involvement.

How to Use It

There are four broad steps involved in holding a roadshow:

1. *Develop the message.* Work out what you are going to say, and for how long (if this is the first time you are doing it, half-a-day is more than enough). Craft the presentations and demonstrations you will use to convey the message, and gather up the real-to-life scenarios and exemplar stories you will talk through.

2. *Schedule the meetings.* Find a lead champion at each roadshow location to help choose a date, and sign up attendees. All the logistics will have to be organized too —booking a room, ordering the coffee and refreshments, booking flights and hotel rooms, and so on.

3. *Go traveling*. If you have compressed the roadshows into a two-week timeframe, pack a large suitcase and hit the road. If you want to be kinder to yourself, make shorter, more strategic trips. If there are multiple offices you need to visit in a far-off place, then try to accommodate all of them during one trip, not multiples.

> **If there are multiple offices you need to visit in a far-off place, then try to accommodate all of them during one trip, not multiples.**

4. *Follow-up*. Collect business cards or contact details while you are on the road, and follow-up when you get back to the office. Find out what resonated with them. Ask whether they are ready for early involvement.

If you decide to run a half-day roadshow, your agenda should cover the business and environmental context, a description and demonstration of the new technology, scenarios and exemplar stories of where the new technology could help or has helped within the organization, and a discussion of how to get involved. As an example, your agenda could look like this:

- *0830-0900*. Coffee and registration.

- *0900-0930*. The challenges facing our business, featuring a 5-minute video from the CEO.

- *0930-1000*. About the new technology, and how it will help us improve our game.

- *1000-1030*. Scenarios from others in our business, with two 5-minute video interviews featuring the people who have been involved.

- *1030-1100*. Coffee, donuts, and discussion.

- *1100-1130*. How to get involved in the pilot programs.

- *1130-1200*. Open discussion.

Clearly there is a cost in undertaking a roadshow, but if the conditions are right, it can be an effective way of winning attention.

A warning. If you run the agenda above, don't schedule another meeting for 12pm or you will miss out on the benefit gained from the post-event mingling. If you leave quickly, you won't get to meet the people who could become your key contacts. Plan on staying around and being available for at least an hour to meet those people who want to talk with you.

When to Use It

There are a couple of instances when roadshows are an effective strategy:

- When there are a lot of people in your organization who could be interested, but you need to discover who to work with first. Roadshows can help to identify them.

- When there are big changes coming up in collaboration technology and work practice, and you need a forum for discussion and engagement with people from across the organization. Roadshows are a great way of saying that something big is about to happen.

Why It Works

Let's face it: People are busy—probably too busy! Cutting through the immediate demands on their time and getting them to focus on important matters is a real art. Face-to-face meetings can be an effective way to gather people together for time to focus on a topic, and by extension, roadshows can be as well.

- Roadshows create a bounded time and space to talk through new ways of working, and to reinforce the importance of doing so. If you have some great presentations, mixed with a great presentation style, it creates a memorable event.

> Face-to-face meetings can be an effective way to gather people together for a time to focus on a topic, and by extension, roadshows can be as well.

- Roadshows are presented in a social context. People within one office building or location attend with their peers and colleagues. The subjects presented will be replayed during subsequent meetings and catch-ups, thereby giving a greater likelihood of being remembered.

- Roadshows give the opportunity for talking through the business and environmental context. Time can be devoted to discussing these contextual factors.

- Roadshows are an efficient way of interacting with many people and groups, when you are unsure who is going to respond to the key messages. By holding one larger event with representation or involvement from many, you can quickly identify the key people to work with further.

Data from Survey 2012

Figure 6-6. Data from Survey 2012 for the Roadshow Strategy

Use of the Roadshow Strategy
Percentage of respondents using the strategy sometimes or frequently

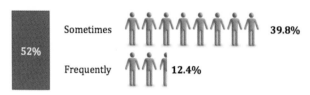

Effectiveness of the Roadshow Strategy
Effectiveness rating by respondents using the strategy sometimes or frequently

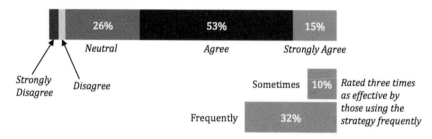

Highest Use in the Adoption Lifecycle
Use of the strategy correlated with length of time working on adoption

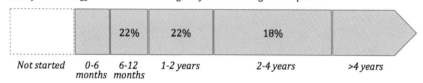

Complementary Strategies
Other adoption strategies most commonly used with Exemplar Stories

1 Executive Sponsorship **50%**

2 Pages on the Intranet **51%**

3 Embedded Champion **44%**

4 Internal User Group **32%**

Comparison with Survey 2010

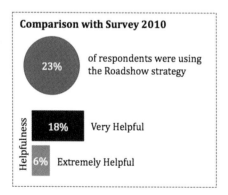

Half of the respondents make some use of the Roadshow strategy, with 12% of respondents using the strategy frequently.

Examples and Case Studies

Here are three examples of the Roadshow strategy in use at different organizations:

- A bank in South Africa ran into problems fairly quickly with its SharePoint implementation. SharePoint had been selected by the IT department and installed with a "build it and they will come" philosophy, but this led to significant problems—such as a system that didn't address user needs, and low user acceptance. In re-thinking how the bank could approach SharePoint, a variety of strategies were used to develop buy-in, win acceptance, and communicate clearly. The roadshow strategy was one of these. It involved visiting selected branch offices and showing staff the capabilities that were coming with SharePoint 2010. Using the roadshow strategy allowed the bank to emphasize its focus on better collaboration between people, rather than the new technology as such.[7]

- One company holds 'Collaboration Days' to describe the new collaboration technologies that are coming, and the opportunities these create for staff. Instead of giving presentations about the various capabilities—such as IBM Connections—the collaboration team sets up stands, similar to what would be used at a trade show. Staff are invited to browse the stands during the day, look at the demonstrations, and talk with the booth personnel. Staff have really liked this informal approach to learning about upcoming opportunities. This approach is taken at various offices across the United States, and staff at global offices are given similar opportunities through virtual approaches.[8]

> Instead of giving presentations about the various capabilities—such as IBM Connections—the collaboration team sets up stands, similar to what would be used at a trade show. Staff have really liked this informal approach.

- The roadshow strategy was used at a chemical company to increase awareness of the new business network and internal communities based on IBM Connections. The collaboration team provided presentations, demonstrations, and opportunities for discussion at important company sites, to which interested executives, employees, community members, and specific teams were invited. The roadshow strategy was one part of the company's overall adoption plan.[9]

One final suggestion—if you are showing live demonstrations during your roadshow events, make sure you have a recorded backup in case it doesn't work due to a network or system failure. Having a Plan B ready to go for such demonstrations is just good planning.

Strategy 1.5 Organizational Chaos

The final "strategy" for winning attention is organizational chaos. In all fairness, it's really a situation or opportunity that can be turned to your advantage for winning people's attention. But so we don't miss the wider benefit, if there is chaos and uncertainty happening within your organization now, it may be possible to introduce additional changes that would be rejected under normal circumstances.

When everything is going along smoothly, the outlook is pleasant, and everyone knows exactly what to do to keep the organization running as it is, it is very difficult—maybe even impossible—to advocate change. While I'm not suggesting that you create organizational chaos and uncertainty for the sake of it, I am saying that if you are facing such chaos and uncertainty now, then make good use of it.

> I'm not suggesting that you create organizational chaos and uncertainty for the sake of it, but if you are facing such chaos and uncertainty now, then make good use of it.

Consider the approach taken by the new CEO of eBay who took over just before the recent worldwide financial meltdown:

> *Although Donahoe had led the privately held Bain & Co. consulting firm before moving to eBay, he says running his first public company, with so many constituencies, required a different approach. It's not a popularity contest: You do what you think is right for the company and resist the attacks from those who prefer the status quo. "When I became CEO, there was an opportunity to take the next step," says Donahoe, 49. "And the next step was making changes that we knew were going to be unpopular in the short term." Donahoe, in fact, found that many employees and investors were more open to dramatic change than they might have been otherwise. "In a crisis, people were scared enough and uncertain enough that I could take action," he says.* [10]

Let's explore organizational chaos in more depth.

Description

There are times in the life of organizations and their people when big changes happen. A new CEO joins the firm, and to shake things up, implements a far-reaching re-organization. Lines of authority and reporting are re-drawn, new executives are brought in to replace those that have left to "pursue new avenues" (a polite spin on being fired for non-performance), and a roster of new initiatives is proposed to replace the current focus areas. Flow-on effects of these changes include new people being added to established teams, new performance management systems, and more. Talk about chaos!

Chaos can arise in other ways too. For example:

- Pharmaceutical companies know all about fast approaching chaos as their drugs approach the end of patent protection, and competitors offering generic replications line up for a feeding frenzy.

- Organizations that drive growth by acquiring both competitors and complementary businesses know about the chaos of trying to integrate the people and systems from the new acquisition into the "way we do things around here." Many things can remain undefined for a long time, causing high levels of stress and inaction.

- Unexpected natural disasters—such as earthquakes, severe weather disruption, and volcanic eruptions—can bring about organizational chaos. Approaches to working together that worked previously stop working, causing immediate challenges for collaboration. This can create the right conditions for a new willingness to explore alternative ways of working together.

During times of chaos, changes in how people work can be implemented as part of the drive to survive. Take Molson Coors Brewing Company as an example. It acquired 10 companies over a decade, but remained a collection of individual businesses. A new CEO, on a recommendation from an employee, gave staff a new way to interact with their peers and colleagues around the world—using Yammer—as part of a multi-pronged approach to developing a new cohesive corporate culture.[11]

How to Use It

The most important aspect of using the organizational chaos strategy as a driver for gaining attention is to show causality! You will need to provide a realistic link between what you are advocating and the eventual betterment of the organization and situation. It's no use proposing minor changes with no linkage to overall improvement. The people hearing what you have to say need to perceive the linkage. For example, for employees at Molson Coors, there was a clear linkage between new ways of interacting and a more cohesive corporate culture.

> When using the organizational chaos strategy, you have to show causality—a realistic link between what you are advocating and the eventual betterment of the organization or situation.

When to Use It

Use the organizational chaos approach for big and fundamental changes—the way people interact, the communications technology people use when working with others, and so on. Don't waste the opportunity on inconsequential things that don't exhibit a clear linkage from the current problem to the eventual solution.

Why It Works

Organizational chaos works to win people's attention about upcoming changes because people are already in a change-ready mode. They have experienced the pain of past ways of working, and know something has to change.

- *People have lower resistance to change.* As a consequence of the wider stress and uncertainty of the environment, people are more willing to embrace change, if they can see a link between the now and something better.

- *People know the old must go.* Organizational structures that used to work, and organizational approaches that were effective in previous times, are not looked on with so much fondness. The old way of doing things has contributed to a real and current problem, and new stuff is required.

I talk about "organizational chaos" as a user adoption strategy in my SharePoint Roadmap masterclass, and when I see that it's the next slide up, I always take a deep breath before clicking. I know there will be people listening who have been through traumatic organizational restructuring, and the mere idea that it could be harnessed for something good can be difficult to swallow.

> People who have been through traumatic organizational restructuring find it difficult to swallow the idea that organizational chaos could be harnessed for something good.

During a recent masterclass, one attendee put up his hand. I thought, "Here we go for the pushback." But he didn't. He related a situation from his organization from the late 1980s, when some major IT changes were introduced during a time of massive environmental and organizational chaos. He summarized the experience by saying, *While we've never been bold enough to do it again, I look back on that experience as one of the best change and transition situations I have ever been involved with.*

Data from Survey 2012

Figure 6-7. Data from Survey 2012 for the Organizational Chaos Strategy

Use of the Organizational Chaos Strategy
Percentage of respondents using the strategy sometimes or frequently

Effectiveness of the Organizational Chaos Strategy
Effectiveness rating by respondents using the strategy sometimes or frequently

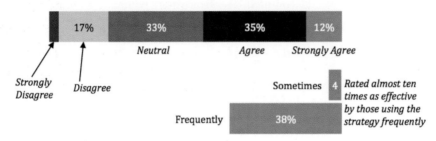

Highest Use in the Adoption Lifecycle
Use of the strategy correlated with length of time working on adoption

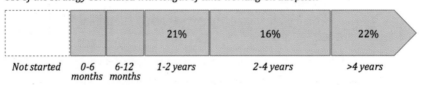

Complementary Strategies
Other adoption strategies most commonly used with Organizational Chaos

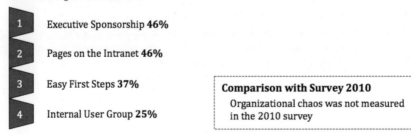

1 Executive Sponsorship **46%**

2 Pages on the Intranet **46%**

3 Easy First Steps **37%**

4 Internal User Group **25%**

Comparison with Survey 2010
Organizational chaos was not measured in the 2010 survey

The Organizational Chaos strategy is only used by one out of three three respondents. Some respondents use the strategy frequently, and rank it as highly effective.

Examples and Case Studies

Here are three examples of organizations that have made use of organizational or environmental chaos to win attention:

- After a serious earthquake an insurance firm received a huge volume of claims. It had previously used multiple claims systems, with no integration between them. Due to the organizational chaos being experienced from the huge influx of claims, decisions were made quickly about developing a unified claims system, and the new system was released within six weeks. While the development of a unified claims system had been on the organizational agenda for some time, no decision had been made. It was always put off as being too hard. But the chaos of the claims as a consequence of the earthquake made it imperative to act—and act quickly.

> When the crises occurred, adoption of SharePoint was immediate, even among people who had shown little prior interest. People now had to use SharePoint to stay relevant.

- During one of the recent Middle East crises, a government agency had to coordinate its response effectively. This involved capturing as much intelligence from the area as quickly as possible, and both formulating and promulgating its strategy rapidly. Previously this work had been done using email messages and attachments, and while there had been some work done on shifting to SharePoint, people had shown little interest. When the crises occurred, adoption of SharePoint was immediate. People had to use SharePoint to stay relevant.

- A consulting firm was in the early stages of introducing various new collaboration tools to its employees, and was planning to use one subsidiary for testing its approach to engagement and adoption. When the financial results for the subsidiary were analyzed before the initiative started, the senior management team was shocked at the poor performance. Since part of the root cause for the shocking results could be tracked to poor information sharing—an area the new collaboration tools would address—the priority and visibility of the initiative rose. The new tools moved from the nice-to-have list to the must-do list.

None of these organizations planned for these situations, but they were able to take action quickly to achieve strategically-aligned outcomes when the need arose.

Two Other Possible Strategies for Winning Attention

Before concluding this chapter, let's talk briefly about two other possible strategies for winning attention. I do not recommend either of these strategies, but note them here because they are used by some organizations.

Incentives

People often ask whether I recommend incentives—like contests or prizes—to encourage user adoption? After asking the question, they usually proceed to relate how they have given away T-shirts, chocolates, or game machines to promote user adoption. Their perspective has been that such an approach has worked really well for their organization. But when I ask what happened after stopping the incentives, their bright smile falls away and they admit that "people stopped using the system."

> If the focus is on the incentives for using the system, while people may do whatever they have to do to win the incentive, their efforts are about the incentive instead of the system.

That's the core of my concern about this strategy—that when the incentives stop, usage stops. If the focus is on the incentives for using the system, while people may do whatever they have to do to win the incentive, their efforts are about the incentive instead of the system. And if incentives are needed to promote usage, perhaps the system itself is an unnecessary add-on to an already over-scheduled day.

I think the real question should be: will the new system help them do their job better? I'd prefer to see people pay more attention to this question, and in exploring where and how the new system actually improves work. While it's less immediate than giving away chocolate, the long-run benefits are much sweeter.

Tell Clients The New System Will Be Used—Forcing Internal Adoption

A couple of IT leaders have asked what I thought about going around resistant internal staff and telling their clients that a particular new system will be used for work. The thinking was that instead of engaging directly with employees, if external clients were sold on the idea of using the new system, that this would force internal adoption.

In my view, the downsides of this strategy outweigh any possible benefits, with a loss of respect being at the top of the list. In an article for The BrainYard, I wrote:[12]

> *As an IT adviser, you could lose the respect of your internal groups if you go behind their backs and stimulate demand for tools or working methods that they fundamentally disagree with. In the worst case scenario, you create conflict between*

people in your company and their clients, because the clients—thanks to your meddling—now demand something that groups within your company have no intention of ever doing.

And offering customers something of this scale for free, especially when you're not the person to pay the internal bill of rewiring how a group works, is dangerous. If there's no cost per se to customers, or no equal change and commitment required on their part, you've struck an unfair bargain, further undermining your relationship with internal groups.

In conclusion, it's not a strategy I recommend.

Summary

This chapter has addressed the first stage of the Four Stages Model of User Adoption: Winning Attention. Before you can talk to second wave people about the basic concepts of the new collaboration technology and work practice, you need to win their attention.

Five strategies for winning attention were discussed and examined:

- Executive sponsorship and support helps with winning attention because it sends social and contextual signals that the new collaboration technology and work practices are important.

- Real-to-life scenarios and exemplar stories provide narrative descriptions of how benefits could or have come to people as a result of embracing the new technology and work practices.

- Roadshows and organizational chaos were the two final strategies under discussion, and both had a place to play in winning attention.

In the next chapter, we turn our focus to the second stage of the model: Cultivating Basic Concepts. The chapter looks at specific strategies for enabling second wave people to understand the basic features and capabilities of the new collaboration technology.

---

[1] Alan is the Professor of Marketing at the McDonough School of Business of Georgetown University and Executive Director of the Social Marketing Institute. This quote is from his writings in the early 1990s. See explore.georgetown.edu/people/andreasa/.

[2] As well as running her own consulting firm (Susan Hanley LLC, see www.susanhanley.com), maintaining an active speaking schedule, and co-authoring a great book on governance and planning for SharePoint, Susan also finds time to write for Network World. This snippet is taken from her October 2009 blog post *A Change Will Do You Good: Lessons from Change Management for SharePoint Solution Architects*, at www.networkworld.com/community/node/43459.

[3] To watch the video of Hexagon Wrench, see *Explaining Sharing and Communities Inside the Enterprise*, at currents.michaelsampson.net/2011/11/dnv.html.

[4] Visit Microsoft's *That's Why I Use SharePoint* resource site at www.iusesharepoint.com.

[5] Susan Scrupski, *Serendity Happens ... to Deliver Million$*, September 30, 2011, see itsinsider.com/2011/09/30/serendipity-happens-to-deliver-million/.

[6] Derek Weeks, *Saving Her Business $500K with SharePoint Part IV of the Profiles in Productivity Series*, March 2011, see www.nothingbutsharepoint.com/sites/eusp/Pages/Saving-Her-Business-$500K-with-SharePoint-Part-IV-of-the-Profiles-in-Productivity-Series-.aspx.

[7] Annelize Jonck presented at the inaugural Share Conference for business users in Sydney, in November 2010. See my notes on her presentation entitled *Overcoming Collaboration Challenges by Inspiring Ownership and Training End Users*, at currents.michaelsampson.net/2010/11/share2010-session11.html.

[8] At Lotusphere 2012, Mitch Cohen from Colgate talked about their approach to the rollout and adoption of IBM Connections. See my notes on his presentation at currents.michaelsampson.net/2012/01/ls12-ccs112.html. Used with permission.

[9] At Lotusphere 2012, Dr. CheeChin Liew from BASF talked about their strategy and approach to business networks and communities. See his slides at www.slideshare.net/basf/socialconnectbasf.

[10] BusinessWeek is one of my all-time favorite business magazines. This quotation is taken from Douglas MacMillan's article called *How Four Rookie CEOs Handled the Great Recession* in the February 18, 2010 edition. You don't have to be subscriber to read it, as it is also available at www.businessweek.com/magazine/content/10_09/b4168032766715.htm

[11] The Molson Coors story is also featured in Douglas's article from BusinessWeek (above). To see my summary of their actions, look at currents.michaelsampson.net/2010/03/ipdt-molsoncoors.html.

[12] Michael Sampson, *A Collaboration Strategy for the Change-Averse*, June 7, 2011, see www.informationweek.com/thebrainyard/news/229402760/a-collaboration-strategy-for-the-changeaverse.

Chapter 7.
Cultivating Basic Concepts

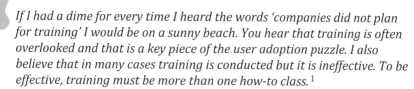

If I had a dime for every time I heard the words 'companies did not plan for training' I would be on a sunny beach. You hear that training is often overlooked and that is a key piece of the user adoption puzzle. I also believe that in many cases training is conducted but it is ineffective. To be effective, training must be more than one how-to class. [1]

Lynn Fraas, Crown Partners

Congratulations on winning the attention of the second wave people in your organization! They are interested in what's on offer, and if you have played your cards right, they have some sense of how the new offerings will help them in their work. Stage 2 of the Four Stages Model of User Adoption is all about Cultivating Basic Concepts—giving your second wave people an understanding of how to transition from a high-level idea of what's possible to the nuts and bolts of how to actually do it. Please note upfront that this stage isn't about being boring! Although there are specific basic concepts you have to get across, Stage 2 must be done in a way that keeps passion and interest alive.

In this chapter, we will:

- Discover the role of Cultivating Basic Concepts in user adoption.

- Explore three target strategies for Cultivating Basic Concepts.

- Consider how each strategy can be used effectively, and get a heads-up about the pitfalls to avoid.

- Examine the effectiveness of the three strategies through the eyes of the survey respondents.

What Can You Do?

Knowing "what" the technology can do or be used for is very helpful when the time comes to apply it to work. When faced with having to use a new collaboration tool, and trying to figure it out at the same time, having that little voice in the back of your head saying "But Jenny showed me how to do this last week, so I know it can be done" is a helpful signal to keep going and not give up. Also knowing it was "Jenny" who showed you is just as helpful, because you can ask her again if you need to.

Now that you have people's attention, you need to demonstrate the basic principles of the new collaboration product or service.

> Don't teach everything. Think of it as "hang your hat" concepts, or "the 5-7 key things you need to know."

The most critical thing to note at this point is that you are not aiming to teach everything. Stage 2 is about cultivating an understanding of enough of the basic concepts of the new collaboration technology so that second wave people can take a more active part in Stage 3. Think of it as "hang your hat" concepts, or "the 5-7 key things you need to know" in order to understand how the new technology works differently from what happens today. For example:

- With SharePoint, basic concepts are the site, lists and libraries, permissions, and integration with Microsoft Office and Microsoft Outlook.

- With Yammer, it's about the short message, free-form group creation through hashtags,[2] and following people.

- With Confluence, it's editable web pages, tags for classification, on-page discussions, and email notifications.

Strategies for Cultivating Basic Concepts

Three key strategies are discussed in this chapter:

1. Classroom Training.

2. Web-Based Training.

3. Pages on the Intranet.

Each of these strategies was probed in the two user adoption surveys, and data on the use and effectiveness of these strategies is presented in this chapter.

Survey Snapshot

Figure 7-1. Snapshot of Survey Results for Stage 2

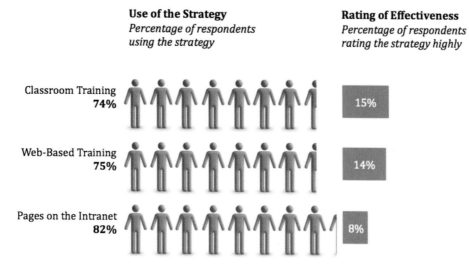

Use of the Strategy
Percentage of respondents using the strategy

Rating of Effectiveness
Percentage of respondents rating the strategy highly

Classroom Training **74%** — 15%

Web-Based Training **75%** — 14%

Pages on the Intranet **82%** — 8%

Highest Use by Size of Organization
Most commonly used strategies by size of organization (number of employees)

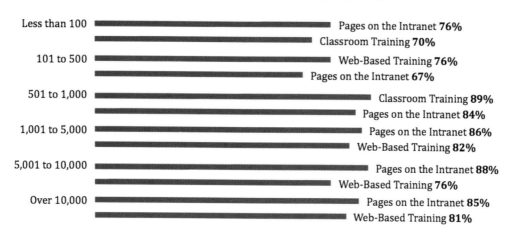

Less than 100 — Pages on the Intranet **76%** / Classroom Training **70%**

101 to 500 — Web-Based Training **76%** / Pages on the Intranet **67%**

501 to 1,000 — Classroom Training **89%** / Pages on the Intranet **84%**

1,001 to 5,000 — Pages on the Intranet **86%** / Web-Based Training **82%**

5,001 to 10,000 — Pages on the Intranet **88%** / Web-Based Training **76%**

Over 10,000 — Pages on the Intranet **85%** / Web-Based Training **81%**

All three strategies were widely used by survey respondents, and all three attracted only a small level of support for their effectiveness.

Strategy 2.1 Classroom Training

One of the most frequently embraced user adoption strategies is the Classroom Training strategy. In this section, we look at the different ways classroom training can be configured, some comments on how to use it effectively, and then we look at the survey data on the use and effectiveness of classroom training around the world.

Description

In classroom training, many people are brought together into a room for classroom-style training (remember your school days?). Basically, someone stands up the front and talks about what the new collaboration technology enables you to do, and the "students" listen and hopefully learn. There should also be some practice thrown in for good measure.

There are various design considerations with classroom training:

- *Internal vs. External Trainer*. For organizations with their own training group, an internal trainer will front up on training day and deliver the training material. Internal trainers may already know some of the people they are training, so their ability to engage and personalize the material is much greater. External trainers can be hired when internal trainers are not available, or when the material requires a depth and breadth of expertise that calls for someone special. Remember, however, that internal trainers have a different outcome in mind than external trainers. For internal trainers—at least the good ones—the outcome is greater understanding and competence for the employees at the organization. For external trainers, the outcome is to deliver the class and get paid well.

> Internal trainers have a different outcome in mind than external trainers. For internal trainers, the outcome is greater understanding and competence. For external trainers, the outcome is to deliver the class.

- *Off-the-Shelf vs. Custom Material*. Staff can be trained with off-the-shelf training material purchased from an external training content provider, or for organizations with in-house capability, through custom-written training material. The latter will give more opportunities for engagement and personalization, but is obviously much more expensive to develop and maintain.

- *Hands-On vs. Workbook*. Classroom training can be delivered in a hands-on way, where each individual student has a laptop or computer available. The trainer talks through a core concept, demonstrates how to do it, and then gives the students an exercise to complete. The alternative is to lecture from the front, and have the trainer demonstrate all the capabilities but not provide students with an opportunity in the classroom to try it out. Students leave with a workbook of slides and examples, and then are expected to try it out at their desks. If the people you will be training are unlikely to read a workbook after the event, condense the key concepts into a one-page "cheat sheet." And yes, it must be a maximum of one page!

- *Work Colleagues vs. Work Peers.* When colleagues are trained at the same time, they hear and work through the material in the social setting in which it will be applied. Everyone on the same group or team is learning together, and this can be used as a way of both giving support and holding people accountable when the training ends and people go back to their "normal" lives. The alternative is to train peers at the same time—people from one location who don't work together. These people are then expected to go back and spread the training around.

- *Train for Starting vs. Training for Everything.* Classroom training can focus on giving people enough information and experience to get going, or it can attempt to give them everything they'll need forever and a day. When training for starting, the ethos is to give them enough to get going with a business critical process or practice immediately, and let them know where they can get more. When training for everything, the ethos shifts to a focus on the different features and functions of the product or service, so students get a broad understanding of what's possible.

- *An Hour vs. A Day.* Recall that the focus of the Cultivating Basic Concepts stage is to provide people with sufficient understanding so they can be more effective during Stage 3. If you can cultivate this understanding in an hour or two, go for it. Don't schedule a one-day training session just because that's the traditional way it's done at your organization. Use as little time as possible.

- *Lots of People vs. Fewer People.* Classroom training sessions can be run with large or small groups. Larger classes have 30 or more people, while smaller groups have 15 or fewer, and there's a middle group of 15-30 too. Larger groups enable you to "get through" the whole organization faster, but this comes at the cost of fewer feedback opportunities, and less ability to engage with specific learners. Smaller sessions enable more personalized attention, but take longer.

> The effectiveness of the Classroom Training strategy will depend on the design of the session, who presents the material, and how they do it.

Coming back to Lynn's comment at the beginning of this chapter, "classroom training" isn't just one thing. The effectiveness of the Classroom Training strategy will depend on the design of the session, who presents the material, and how they do it.

How to Use It

Classroom training is best used under the following conditions:

- The material is fresh and presented in a bright and interesting manner. The greater the level of personal and work relevance, the better. In terms of presentation style, the trainer needs to enjoy what they're doing and exhibit a passion for the topic. In other words, it's not boring.

- Students can try things out for themselves. The more they can do inside a classroom, the better. Being able to try it out, asking questions, probing the trainer for more information and help, and getting assistance from their fellow students, all helps.

- Classroom training is treated as part of a larger process, not a one-time event. By itself, classroom training has little ability to reform the way people and groups work, but in conjunction with other strategies, it can be highly effective.

> Treat classroom training as part of a larger process, not a one-time event. By itself, classroom training has little ability to reform the way people and groups work.

- It's used for establishing a capability baseline, which can then be extended through additional user adoption strategies. Don't take a "train, then blame" approach where after a one-time how-to session has been run, any failure is the user's problem. That doesn't cut it.

- It's more effective to train people in smaller increments—train for starting— rather than attempting to train for everything. Give them something they can go back and do immediately and successfully, and tell them where to find more training material when they are ready to push the boundaries on what they know.

- Don't let too much time disappear between classroom training and the follow-on activities in Stage 3. A few days is best, because people will have a greater likelihood of recalling what they started learning. If a month goes by, they will have forgotten pretty much everything. You will have wasted their time and yours.

Finally, create space during and after the classroom training session to talk with and listen to the participants. They will have ideas that can be used to improve the way collaboration technology is used at work, as well as feedback on the presentation of the classroom session.

When to Use It

Classroom training makes a lot of sense when you have many people at particular locations. For example, if there are hundreds or thousands of people working at a given office, classroom training provides a cost-effective way of Cultivating Basic Concepts. If people are spread out over many locations, then web-based training (see the next strategy) would be more relevant and cost effective.

> Classroom training makes a lot of sense when you have many people at particular locations. But it can work for more distributed teams and groups too.

Classroom training can work with more distributed teams and groups, but someone has to make the effort to make it happen. An attendee at one of my user adoption workshops said she carried multiple laptops to far-flung offices to provide classroom training. For her, the benefit was in gaining feedback she otherwise would not have received.

Why It Works

Classroom training works for the following reasons:

- People learn together, and therefore create the social support structures necessary for continuing with the tool once the class has finished. When the trainer has left, Bob knows he can talk to Sue for reminders about how to use the new tool.

- People have an opportunity to move quickly from ignorance of the technology to early stages of mastery. They don't have to figure it out for themselves. The training group has blazed a trail, and has now provided insight in condensed and quick-to-understand ways.

- People can try the technology out in a test environment, without impacting the real system. They don't have to feel constrained about creating test projects, or sending their first micro-blog status update, because it's done within a learning social context.

- People learn about how the new collaboration technology will be applied at their organization. The classroom training events set the scene for how the specific organization will approach the collaboration technology. People also hear this in conjunction with their peers or colleagues, which reinforces the approach at a social level.

Data from Survey 2012

Figure 7-2. Data from Survey 2012 for the Classroom Training Strategy

Use of the Classroom Training Strategy
Percentage of respondents using the strategy sometimes or frequently

Effectiveness of the Classroom Training Strategy
Effectiveness rating by respondents using the strategy sometimes or frequently

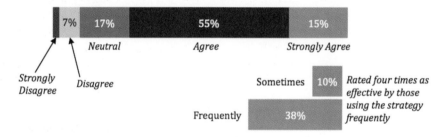

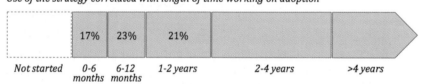

Highest Use in the Adoption Lifecycle
Use of the strategy correlated with length of time working on adoption

	17%	23%	21%		
Not started	0-6 months	6-12 months	1-2 years	2-4 years	>4 years

Complementary Strategies
Other adoption strategies most commonly used with Classroom Training

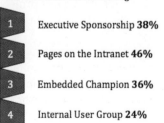

1 Executive Sponsorship **38%**

2 Pages on the Intranet **46%**

3 Embedded Champion **36%**

4 Internal User Group **24%**

Comparison with Survey 2010

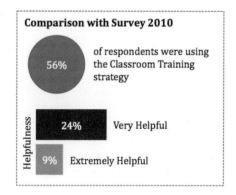

56% of respondents were using the Classroom Training strategy

Helpfulness

24% Very Helpful

9% Extremely Helpful

Half of the respondents use the Classroom Training strategy sometimes, and a further quarter use the strategy frequently. It's not rated as a highly effective strategy.

Examples and Case Studies

Here are some examples of how different organizations have made use of classroom training during the cultivating basic concepts stage of user adoption:

- A global pharmaceuticals company was switching from eRoom to SharePoint. Classroom and one-to-one training had been critical to its success with eRoom, but this lesson was not being carried forward with SharePoint. The collaboration manager commented, *With eRoom (our previous tool) we had grass-roots support, since at the time, it was our company's first and only technical solution for team workspaces, and therefore was eagerly adopted. We required mandatory training before users could have access—initially performed in classroom or in 'over-the-shoulder' settings, and eventually available through web-based training (both self-paced and WebEx style) which we considered key in successful user adoption. By requiring that users learn what was possible with the tool, we enabled and empowered them to do their jobs better. For our current adoption of SharePoint, due to our company's global strategy, we will not enforce the requirement for training prior to access. I do have concerns that this will have negative implications on how successfully the tool is used. I think users will simply use the file storage features, rather than embracing it for full team collaboration tasks, and this will create support issues as well.*

- Jenny works for a research firm, and in her response to the survey she wrote: *User adoption has worked really well when we have taken the time to first of all inform staff of the why and what we were trying to achieve through communications and roadshows, and then following that with hands-on classroom training sessions. We have also benefited from having dedicated trainers, and a logistics person to organize the attendees. This has allowed people to gain a sense of the importance of the training that they were being invited to—it wasn't just something 'someone in IT was running.'*

> We have benefited from having dedicated trainers, and a logistics person to organize the attendees. This has allowed people to gain a sense of the importance of the training that they were being invited to.

- A government department discovered two keys to making training work. The first was to call the initial sessions "Introductions," rather than "Basics." Staff didn't want to attend a session on the basics. The second was to tailor the material to specific roles, so staff learnt only what they needed to do their work.

Strategy 2.2 Web-Based Training

There has been high interest in web-based training over the past decade, and that's no surprise. It's costly to hold classroom training events, once you calculate the investment for trainers, travel and time off work. Web-based training offers the potential to greatly reduce the cost of running training events, while being as effective (and sometimes more effective) as classroom training.

Description

Web-based training involves delivering training material over the web. In practical terms, this means the training materials are generally "stored" on a web server somewhere, and can be accessed by authorized people from the web browser on their computer. However, web-based training can also be conducted "live" with a person presenting to a group of attendees.

> It's costly to hold classroom training events, once you have added up the investment in trainers, travel and time off work. Web-based training offers the potential to greatly reduce the cost of running training events.

There are a few variations on a theme with web-based training:

1. *Live Remote Training*. A meeting is scheduled and a trainer presents the material, but over the web. The trainer sits in their office, probably with a headset on, and walks through a presentation of capabilities, along with a demonstration of how to use the product or service. Meeting attendees sit at their desks, and "join" the meeting by opening their web browser to a particular page so they can view the trainer's presentation and demonstration in real time. Training events of this nature are usually called "webinars," or "web seminars." Remote training of this nature also offers opportunities for attendees to ask questions, so the trainer is able to gauge if people understand what they are being told. Such web seminars offer much of what can be accomplished with classroom training on the content side, but because people are normally sitting at their own desks, they are less effective at the social cultivation of learning.

2. *Recorded Web Seminars*. Web seminars, as above, can be recorded and made available for subsequent viewing on an on-demand basis. Whenever one of the original attendees wants to go over the material for a second time, they can view it whenever they want. In addition, people who didn't attend the original web seminar can be provided with access to the recording. This means that recorded web seminars can be a very cost effective way of spreading learning throughout the organization: a trainer gives a one-time presentation to a group of people, they ask questions to show engagement and help clarify the information, and then everyone else can be pointed to the recording when they have time available. If

greater engagement is required, or there's a need for further clarification, a discussion forum can be associated with the original web seminar.

3. *Full e-Learning Courses*. E-learning courses are special purpose learning events created for individuals to take at their own pace. E-learning materials will generally include content delivery—telling the learner about what they are learning—along with screenshots, recorded demonstrations, self-paced tests, downloadable worksheets, and more. In terms of training people at their pace, e-learning is the gold standard, but it comes with a golden price tag too! It's expensive to develop e-learning materials, which is why most organizations purchase off-the-shelf materials.

How to Use It

Web-based training can be used effectively for cultivating the basic concepts of the new collaboration technology. You can use web-based training in the following ways:

- *Introducing the New Technology*. An initial webinar to introduce the new collaboration technology to a large group of people can be an effective replacement for classroom training. An invitation to attend the webinar can be distributed through multiple avenues—email distribution lists, an announcement on the intranet home page, posters in the café, and word-of-mouth—and those who want to come are invited to register. At webinar time, the live attendees hear what's going on, and receive training on the key capabilities. The webinar is recorded and made available for subsequent viewing by people who couldn't attend the live event.

- *Training by Feature*. Develop just-in-time, at-your-desk, training videos on how to use particular features of the new technology. For example, organizations using SharePoint should have a training video on the document management features in a SharePoint document library. It's Fred's first time using SharePoint for check-in and check-out, and as a result he is shown a 6-minute recorded presentation and video about the steps involved.

> You can use web-based training to develop just-in-time, at-your-desk, training videos on how to use particular features of the new technology.

- *Training by Business Process*. Develop web-based training materials to demonstrate how a core business process is going to be done using the new technology. For example, managing the approval of new suppliers used to be done by exchanging emails and documents inside and outside of the organization, but with the recent purchase of Lotus Quickr, the process will be managed out of Quickr places. In rolling out the new offering, Sally needs to see how to run the process using Quickr—and she watches a training presentation and demonstration at her desk.

- *Training by Collaboration Scenario.* Co-authoring of documents by many people is a common collaboration scenario in many firms. This used to be done by exchanging emails and attachments. With the recent purchase of PleaseReview, all co-authoring is going to take place through this medium—including the initial feedback cycle where reviewers don't get to see the comments of others (while still contributing to the master copy of the document), and subsequent feedback cycles where comments are open to everyone.[3] Web-based training materials in this scenario provide a way for people to quickly see the steps and stages involved in setting up a new review, requesting feedback, and working through to approve or reject particular points of feedback.

When to Use It

Web-based training has high applicability during the second stage of the Four Stages Model of User Adoption. But it should also be part of your ongoing strategy for embedding the ideas in your organization. The following are examples of when to use the strategy:

- When you have employees or staff spread across many office or work locations. Web-based training—the live webinar variety as well as the recorded web-based training courses—are a very cost effective way to pass on core concepts.

- When you can't justify the cost and expense of classroom training. Hold a multi-hour web seminar instead, but keep the focus both on communicating core concepts and engaging with the attendees about how they can apply the core concepts in their work.

- When classroom training has been run (successfully), and it's time for people to get back to work. Complementary web-based training materials can help classroom students recall what they learnt.

> Use web-based training when classroom training has been run (successfully), and it's time for people to get back to work. Complementary web-based training materials can help classroom students recall what they learnt.

- When you don't have training classrooms available, and you don't want to carry multiple laptops to far-flung offices to set up a temporary training room for a day or two.

- When inducting new people into the organization. Classroom training can be cost-effective when you have enough people to train in one location, but if your organization is hiring new people in small numbers throughout the year and at different locations, classroom training is hard to justify. In addition, some people would have to wait weeks before a required quorum could be put together. Offering web-based training as part of the induction program gets new people up-to-speed much faster.

Why It Works

Web-based training works for the following reasons:

- *It's multi-sensory.* People can hear the message, see the message, and depending on the nature of the web-based training, try it out for themselves through scripted tests. Multi-sensory learning experiences are more effective than single sensory experiences.

- *It's self-paced, except for the live webinars.* People can work through the training material when they want to, at their own pace. If they already know a particular concept, they can skip over that section and focus on what they need to learn next.

> Web-based training is multi-sensory. People can hear the message, see the message, and depending on the nature of the web-based training, try it out for themselves through scripted tests.

- *It's constantly available.* People can look over the training material when they need it. Training isn't constrained to a class at 4pm on Thursday (which may happen to conflict with another appointment).

- *It offers opportunities for engagement.* In live webinars, people can ask questions and get answers from the trainer. With self-paced training, discussion forums can be provided, or the contact details of the trainer can be listed so people can ask follow-on questions.

- *It provides feedback that can be used for improvement.* If people ask the same questions at every live webinar, you can change the training to give a better description. Or if people are watching the same recorded snippet multiple times, that could signal that the video needs to be re-recorded—it's too unclear and people aren't getting it. If you pay attention to what people ask and do, you can quickly get ideas on how to improve your game.

Finally, in comparison with classroom training, the Web-Based Training strategy can decrease class time by up to 50%.

Data from Survey 2012

Figure 7-3. Data from Survey 2012 for the Web-Based Training Strategy

Use of the Web-Based Training Strategy
Percentage of respondents using the strategy sometimes or frequently

Effectiveness of the Web-Based Training Strategy
Effectiveness rating by respondents using the strategy sometimes or frequently

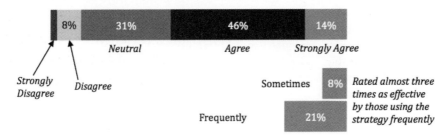

Highest Use in the Adoption Lifecycle
Use of the strategy correlated with length of time working on adoption

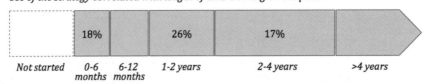

Complementary Strategies
Other adoption strategies most commonly used with Web-Based Training

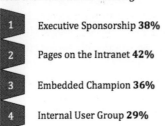

1   Executive Sponsorship **38%**

2   Pages on the Intranet **42%**

3   Embedded Champion **36%**

4   Internal User Group **29%**

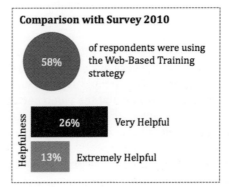

Comparison with Survey 2010

58% of respondents were using the Web-Based Training strategy

Helpfulness

26% Very Helpful

13% Extremely Helpful

Web-Based Training is a commonly used strategy among the survey respondents. It's not rated as a highly effective strategy.

Examples and Case Studies

Here are some examples of how different organizations have used web-based training for cultivating basic concepts:

- One of the divisions at a biopharmaceuticals company was using a very customized approach to SharePoint, and therefore off-the-shelf training curricula was not appropriate. Training materials for site members were developed internally, covering an overview of SharePoint, an introduction to lists and libraries, and a couple of advanced topics. These materials were initially delivered using Microsoft Live Meeting, but since January 2012, the four courses for site members have been offered as online courseware, allowing people to work through the material at their own pace.[4]

> Due to using a very customized approach to SharePoint, off-the-shelf training curricula was not appropriate. Training materials for site members were developed internally, and are offered online.

- At a defense and aerospace company, the collaboration manager uses web-based training with the engineers. He says: *I work in an extremely technical environment with engineers. Anything that isn't engineering is a waste of time. And a lot of what they're asked to do in engineering they consider a waste of time. So I essentially created an online environment to meet their needs of being able to share formal knowledge (work instructions, definitions, process, training) and "market" their projects to other engineers. I created bite-sized training sessions—complete with engineering examples—to help the engineers use the system.*

- The Australian division of a global consulting firm offers live webinars every three weeks on the basic concepts of using SharePoint. For example, one session is a 45-minute webinar on using lists and libraries. New staff are invited to attend, and existing staff can attend if they want to. The internal trainer says staff have become accustomed to online meetings within the organization, and since there are no computer training rooms available, she has no choice but to run the sessions online. There's a key advantage gained by running the sessions in a live format: she gets to hear the questions people are asking, and can make proactive adjustments in her courseware and delivery.

People who have used the web-based training strategy note the importance of monitoring engagement levels. Attendees will tune out if a live session is too long, or presented in a boring way. Asking appropriate questions throughout the session can help with keeping attendees engaged, and offering alternative recorded methods of learning can provide another approach for people who learn best at their own pace. Finally, remember that web-based training is just part of the user adoption journey rather than the sole approach.

Strategy 2.3 Pages on the Intranet

The third strategy for Cultivating Basic Concepts is descriptive Pages on the Intranet.

Description

The Pages on the Intranet strategy involves publishing user-oriented help information to a specified location on the corporate intranet. When people need to know how to perform a particular task, or use a particular function of the new collaboration technology, they visit the help pages. The help pages contain clear instructions on how to perform the steps involved in the task or function, meaning a user can quickly get on with the task or function without having to interrupt a work colleague.

How to Use It

Write help pages on the tasks or functions people will be doing regularly. The task-focused pages explain how to carry out one of the tasks in a business process—perhaps it's how to set up an idea creation space for an upcoming business planning event, how to start a review of the next press release with input from the external marketing consultancy firm, or how to create a collaboration space for a new team project in the Product Development Group. Task-focused pages demonstrate a function of the collaboration technology within the context of a common business process. Whatever you decide to write, make it about the work people are doing, and the questions they are asking.

> The help pages contain clear instructions on how to perform the steps involved in the task or function, meaning a user can quickly get on with the task or function without having to interrupt a work colleague.

The function-focused pages talk about the basic capabilities of the collaboration technology, but do not discuss how those capabilities can be used in a business process. For example:

- Team projects can be run in a collaboration space. The page on the intranet would describe what a collaboration space was, and note which tools could be used inside a collaboration space (document sharing, discussion forum, risks and issues register, for example).

- Blogs can be used to share updates with team members and the wider organization. The page would talk about what a blog is, how people get notified, and include links to key internal and external blogs as exemplars.

- Document reviews end when the lead author closes the review cycle and works through the master document to approve or reject proposed changes. The page on the intranet would talk about how to approve or reject changes.

The two other strategies we have discussed in this chapter derive part of their effectiveness from multi-modal learning and social interaction with others. Both of these effectiveness factors can be addressed as part of the strategy:

- Multi-modal learning can be offered through embedded videos or recorded demos of particular tasks or functions. Software to record short videos and demonstrations is inexpensive these days (a few hundred dollars will do it), and will contribute greater learning effectiveness. Pages on the Intranet don't just have to be composed of text. For a great example of multi-modal learning, take a look at what Transfield Services in Australia did when rolling out SharePoint to its employees.[5]

> Multi-modal learning can be offered through embedded videos or recorded demos of particular tasks or functions. Software to record short videos and demonstrations is inexpensive these days, and will contribute greater learning effectiveness.

- Social interaction with other people can be offered in a couple of ways. The minimum is to name the author of the page so people know who to contact when they have a question. If greater interaction would be beneficial, a discussion forum related to the particular topic could be added.

Finally, while the pages don't have to look beautiful, they shouldn't be ugly either. Prepare something that works for the people in your organization, avoiding the extremes of presentation. Some people find that preparing two versions of the material works well—a "cheat sheet" for quick reference, and a longer description.

When to Use It

The Pages on the Intranet strategy has wide applicability for user adoption, but it has a particular role to play when Cultivating Basic Concepts. Classroom training and web seminars will not be able to cover all the required material, and even if they could, people would be unable to retain it. Thus Pages on the Intranet can be used for follow-on descriptive material that will both reinforce the ideas taught through classroom or web seminar methods, as well as extend the learning beyond what either of those modes can do. Trainers in both the classroom and remote situations should make it part of their role to point people to the pages on the intranet that will help them once they are back in their own work roles.

Why It Works

Pages on the Intranet that explain the basic concepts of the new collaboration technology work for the following reasons:

- *People can set their own learning pace.* Some people will prefer to "eat everything" in one sitting—they will go through the complete set of pages over a couple of hours so they can see what's there and rapidly learn the basic skills. If the pages have been well-written, they give the high-level view of what's possible, as well as the more detail-oriented view of specific tasks or functions. Other people prefer the "snack and digest" approach to learning the basic concepts, and learn in smaller chunks by reading or reviewing one page at a time—when they have a specific need for that information.

> Some people will prefer to "eat everything" in one sitting—they will go through the complete set of pages over a couple of hours so they can see what's there and rapidly learn the basic skills.

- *People can focus on what they need to learn.* If Christopher already knows the principles in one of the topics, he can skip it and move onto another topic. He is able to focus on the learning he needs to do for the particular tasks he carries out as part of his job. Christopher isn't inconvenienced in his learning by having to wait for a trainer to explain a particular topic to other people, as happens in a classroom or live web seminar environment.

- *People can learn when they need to.* The pages on the intranet are available at any time for Christopher to review. He isn't limited to learning new material when resident expert Sally is in the office, and he doesn't have to wait until the next scheduled classroom training session comes around. He can learn what he needs to learn when he needs to learn it.

Directing people to pages on the intranet can be a useful part of an overall user adoption approach, but as we explain in Chapter 10, don't make it your only approach.

Data from Survey 2012

Figure 7-4. Data from Survey 2012 for the Pages on the Intranet Strategy

Use of the Pages on the Intranet Strategy
Percentage of respondents using the strategy sometimes or frequently

Effectiveness of the Pages on the Intranet Strategy
Effectiveness rating by respondents using the strategy sometimes or frequently

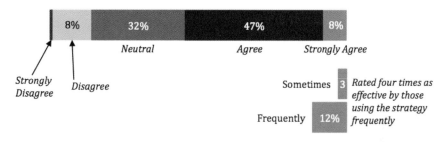

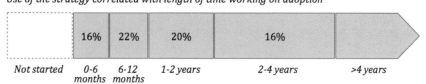

Highest Use in the Adoption Lifecycle
Use of the strategy correlated with length of time working on adoption

Complementary Strategies
Other adoption strategies most commonly used with Pages on the Intranet

1 Executive Sponsorship **37%**

2 Web-Based Training **38%**

3 Embedded Champion **34%**

4 Internal User Group **26%**

Comparison with Survey 2010

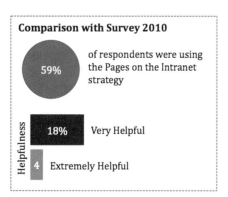

The Pages on the Intranet strategy is the most widely used strategy in Stage 2, but achieves the lowest ranking for effectiveness from the three strategies in Stage 2.

Examples and Case Studies

Here are two examples of how different organizations have made use of pages on the intranet for cultivating basic concepts:

- An organization was introducing a new way for handling documents, and the IT team tried three strategies: a written manual (Pages on the Intranet), video training (web-based training with video), and one-to-one coaching (which we will consider in the next chapter). The team tracked the time it took people to learn how to use the new system, and found that it took four hours with the written manual, two hours with video training, and only 10 minutes with one-to-one coaching. Assuming that the people knew all they needed to know from each of the three approaches (and that is a big assumption), that's an huge difference.

  > Although the senior managers said no training would be required, when the new technology was made available, the internal collaboration manager used Pages on the Intranet when he discovered that staff didn't know what to do.

- The senior managers at a professional services firm declared that no training would be needed with the roll-out of a new collaboration technology. They felt the staff would be able to embrace the new way of working without any training. When the new technology was made available, the internal collaboration manager discovered that the staff did need training—they didn't know what to do. In response he used the Pages on the Intranet strategy to rapidly publish help documentation on the key activities, such as uploading documents and writing blog posts.

In her response to the 2012 survey, one change consultant commented on why this strategy was frequently used:

> *I consult in this space, and am therefore always starting my User Adoption Strategies again. Each time I am engaged for User Adoption work with collaboration technologies I prepare a new strategy specifically designed for the opportunities and constraints in each environment. Overall, my observation would be that the more effective adoption methods are usually the least scalable and cost effective, and are therefore rarely resourced to the requisite level. As a result, the less successful methodologies that are more scalable and visible—such as help & how-to pages on the intranet, self-help videos and other instructional courseware, and online FAQs— tend to be the strategies that clients demand and are prepared to resource, whatever the evidence that may be presented for or against. What I always try to do these days is educate my clients on the realities of user adoption and set expectations about the relative efficacy of their chosen strategies.*

A Final Comment

Remember that people need the capability to absorb the ideas and put them to use. If too much information is given at once, people won't be able to absorb what they are hearing. You can use the complementary nature of the three strategies to overcome this challenge. For example, start with a two-hour classroom training session, or a 45-minute web-based training session, and then point the participants to pre-recorded online training materials or help pages on the intranet. They get the initial learning kick-start, and know where to find more depth or help in the days to come.

> If too much information is given at once, people won't be able to absorb what they are hearing. You can use the complementary nature of the three strategies to overcome this challenge.

For example, a global biotech firm focused their adoption program for SharePoint on site owners, who were seen to be people of influence for particular teams and groups. The first two parts of their adoption approach fitted within the cultivating basic concepts stage. The central IT business team wrote a series of wiki pages about the basic concepts in SharePoint sites (the Pages on the Intranet strategy). This was followed by two half-day onsite training sessions—held back-to-back in various offices around the world—where these basic concepts were discussed along with how to apply them for particular teams and groups (the Classroom Training strategy). Once these training sessions had been completed, further engagement was based on an expression of interest from site owners to learn more. This was provided remotely by the IT business team instead of traveling to the far-flung offices a second time.

Summary

This chapter has looked at three key strategies for cultivating the basic concepts required before staff are able to see how new collaboration technology could be used effectively in your organization. Each of these strategies can be used in effective ways, and the factors required to do so have been highlighted throughout the chapter. Data on the use of these strategies has been provided based on two user adoption surveys.

In the next chapter, we turn our attention to Stage 3 of the Four Stages Model of User Adoption: Enlivening Applicability. As people take what they learnt during Stage 2 back into their day-to-day work, they will need support to use the ideas effectively. There are ways of achieving this, as we discuss in Stage 3.

_____

[1] Lynn Fraas is a Partner at Crown Partners, an international hybrid Software and Professional Services firm specializing in information management. Lynn is active in the industry and is currently the Chair of the AIIM Board of Directors. This quote is drawn from her blog post, *8 Ways to Increase User Adoption of ECM and ERM Systems.* See aiim.typepad.com/aiim_blog/2009/06/8-ways-to-increase-user-adoption.html

[2] For an interesting look at how hashtags can be used for forming online groups, see Simon Goh's April 2010 blog post, at www.ambientkm.com/2010/04/forming-organic-online-communities-on.html.

[3] The social dynamics of reviewing and providing feedback on documents and other items are fascinating, and worthy of some thought. For example, in the early stages of a document review cycle, what you want are honest opinions and constructive advice. Showing the reviewers what others have said too early can lead to free-riding and a loss of quality. For more on this topic and possible approaches to solving the riddle, see currents.michaelsampson.net/2010/03/coauthoring-conformity.html.

[4] Angela Chionchio from Bristol-Myers Squibb presented at the SHARE 2012 conference in Atlanta on their approach to training. See my notes on her talk, *Case Study: Implementing an Effective SharePoint Training Program*, at currents.michaelsampson.net/2012/04/share2012-6.html.

[5] Transfield Services won a Gold Award in the 2008 Intranet Innovations Awards program, run by Step Two Designs. The Step Two people say, *Transfield's key innovation was productizing their approach to collaboration spaces with 'Team Sites in a Box', and compiling a near-perfect design, support and governance methodology and model, which then saw rapid, but controlled uptake within the organization.* Learn more about Transfield's approach, at www.steptwo.com.au/products/teamsites.

Chapter 8.
Enlivening Applicability

End users don't care about all the grand philosophizing; they just want a smarter, faster, better way to work. Whether you call it a wiki, a blog, or a whoozit, people just want an easier way to do their job. Make solutions for specific, concrete use cases, rather than tools for general purposes.[1]

Chris Yeh, PBWorks

Enlivening Applicability means working alongside a group or team and helping them discover the applicability of the new collaboration technology for their work. If you have won their attention using Exemplar Stories or Real-to-Life Scenarios, you have basically portrayed the applicability of the new collaboration technology to another or imagined reference group. Stage 3 shifts the lens from these external reference groups to a particular and certain group in your organization.

In this chapter, you will:

- Discover the role of Enlivening Applicability in the user adoption process.

- Find out about some strategies to help groups and teams explore the applicability of the new collaboration technology to their work.

- Review the use and effectiveness of different strategies, as reported by the survey respondents.

- Learn why Lee Reed argues "communication, not technology, is the success" in new technology implementations.

Coming Back to Purpose and Intent

Knowing that something is beneficial for someone else can provide sufficient impetus to get people interested. Hopefully, they will jump in and try it out themselves. However, that's usually the case for first wave people, not second wave people. Stage 3 of our model focuses on bringing second wave people to an understanding of where and how new collaboration technology and approaches can make a difference in their work.

The two previous stages have laid a vital foundation for the activities you will do in Stage 3. In order to explore the applicability of the new technology, people need to share some common language before an effective discussion can take place. The Stage 1 activities gift this at a high-level, and the Stage 2 activities complement the high-level overview with a grounding in the basic concepts of the new collaboration technology. The Enlivening Applicability stage brings both together for a particular group or team.

> The Enlivening Applicability stage brings together your earlier efforts for a particular group or team.

Before we dive into evaluating the different strategies, think back to Chapter 2. There we discussed the wider organizational context in which your work takes place. We discussed the process of engagement, where the focus is on working with a small number of representative groups to understand their work, and develop an understanding of how new collaboration technologies and approaches to work could fit. The other model talked about scenario development, which focused on the same end. Therefore, remember that your Stage 3 activities are constrained by the overall vision. You don't have an open book.[2]

Strategies for Enlivening Applicability

Let's look at six major strategies for Enlivening Applicability:

1. Facilitated Group Re-Imagining

2. One-to-One Coaching

3. Embedded Champion

4. Sandbox for Experimentation

5. Easy First Steps

6. Build It And They Will Come

The chapter finishes with a brief look at three supporting strategies.

Survey Snapshot

Figure 8-1. Snapshot of Survey Results for Stage 3

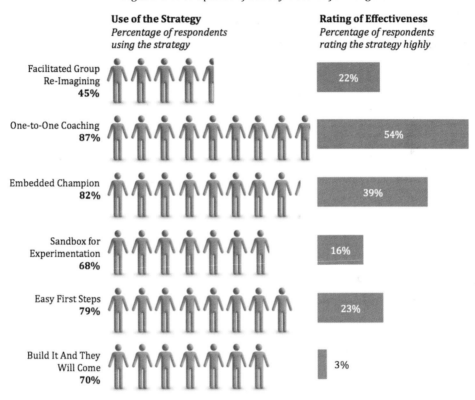

Use of the Strategy
Percentage of respondents using the strategy

Rating of Effectiveness
Percentage of respondents rating the strategy highly

Facilitated Group Re-Imagining **45%** — 22%

One-to-One Coaching **87%** — 54%

Embedded Champion **82%** — 39%

Sandbox for Experimentation **68%** — 16%

Easy First Steps **79%** — 23%

Build It And They Will Come **70%** — 3%

Highest Use by Size of Organization
Most commonly used strategies by size of organization (number of employees)

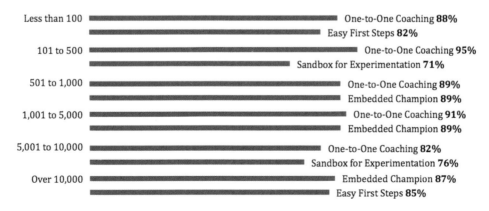

Less than 100 — One-to-One Coaching **88%** / Easy First Steps **82%**

101 to 500 — One-to-One Coaching **95%** / Sandbox for Experimentation **71%**

501 to 1,000 — One-to-One Coaching **89%** / Embedded Champion **89%**

1,001 to 5,000 — One-to-One Coaching **91%** / Embedded Champion **89%**

5,001 to 10,000 — One-to-One Coaching **82%** / Sandbox for Experimentation **76%**

Over 10,000 — Embedded Champion **87%** / Easy First Steps **85%**

Of the six strategies in Stage 3, one-to-one coaching is highly used and ranked highly for effectiveness. Built It And They Will Come is also highly used, but ranked as ineffective.

Strategy 3.1 Facilitated Group Re-Imagining

While "facilitated group re-imagining" makes for a jaw-breaking phrase, the concept is actually quite simple: work with a group or team and explore how they could apply the new collaboration technology within the context of their work. If you don't like the phrase itself, don't let that put you off. Call it the Facilitated Workshop strategy instead.

Description

The way a group or team carries out its work is frequently predicated on ways of working and technologies that are 10-15 years old. Even if the group has had new members join in the intervening years, they have been inducted into a particular way of working, and the overall work practice remains rooted in now outdated ideas. The work practice has not been revisited in light of new technological advances.

> The way a group or team carries out its work is frequently predicated on ways of working and technologies that are 10-15 years old. The work practice may not have been revisited in light of new technological advances.

While on the one hand it's highly efficient for people to continue with their current way of doing things, they may also have become highly efficient at doing unnecessary things.

Consider the typical way a group works together today:

- A group uses an elaborate mechanism for collecting feedback on documents, complete with version numbers appended to files. The group doesn't even know about collaborative document co-authoring using PleaseReview.

- Meetings are scheduled using a combination of phone calls and group email messages. No one has ever heard of alternative approaches for streamlining the scheduling process.

- Excel spreadsheets are swapped back-and-forth by email to document and communicate the current status of risks and issues. A complex script was written some years ago to roll-up the different spreadsheets into an overall summary. The group has never been told about using a SharePoint list for project-level tracking, with aggregation to get a programme-level view.

- People doing the work experience the pain, but they don't realize that something can be done about it. It's not even a matter of being comfortable or at peace with the pain—it's just there, but no-one knows that there is a different way.

How to Use It

The Facilitated Group Re-Imagining strategy involves working with an intact group or team of people to discuss how they get work done today, and leading them through a process of discovery and discussion to understand how work could be done in the future with new collaboration technology capabilities. It's important this process is done with a group or team, rather than an individual, because the collaborative nature of the new technology means that multiple people have to change their work practice at the same time in order for the new technology to have an impact.

Using this strategy involves the following steps:

- *Understand the main work activities of the group.* Whether through structured focus groups, more free-range group discussions, facilitated workshops, or any other mechanism that gets the same outcome, develop an understanding of what activities the group does on a regular basis. You should be able to get some appreciation of the main work activities in advance of any meeting or workshops, by looking at their place within the organization and what they are expected to produce. Whatever approach you take, the emphasis is to build an understanding directly from the members of the group.

> Whether through structured focus groups, more free-range group discussions, facilitated workshops, or any other mechanism that gets the same outcome, develop an understanding of what activities the group does on a regular basis.

- *Demonstrate alternative ways of doing the work.* In understanding how the work is done, look for the particular technologies currently being used. Once you can see what's happening, look for opportunities to achieve the same outcome with the new collaboration technology. Ideally, you will be able to demonstrate the alternatives, and compare and contrast the different alternatives with the current approach.

- *Do small experiments to explore fit.* Working with the group, set up small experiments to try out a new way of doing things. Perhaps it's one document that is co-authored using a different approach and technology. Perhaps it's one key event scheduled using new tools. Perhaps it's the tracking of risks and issues for one project. Identify particular people in the group willing to try out the new approach.

Let's be clear about how to be effective with this strategy. People's understanding is constrained by what they know, what they have experienced, or what they have heard from others. This extends to how they can envision doing their work—if they don't have an awareness of what could be, it's very hard for them to state that they want it. Thus there is a dual role to play in the re-imagining strategy: probing team and group members for an understanding of what they do today, plus an educational role to demonstrate what's possible with the new technology.

One way of doing this is to present a series of short scenarios about what could be done with the technology. Take meeting scheduling as an example. For most people today, meetings are scheduled in one of two ways. Either a series of emails or phone calls are placed to find out when people are available for a particular meeting, or if the meeting is only with people inside one organization, a free-busy search is done to find out the next available time to meet. The first approach is time-consuming and error-prone,[3] and the second approach relies on everyone having up-to-date electronic calendars, which may or may not be true. Here's the point: if you ask people in a group that schedules many meetings if there could be better ways of scheduling those meetings, you will get responses reflecting the two standard approaches.

- People should reply faster to our meeting enquiries.

- We should use instant messaging to query people about meeting times, because we'll get a faster response.

- We should make it mandatory to keep our electronic calendar up-to-date.

- People should not be allowed to block off large segments of their day for their own projects, because this signals that they aren't available for the meeting, thus delaying a lot of stuff from happening quickly.

What such people won't realize is that much has been done recently to drastically improve meeting scheduling, and these ideas have been encapsulated into new meeting scheduling services on the Internet. If you haven't told them about newer services that provide a different way of scheduling meetings, they will only see improvements within the constraints of what they know.

> People's understanding is constrained by what they know, what they have experienced, or what they have heard from others. If they don't have an awareness of what could be, it's very hard for them to state that they want it.

Another example of where re-imagining is required is the use of SharePoint. Due to its ability to store files, many new users merely see it as the new file server. But it can be much, much more than that. To see the new possibilities and opportunities, teams and groups need help to shape their thinking.

It's for this reason that "re-imagining" is included in the title of this strategy! It's not about small changes or tucks around the edges, but rather about how core work practices within intact groups and teams can be re-imagined in light of new technology.

When to Use It

The Facilitated Group Re-Imagining strategy should be used with intact teams and groups. That is, the team or group is well-established, they have been working together for a while, and they have an existing way of doing things.

If you ask people in a group that schedules many meetings if there could be better ways of scheduling those meetings, their responses will be constrained by the technologies they currently know.

The second prerequisite is that from an outsider's viewpoint, there are clear benefits in working differently. Perhaps certain group members have started voicing their dissatisfaction with the manual and labor-intensive processes they are stuck in today, and have approached you for support in changing things. You can see clearly how work could be done better, and the Facilitated Group Re-Imagining strategy provides you with a way of exploring this.

Why It Works

Collaboration technology is different from individual software. Think about it this way. How I use my email client software has little impact on how you use email (and for that matter, which email client I choose to use). I use folders to sort and organize my messages; and over the past few years I have developed quite-a-nice-thank-you-very-much set of folders for tracking projects and managing clients. You, on the other hand, don't use folders for organizing messages at all—you prefer to keep everything in one folder and use *search* to find what you are looking for.

Collaboration technology is different because the choices I make about how I used the technology impacts on you. If I start a document as a wiki page, you have to keep going with that. If I create a task list in a collaboration space, you need to keep it up to date (or alternatively not play).

In other words, there is a much greater degree of interdependence with collaboration software than with individual productivity and work planning software.

As a result, as a member of an intact group, Jill can't suddenly decide by herself, with no reference or buy-in from others, to start doing document reviews through Lotus Quickr. Scott can't suddenly decide to use Yammer for keeping everyone up-to-date, if no one has the Yammer client installed or open during the day. Making the transition in work practice from one way of doing things to another requires agreement and commitment from a quorum within the group. Thus a group "sale" is required—multiple people have to buy into the idea.

Data from Survey 2012

Figure 8-2. Data from Survey 2012 for Facilitated Group Re-Imagining

Use of the Facilitated Group Re-Imagining Strategy
Percentage of respondents using the strategy sometimes or frequently

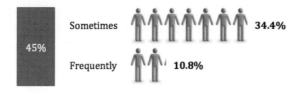

Effectiveness of the Facilitated Group Re-Imagining Strategy
Effectiveness rating by respondents using the strategy sometimes or frequently

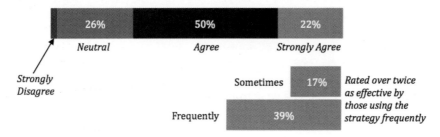

Highest Use in the Adoption Lifecycle
Use of the strategy correlated with length of time working on adoption

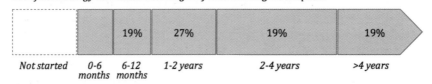

Complementary Strategies
*Other adoption strategies most commonly
used with Facilitated Group Re-Imagining*

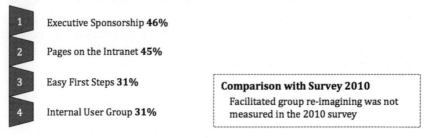

1	Executive Sponsorship **46%**
2	Pages on the Intranet **45%**
3	Easy First Steps **31%**
4	Internal User Group **31%**

Comparison with Survey 2010
Facilitated group re-imagining was not
measured in the 2010 survey

*The Facilitated Group Re-Imagining strategy is used frequently by only 11% of respondents.
Another 35% make some use of the strategy.*

Examples and Case Studies

Here are some examples of how various organizations use the facilitated group re-imagining strategy:

- In her foreword to this book, Nancy White tells a story of the Facilitated Group Re-Imagining strategy in action. *"A research organization had a support team who recognized early on the possibilities of the use of social media for their scientists. So they installed blog and wiki software, created training sessions and thought that it would be a quick and obvious adoption. It was SO clear to these smart individuals. Their scientists were clever. Easy.*

  Not so. After some missteps, the team changed their strategy. They were not scientists. They needed the scientists to define the rules of the game. Instead of training sessions, they convened conversations about research, not about social media. As real collaboration needs surfaced, they offered suggestions and experiments between them. The technology folks created prototypes for experimentation, taking a page from the very practices the scientists used on a daily basis. Prototypes were set up, feedback offered and applied and tools and practices subsequently adjusted. What happened? Practices to enhance collaborative research emerged. They just happened to use technology as part of the process. The scientists did science, not "blog and wiki" classes that they felt were a waste of time. To follow up, the technology team readjusted their roles to stewarding the technology— keeping an eye on how the scientists were using the tools, making adjustments and looking out for new options."

  > Instead of training sessions on social media, the support team convened conversations with the scientists about research.

- An insurance firm in the United States uses the Facilitated Group Re-Imagining strategy when working with internal teams. For example, a collaboration coach worked with a small group that had not previously seen SharePoint, and nor did they understand the opportunities. Over a couple of weeks, using one-on-one observations, interviews, and workshops, the coach came to understand the way work was done in the group, and the opportunities for using SharePoint. One new approach was to use a document library for draft documents, rather than email and attachments. Since the group members were intimately involved in the initiative, this wasn't a matter of the IT group "doing SharePoint to them."

- A firm in Europe uses the Facilitated Group Re-Imagining strategy with teams that have unique requirements. Sitting down with the team and discussing how work is done today provides a mechanism for beginning to understand the current approach, and to highlight common pains and needs. As these are identified, new possibilities for working together are explored.

Strategy 3.2 One-to-One Coaching

Spending time one-to-one with someone in their office or cubicle is a great way to cultivate insights about how they really work. It is also a key strategy for user adoption.

Description

One-to-one coaching provides a way to see how an individual is working today, and to encourage them to explore new collaboration technology capabilities to overcome current pain points, to do things in better and more efficient ways, or to greatly increase effectiveness. By becoming immersed in someone's real work world, you are able to see what they are doing, and can tailor your advice and direction in appropriate ways. Doing one-to-one coaching requires a delicate balance of observing how they work and directing them to work in new ways. It's one form of coaching, for the modern age.

This strategy was called over-the-shoulder watching in the first edition of *User Adoption Strategies*, but I have renamed it in this second edition. The renaming is intended to portray the dynamic give-and-take during one-to-one coaching, and to minimize the passivity conveyed by the word "watching."

How to Use It

The one-to-one coaching strategy involves a combination of two things. First, the ability to watch someone at their work, and observe what they are doing. When watching them—sitting in their office ideally—you are looking out for the common activities they do on a regular basis, and in particular, the activities they do in conjunction with other people.

> One-to-one coaching involves watching someone doing their work, and discussing what you are observing with them.

The second aspect is the permission to interrupt the person during the time you are observing their work, so you can ask for clarification on what you are observing. This will assist you in developing a deeper understanding of why they are doing particular things. The coach will use various questions to build understanding, explore meaning, and consider alternatives—such as:

- *Can you please describe what you are doing here?*

- *Why are you using the old system for those activities?*

- *I noticed you are doing (current approach). Have you considered doing it this way?*

Finally, note that an outsider may be required to do this work. Someone too closely tied to the way work is done today—the workarounds, the excuses, the established way of doing things—will miss things an outsider will pick up quickly.

When to Use It

The one-to-one coaching strategy can be used for many types of IT projects, is very effective (see the survey data results), but is perceived as being very expensive. Here are some times when it may be worth spending the money:

- *When you are trying to understand the group.* Early investments in one-to-one coaching will provide a clear sense of the type of work being done by people in the group. These insights can be used during subsequent engagement sessions.

- *With opinion leaders within a team or group.* Working with opinion leaders to understand their work and give coaching may result in them taking the message to the rest of the team or group. Sally is an opinion leader for her group, and as a result of your coaching, she starts advocating for working in new ways, and wants to set up a broader discussion session with the group so everyone can see the new thing.

> Personal attention and coaching may be the tip-them-over-the-edge approach that helps people who have stood against the changes to get on board.

- *With people who are hard to convince.* Personal attention and coaching may be the tip-them-over-the-edge approach that helps people who have stood against the changes to get on board. While doing one-to-one coaching, be sure to connect the work they're doing, and the coaching you're giving, with the wider organization. For example, mention how the executive team is using these new capabilities, or how the sales and marketing groups have started to do so. On the other hand, giving personal attention to such people may be seen as a reward for bad behavior—stay alert to whether the people you're working with are actively changing or merely creating roadblocks to impede the introduction of new collaboration technology and approaches.

- *When you have permission from the people themselves.* The athlete in a sports coaching situation gives explicit permission for the coach to direct them to higher levels of performance. This same principle of granting permission equally applies in the work setting. The people you are coaching in a one-to-one situation have to grant you permission to enter their work space, observe their work habits, and give ideas for higher levels of performance. If you don't have their permission, avoid one-to-one coaching.

Regarding the perception of expense, one-to-one coaching can be much more effective than alternative approaches, and thus less expensive overall. For example, the regional offices of a large global organization were implementing new capabilities for handling documents, and it was felt that there was no time for classroom training. They tried three alternative approaches: a written document, video training, and one-to-one coaching.

Users took four hours with the written document to understand what they had to do, two hours with video training, and only 10 minutes with one-to-one coaching.

Figure 8-3. Time Required for Learning and Capability Development

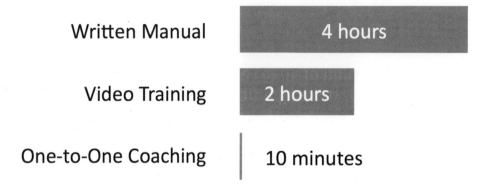

Written Manual	4 hours
Video Training	2 hours
One-to-One Coaching	10 minutes

When introducing a new way of handling documents, one organization found that people learnt how to use the new system much faster through one-to-one coaching.

Regardless of whether there was 100, 1,000, or 10,000 people involved, one-to-one coaching would always be more cost effective assuming that the time-to-learn difference remained the same across the larger population.

Figure 8-4. Comparative Effectiveness and Cost of Different Approaches

	Written Document	Video Training	One-to-One Coaching
Time required for learning and capability development (per person)	4 hours	2 hours	10 minutes (plus 20 minutes for a coach)
Time for 100 people	400 hours	200 hours	50 hours
Time for 1,000 people	4,000 hours	2,000 hours	500 hours
Time for 10,000 people	40,000 hours	20,000 hours	5,000 hours

One-to-one coaching can be more cost effective for capability development than alternative approaches—because people understand the ideas faster. The figures above exclude content development time, cost, and effort.

Finally, due to the time commitment from the person in the coaching role, it's easy to let excuses put you off because you don't have enough time. An attendee at one of my public seminars said they followed a 10-10-10 approach: 10 one-to-one coaching sessions before introducing the new technology and approach, 10 sessions just after the introduction, and

10 sessions after a couple of months to check up on how the new approach and technology were being assimilated into the working habits of the teams and groups.

Why It Works

One-to-one coaching works for many reasons:

- *It gives personal attention.* One person (the watcher/coach) spends some time—from 30 minutes up to a couple of hours—sitting with one person (the watched) and observes what they do. What tasks are they working on? How do they handle working with others? What tools are they using today? How well are they using them? Based on what the watcher sees, coaching is provided about next steps.

- *It conveys importance.* Having a watcher/coach actually show up at your desk and sit to observe and provide helpful comments conveys the tremendous importance of what's going on.

- *It provides tangible next steps for the coached.* The lessons learned by the watcher/coach can be translated into tangible ideas for a particular person to work on. It essentially gives the person an individualized development plan to work on in relation to the new collaboration technology.

- *It offers a validation and feedback loop.* Spending time in one-to-one coaching gives an opportunity to gauge the effectiveness of earlier training and engagement sessions. Are people getting the message? Are they recalling the steps involved? Are they making the transition to the new approach and technology? If not, improvements can be implemented systemically, so that future training and engagement sessions are more effective. This might involve adding a module to a classroom training session, or seeking out additional exemplar stories to help with understanding why the changes are necessary.

> Spending time in one-to-one coaching gives an opportunity to gauge the effectiveness of earlier training and engagement sessions. If they are not effective, systemic changes can be made.

Harmon.ie, an independent software vendor that makes add-on software to link SharePoint with Outlook and Lotus Notes, took a one-to-one coaching approach at a recent conference. It believed its software would make SharePoint more attractive for the average user, by speeding up common, everyday tasks. To prove the point to SharePoint influencers, it invited them to try uploading a document to SharePoint with and without its software. And it timed the difference. The result—a five times reduction in the time required to complete the task.[4]

Data from Survey 2012

Figure 8-5. Data from Survey 2012 for the One-to-One Coaching Strategy

Use of the One-to-One Coaching Strategy
Percentage of respondents using the strategy sometimes or frequently

Effectiveness of the One-to-One Coaching Strategy
Effectiveness rating by respondents using the strategy sometimes or frequently

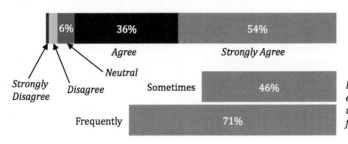

Highest Use in the Adoption Lifecycle
Use of the strategy correlated with length of time working on adoption

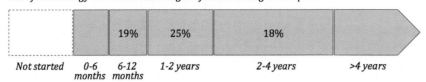

Complementary Strategies
Other adoption strategies most commonly used with One-to-One Coaching

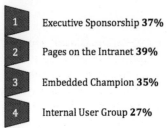

1 Executive Sponsorship **37%**

2 Pages on the Intranet **39%**

3 Embedded Champion **35%**

4 Internal User Group **27%**

Comparison with Survey 2010

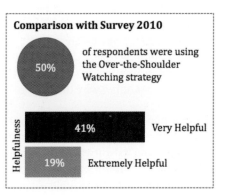

One-to-one coaching is a commonly used strategy, with 30% of respondents using it frequently. It is rated highly for its effectiveness.

Examples and Case Studies

Here are some examples of how organizations are using the one-to-one coaching strategy:

- In the mid-1990s, BP experimented with virtual teaming approaches and technology. Five projects were set up during the experimentation phase, and all but one of those projects receive coaching on how to make use of the new technology. The only project that failed to deliver business value was the one set up with no coaching. Reflecting on the experience, Don Cohen wrote: *"The problem was not that the group couldn't make the technology work — it was fairly simple to operate. What they lacked was an understanding of why they should bother. Remarks from the team ("I don't see how this fits in with my work." "The people I want to talk to are not on the network.") were similar to those made initially by other teams. In part because there was no one to help the group explore the value of the system and overcome their skepticism, their virtual teaming network declined and eventually fell silent."*[5]

- The one-to-one coaching strategy has proven its effectiveness over the long haul. In a comment on a blog post about user adoption, Patti Anklam wrote: *At a conference in Boston in the early 1990s, I attended a session with a consultant who was helping companies with the earliest generations of collaborative tools (think BEFORE SharePoint, eRoom, etc.). He was asked about how he actually got people to use the new tools. His response was "1,000 cups of coffee." In other words, one conversation at a time to help people see whether they might have a reason.*[6]

> How did he get people to use the new tools? "1,000 cups of coffee." In other words, one conversation at a time.

- In her response to the 2010 survey, one respondent wrote: *After a series of instructor-led classes on how a team could use SharePoint to organize their information and communicate with team members, most participants seemed mildly interested and a few went on to establish a team site (from a standardized template). Of those, a few have grown more interested and asked for one-on-one coaching and training. Those who received the special attention really got it and you could see the light bulbs going on in their head.*

- At a university in the United States, Judith used one-to-one coaching in person and by using the technology. *My approach was to mentor and coach people who had some experience with Yammer or a willingness to participate. Using Yammer has been our greatest success. We grew from ten people to 120 in less than three months, and all for professional posts. I needed to post frequently in the beginning, coach and encourage some people in person, and also do some training by posting. People have taken to it very well. We've had better luck with Yammer than we have had with SharePoint.*

Strategy 3.3 Embedded Champion

An embedded champion is a locally known and available semi-expert on how to use the new collaboration technology. The person is a peer (a member of the same organization) or a colleague (a member of the same team or department) who regularly advocates for the use of the new technology, and is clearly committed to its use. While embedded champions are frequently used as a first line of support when people have questions about how to use software features, they can also be used to advocate for doing work in a different way during the Enlivening Applicability stage.

Description

The Embedded Champion strategy involves giving extra training and personal coaching to certain people who work in selected teams and groups across the business. The intent is to increase their capabilities so they have a greater depth of understanding about how to use the new collaboration technology within the context of business processes, as well as how to advocate within their group for that use. It's a bit like the executive support and sponsorship strategy, but instead of being messages and observations from the executives, it's from "Jim who sits over there in that cubicle."

How to Use It

The embedded champion strategy creates people in local offices, groups or teams who can point the way forward with the new collaboration technology. They will be seen as the go-to person. They will frequently advocate for using the new collaboration technology instead of current tools. Because they are local, they will see things that outsiders will miss, and they are likely to have sufficient kudos within their local environment to propose how things could be done in better ways. However, note that it takes a special kind of person to be able to work within the current way of doing things, while also being able to imagine the possibilities for doing it differently. If you have such people at your organization, you have a great opportunity.

> The embedded champion strategy creates people in local offices, groups or teams who can point the way forward with the new collaboration technology.

You use the embedded champion strategy in the following ways:

- *Find the opinion leaders*. Recruit energetic champions who are willing to take a stand and encourage adoption of a particular use case. In your own work with the new technology, you will come across particular people who "get it" and start agitating for wider use.

- *Convert key users into champions.* Find key users in certain groups or teams and give them special coaching to become champions. Perhaps this is the person who is always calling you and asking for help in solving a problem. Or they're the person who asks all the questions in the workshops. When you find them, give them what they need to improve the performance of their group or team.

- *Provide extra training and assistance.* Local champions need a deeper level of awareness about the new technology and how it can be used effectively. Provide extra training and assistance to them—quickly share new exemplar stories with them, invite them to any onsite or online training sessions you are running, and get them involved in an online community of like-minded people. In the latter, the group will be able to share success stories and provide support to each other.

> Local champions need a deeper level of awareness about the new technology and how it can be used effectively.

- *Share the greater vision.* Talk to the local embedded champions about the greater vision. Don't make it just about improving work practice; make it about rewiring the way the organization collaborates so it can serve its customers better. Extrapolate from the immediate concerns to the final outcomes.

- *Don't forget the under-study champion.* The sudden loss of an embedded champion can ruin the momentum behind the new collaboration technology and approaches. Having another person in the role of an under-study can help with mitigating this havoc, because they are ready-to-go when the primary champion leaves.

Becoming a champion offers benefits to the selected individuals—improved communication skills, a deeper understanding of the new system and its possibilities, new career opportunities. There are examples of where an internal champion has gone on to work for the vendor of the collaboration technology involved, and used their organizational know-how to help people in similar organizations make great progress.

When to Use It

The most important signal that you can use this strategy is when you can identify appropriate people would could be embedded champions within your organization. They need the ability to work effectively within the current systems, combined with the ability to imagine different ways of achieving the same outcome. If you can find such people, it is particularly effective when:

- There are concentrations of people at particular offices. Having a local embedded champion is very helpful for gaining insight into where the new technology could be used.

- There is a small collaboration team, they are located in one place, and the collaboration project is for a short period of time. The Embedded Champion strategy provides a way of getting people in the business to advocate for new ways of working.

It is important to find the right people to be your embedded champions. They need to be viewed as credible in the eyes of the people they work with; you don't want to entrust the success of your collaboration initiative to someone who is viewed with distrust by the group they work with. Good attributes to look for include trustworthiness, a good work ethic, a vision for improvement at a business or functional level (rather than a love of new technology toys), and an ability to work well with other people. In short, take your time in choosing your initial champions. Don't jump at the first people who put up their hands. Look around, consider the evidence, and then make your move.

> You don't want to entrust the success of your collaboration initiative to someone who is openly viewed with distrust by the group they work with.

Why It Works

There are many reasons why the embedded champion strategy works:

1. The champion is relevant and credible to the team or group. He or she is an active member of the team or group, not an outsider. He or she intimately knows the work that has to happen because they are accountable for a part of it.

2. The champion is an ever-present reminder of the possibilities of the new technology, what's been talked about, and what's been proposed as a way forward. He or she attends the meetings, sits in the coffee room, meets around the water cooler, and sets up conference calls.

3. The champion is alive and present, and will talk back to doubters—quite unlike Pages on the Intranet or a recorded webinar. If they hear other people deriding the new approach, they are there to probe reasoning and explore applicability.

4. The champion will be an active voice for accountability, reminding their fellow team members that work is being done in a new way. They are a force for change within the group, rather than that task being driven by the IT department.

Data from Survey 2012

Figure 8-6. Data from Survey 2012 for the Embedded Champion Strategy

Use of the Embedded Champion Strategy
Percentage of respondents using the strategy sometimes or frequently

Effectiveness of the Embedded Champion Strategy
Effectiveness rating by respondents using the strategy sometimes or frequently

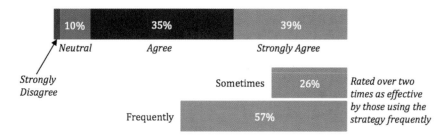

Highest Use in the Adoption Lifecycle
Use of the strategy correlated with length of time working on adoption

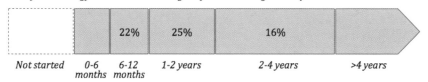

Complementary Strategies
Other adoption strategies most commonly used with the Embedded Champion strategy

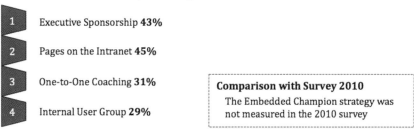

1 Executive Sponsorship **43%**

2 Pages on the Intranet **45%**

3 One-to-One Coaching **31%**

4 Internal User Group **29%**

> **Comparison with Survey 2010**
> The Embedded Champion strategy was
> not measured in the 2010 survey

The Embedded Champion strategy is commonly used, and ranked highly for its effectiveness. Over one in three respondents say the strategy is used frequently at their organization.

Examples and Case Studies

Embedded champions have been used by many organizations. Here's an insight into some recent experiences:

- At a bank in the United States, IBM Connections was the tool of choice. The value of an embedded champion was evident. One such champion says: *I spent a year as the designated Collaboration Consultant for a line of business with approximately 600 employees. I evangelized the tool, held one-on-one training, facilitated team learning sessions, and answered questions that people had. The department had excellent adoption of IBM Connections and continues to enjoy much success with it. I'm now in a new role, and my successor has continued to find that she's adding value with her work and people appreciate having a friendly human face to help them navigate the tools.*

- A different bank—this time in Europe—were also using IBM Connections, and also found the benefit of the champions strategy, albeit that they didn't plan for it. The adoption specialist says: *As we were implementing, we didn't really focus on supporting and finding ambassadors or champions, but they popped up in different places and started convincing their colleagues that IBM Connections really has an added value in daily work situations. We did a roadshow to show people what they could use Connections for. Though not every participant was convinced right away, it was really interesting for us to also get some feedback from the not-so-early adopters.*

> Champions popped up in different places and started convincing their colleagues that IBM Connections really has an added value in daily work situations.

- A mid-sized software development firm using SharePoint found embedded champions an effective strategy. The adoption specialist says, *Embedded champions have worked very well for us, especially as we have paired that strategy with a high-performing internal user group. Monthly meetings of this group in which best practices, lessons learned and new ideas are shared are excellent vehicles for driving adoption.*

Finally, echoing the earlier comments about choosing the right people for the embedded champion role, a change management consultant in Australia says, *Embedded champions can also deliver results, but only when the champion is the right person, both in terms of technical skill and attitude. They can be hard to find, co-opt and up-skill, and clients can find it difficult to maintain and nurture these people over time.*

Strategy 3.4 Sandbox for Experimentation

In nursery school, a sandbox provides a place for little children to play together. There are lots of toys for joint play—like trucks, diggers, and cranes—enabling children to construct cities and roads out of sand. The idea is to provide a safe place to learn about building things, using a cheap and easy-to-reconfigure ingredient. A "sandbox for experimentation" with collaboration technology works with the same intent, without the sand.

Description

A collaboration technology sandbox provides a place where people can try out the different tools and features of a new collaboration technology, in a safe environment. The technology is provided to "play with," and is separate from the main production environment. What happens in the sandbox doesn't cross over to the production system, except for special cases. These special cases include systems that business users have developed that make real sense for a specific business group, and where the IT group have analyzed the system and signed off on its design, security approach, and any compliance requirements.

> A collaboration technology sandbox provides a place where people can try out the different tools and features of a new collaboration technology, in a safe environment.

The sandbox provides a place for learning, and trying things out. Not everyone will use it, but some will. They will be your local champions or lead users.

How to Use It

Consider this scenario. Your organization has decided to buy and use Atlassian Confluence, an enterprise wiki. There are a whole raft of Real-to-Life Scenarios that can be developed —around co-creation of documents, drafting of presentations, planning upcoming projects, and so on—but the decision is made to see what other uses people want to put Confluence to. In other words, the collaboration team wants to create a space for local ideas to percolate and find their way into Confluence.

So the collaboration team does two things:

1. It creates a production environment for Confluence, where all of the current business things will happen. It's accessible internally at confluence.mycompany.com.

2. It creates a separate sandbox environment for Confluence, where testing can take place. No current business projects or activities take place here. It's the place to try things out, not to get work done. It looks very similar to the production

environment, except for different branding at the top to remind users that it's the sandbox version. It's accessible internally at <u>confluence-sandbox.mycompany.com</u>.

People get an invitation to both environments. Soon work starts to happen on the production environment, while testing of ideas starts to happen in the sandbox. In order to set clear expectations, a few simple guidelines are posted in a prominent location in the sandbox. People are reminded via visual cues that this is not for critical business projects, it's a safe place to try things out, and there is a 30-day lifespan for wiki pages. Simple rules like this are essential for the sandbox to work.

Over the subsequent weeks, the following takes place:

- A group in marketing uses the sandbox to brainstorm a new campaign. They used to do this process using email and a whiteboard, but try it out using Confluence. As a result, they see how it could work for them, and now want to do all future work like this. They will start all future brainstorms in the production edition of Confluence.

- A group in product development has been using an Excel spreadsheet for tracking the status of beta customers. This has been an error-prone process, resulting in some mix-ups and leading to the inadvertent loss of several expensive beta products. The group experimented with using Confluence instead, and found the errors disappeared because everyone was working off the same page. Now they want to commit to Confluence for this and similar processes.

- The executive assistants (EAs) have always had a strong sub-group culture of supporting each other, and really making the organization hum. But their discussions via email were starting to become overwhelming—too much disjointed discussion and conversation. A few key EAs tried out Confluence as a way of streamlining their discussions, and making previous discussions searchable. The benefits have been immediately obvious, and they want to shift the entire EA community into Confluence.

> You could use the sandbox to show proof-of-concept demonstrations in which the various capabilities of the new technology are brought together for current business processes.

The sandbox can be left as a "try-it-and-see-if-you-like-it" place, but that approach can lead to little being explored. You would need the right people in the groups and teams you are working with to make this approach work. To overcome this risk, one way is to use the sandbox as a place for featuring proof-of-concept demonstrations in which the various capabilities of the new technology could be brought together for current business processes. This gives groups something tangible to explore, and may spark ideas about applicability.

When to Use It

The Sandbox for Experimentation strategy is most appropriate when the technology is a broad-based platform that could be used for many different activities. As a result, experimentation is needed to explore where and how the different options could come together for a certain group.

A second signal is where people in a group have expressed an interest in trying it out first, before committing to using it in their day-to-day work. The sandbox provides a safe place for them to experiment and learn more about the use of the technology, without jumping immediately to real business-critical projects.

Why It Works

The Sandbox for Experimentation strategy works for the following reasons:

- *It's a place to try things out.* A sandbox provides a safe place to try out the new capabilities, and to explore how they could be put together for addressing current business concerns. If someone does something wrong in the sandbox, business operations are not compromised.

- *It enables people to build competence.* Within a test scenario, people can build competence on using the capabilities—where to click, how to put something together, and how to create links. This competence is directly transferrable to the production system.

- *It reduces the perception of risk.* Since the sandbox is approached from the mindset of exploration and experimentation, people can look at how their current work might be improved using the new technology, without having to formally commit to using it first. This reduces perceived risk of failure. If it doesn't work, nothing is lost.

People can look at how their current work might be improved using the new technology, without having to formally commit to using it first.

- *It provides a place for social learning and group re-imagining.* Before committing to a major change, many people like the opportunity to try things out first. A sandbox provides a group with the ability to sit down together and explore what could happen if they worked in a different way. Their current process has not been changed, and they haven't committed to the new way. But they have taken a significant first step towards that future state.

Data from Survey 2012

Figure 8-7. Data from Survey 2012 for the Sandbox Strategy

Use of the Sandbox for Experimentation Strategy
Percentage of respondents using the strategy sometimes or frequently

Effectiveness of the Sandbox for Experimentation Strategy
Effectiveness rating by respondents using the strategy sometimes or frequently

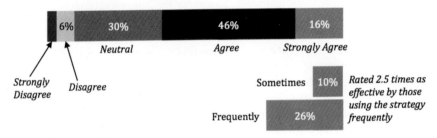

Highest Use in the Adoption Lifecycle
Use of the strategy correlated with length of time working on adoption

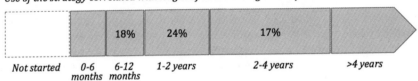

Complementary Strategies
*Other adoption strategies most commonly
used with Sandbox for Experimentation*

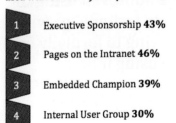

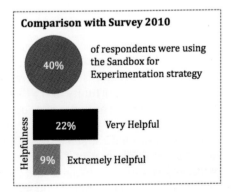

The sandbox strategy is commonly used as a way of providing opportunities for learning and experimentation. One in four respondents use the strategy frequently at their organization.

Examples and Case Studies

The sandbox strategy has been used by various organizations to encourage user adoption. Here are some examples and case studies:

- At a state government agency in the United States, Central Desktop was the tool of choice. The sandbox strategy was used to enliven applicability: *We set up the sandbox first so people could "play" with Central Desktop, and held a demonstration to show them how the new tool would be used to improve their current operations. We solicited feedback and incorporated changes when things didn't work the way the users needed them to. We collected input from the external user community on its effectiveness and demonstrated an actual cost savings on travel expenditures. Usage is increasing as users are becoming more familiar with the tool and gaining confidence in using it.*

- At a small firm in the United States, the sandbox strategy has played an important role in encouraging user adoption. The collaboration manager says, *In our user adoption strategies, building a sandbox and inviting users in worked remarkably well to increase adoption. Team members felt like they had a say in the design of the system prior to the entire system being built. In addition, we had a strong executive sponsor which helped push the system forward. I think most importantly, we utilized the power of social influencers (not necessarily managers) in the team and made sure to invite those into the sandbox first. After they had experience in the system, we asked them to help spread the word in their individual departments. This strategy built excitement about our platform and really boosted long-term (over 6 month) user adoption.*

> Building a sandbox and inviting users in worked remarkably well to increase adoption. Team members felt like they had a say in the design of the system prior to the entire system being built.

- A brewing company uses the sandbox strategy to provide new teams with a way to try out a SharePoint team site without affecting the production environment. Teams can get a sense of what is possible in SharePoint, and then request a team site for production purposes.

Attendees at the User Adoption Strategies workshop says that it's important to use the sandbox strategy with people who have a real reason to use it. People should have a specific set of tasks to accomplish, or a clear objective when using the sandbox. It shouldn't just be made available to anyone without any oversight, guidance, and the availability of coaching support.

Strategy 3.5 Easy First Steps

It can be pretty mind-blowing to hear about all the things you can do in a new system, but mind-blowing is a big turnoff to second wave people. Too many options and configuration choices decreases their interest. An Easy First Steps strategy provides a way of addressing this risk.

Description

New systems appear overwhelming to new users, even after they understand the basic concepts. Thus you need to make the first steps into the new system as easy as possible. This strategy makes a conscious decision to downplay all the possibilities of a new system—"It can do this," "It can do that," "It can also do this other thing!"—and instead lay out four to seven must-do activities. The approach works because it breaks down the perceived barriers to taking that first step. This strategy can also be used as a Making It Real strategy in Stage 4, but it is put here because its role starts in Stage 3.

> The Easy First Steps strategy represents a conscious decision to downplay all the possibilities of a new system, and instead lay a few must-do activities.

How to Use It

Create a set of "Easy First Steps" that people can do quickly and easily. Let's use IBM Connections as an example when considering how the strategy could be used. IBM Connections offers capabilities that can be used across a broad variety of business scenarios, but this breadth can also be intimidating. Following the Easy First Steps strategy would mean that a new user—Victoria—follows a narrow range of instructions on how to:

- Upload a recent picture into her Profile, if one hasn't been automatically loaded.

- Write a few lines in her Profile about the focus of her work, and if appropriate, her non-work life.

- Invite a colleague to join her in IBM Connections.

- Use search to discover and join a community in IBM Connections that holds professional interest.

- Contribute a Web page to the shared bookmarking portion of IBM Connections, and add descriptive tags so others can find the page easily.

These Easy First Steps provide the initial pull for Victoria to start using IBM Connections, give her some real-world exposure to the different capabilities, and enable her to benefit quickly from what other people are already doing in IBM Connections. While the five examples above are generic activities, they are broadly applicable within Connections and similar collaborative systems. A more tailored list could be created for particular needs.

Gamification approaches can be used within the Easy First Steps strategy. ISW Development, an IBM Business Partner in Australia, offers an add-on gamification tool for IBM Connections called Kudos Badges.[7] The design intent is that Connections administrators can set up badges for people to earn, by doing various activities in Connections. For example, if they make an activity update, create a blog post, and join a community in Connections, they can earn the "New Users Badge." Within the context of the Easy First Steps strategy, ISW's Kudos Badges could be used to show new users when they have completed the four to seven first step activities. Speaking more strategically, a well-constructed gamification approach can be used to focus people on creating value for other people and the organization through how they use the system—for example by reinforcing the need to tag files to ease findability.

When to Use It

With its emphasis on "first steps," this strategy is ideal when people return to their own work environment after the Stage 2 activities have been completed. They have an appreciation of what can be done, and the Easy First Steps gives them a place to start.

The strategy can also be used when new functionality is added to the current technology, and there is value and benefit seen in embracing it. Make it easy for people to start using the new capabilities, by laying out the first steps.

Why It Works

The Easy First Steps strategy works because it breaks the conceptualization of the system as something "out there and unknowable and so wildly complex that I'm not going to even try" into a set of defined, closed-ended activities that someone can do, and clearly see they have done. By following the easy first steps, the person gains a sense of accomplishment—"I did it!." They may also gain a boost in confidence—"Perhaps I can use this new system after all." This lays an essential foundation for wider exploration about how the new technology can be used within the context of group and team activities.

> The strategy works because it breaks the conceptualization of the system as something "out there and unknowable and so wildly complex that I'm not going to even try" into a set of defined, closed-ended activities.

Data from Survey 2012

Figure 8-8. Data from Survey 2012 for the Easy First Steps Strategy

Use of the Easy First Steps Strategy
Percentage of respondents using the strategy sometimes or frequently

Effectiveness of the Easy First Steps Strategy
Effectiveness rating by respondents using the strategy sometimes or frequently

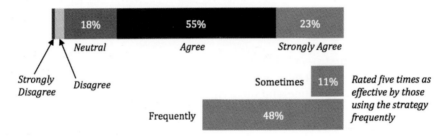

Highest Use in the Adoption Lifecycle
Use of the strategy correlated with length of time working on adoption

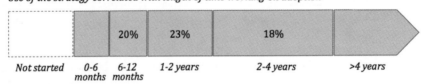

Complementary Strategies
Other adoption strategies most commonly used with Easy First Steps

1   Executive Sponsorship **42%**

2   Pages on the Intranet **43%**

3   Embedded Champion **37%**

4   Internal User Group **30%**

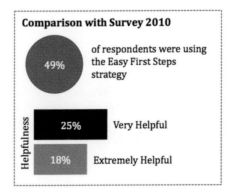

Comparison with Survey 2010

49% of respondents were using the Easy First Steps strategy

Helpfulness

25%   Very Helpful

18%   Extremely Helpful

Four out of five respondents make some or frequent use of the Easy First Strategy. It provides an effective approach for getting users into the new collaboration technology.

Examples and Case Studies

Here are some examples of how different organizations are using the Easy First Steps strategy:

- *We assign tasks—very simple tasks—to individuals who are challenged with these tools to quickly increase their confidence. This has led to early adoption.*

- *We focus on making it easy to use. In fact all steps have to be easy-to-use, otherwise the first major problem the user experienced could negate adoption. We had to return to the user often, especially early in the process to assess usage. Early acceptance is important.*

- *As a small team, informal communication of what, why and how was sufficient. It is important to have a tool with a relatively low learning hurdle to minimize frustration, as well as integrating into existing ways of doing things, such as email. Using the tool for simple tasks like document sharing and using email notifications draws people into the tool.*

> It is important to have a tool with a relatively low learning hurdle to minimize frustration, as well as integrating into existing ways of doing things, such as email.

- In rolling out SharePoint, a firm in the United States took the approach of "Start Personal," with a focus on activities that staff members could do. For example, they didn't turn on all of the features when they released My Site, but made enough capabilities available so people could start using it.

As you can see from the above experiences, some organizations also focus on making the first uses of the tool easy to do. Simple activities like new ways of sharing documents or profile information are emphasized early in the adoption journey, paving the way for more complex activities later on. As people learn what they can do with the tool and gain personal hands-on experience, this creates a willingness to consider more advanced applications, along with the competence to go with it. In the final analysis, this approach shows respect for people's current understanding and abilities, and gives them an easy way to start using the new technology. It doesn't start with highly complex activities, nor activities that are far removed from the current day-to-day activities of people.

Strategy 3.6 Build It And They Will Come

The final major strategy we will discuss for Enlivening Applicability is "Build It And They Will Come." For all the bad press I've given this strategy earlier in the book, it can actually work—if done right, within the right environment, and if the prerequisites are met. Let's stand back and discuss when this strategy can work.

> The desire is for grassroots adoption and advocacy of the new technology, fueled not by directives or encouragement from IT but rather from loud and persistent advocacy from people in the business.

Description

The Build It And They Will Come strategy for new collaboration technology involves a light-handed approach. The desire is for grassroots adoption and advocacy of the new technology, fueled not by directives or encouragement from IT but rather from loud and persistent advocacy from people in the business. It's the strategy that everyone in IT wishes would work, and it can—sometimes.

How to Use It

The Build It And They Will Come strategy can be used, but there are major prerequisites before it will be successful.

1. *Reputation of Greatness*. You can use it to encourage user adoption, but you must have a reputation within the business of being amazing. Specifically, this means you have introduced new systems, technologies, and approaches that have worked fantastically well, and people actively talk about it. This reputation is built over time from your previous feats.

2. *Rabid Fan Base*. You can use the strategy to encourage user adoption if you have created a set of rabid fans within your organization who will actively embrace what you put out. They will champion the cause, advocate for its use, and lead the charge against the ingrained ways of doing things and the people opposed to the change. Your fan base will pick up the new things you offer, and make it happen.

3. *Relevant Broadly Spread Conceptualization*. You can use it to encourage user adoption if your users have clear experience with a previous generation of the same product category, either within your organization or from previous employers or their private lives, and they are able to see a clear picture of where and how they could use it now. Your users understand what could be, and intuitively "get it."

4. *Proximity to Where Business Gets Done*. You have deep connections with the people in your organization who are on the front lines of business. Based on your

engagement work with them, you have a clear understanding of what they need to work in better and more enhanced ways, and this understanding is shared jointly with them. You know what can make their work easier. They know that you know. You are both working towards the same goal.

Those are four major prerequisites. Given that these conditions are not generally met, one of two things usually happens:

- *Absolutely Nothing.* The new system is ignored. No one uses it, because they can't see the benefit or value. This is a massive failure.

- *Absolutely Everything.* Everyone embraces it, but in different ways, with no oversight, resulting in overlapping and conflicting ways of using the new technology. The environment becomes a mess. This is also a massive failure.

When to Use It

If you meet the four prerequisites above, feel free to try the Build It And They Will Come strategy. If not, don't even think about it. Work with other Stage 3 strategies instead, building competence, results, and reputation. Perhaps in future years you can come back and try this strategy.

Why It Works

The Build It And They Will Come strategy works in particular situations only, and usually only when people already have a high degree of maturity in their understanding about what's possible and how to use the new technology. In such a context, the strategy works because:

The strategy only works in particular situations, and usually only when people already have a high degree of maturity in their understanding about what's possible and how to use the new technology.

- It's treated as business as usual. Apart from the technology, nothing else is changing. It's just a new set of technologies for a pre-existing process.

- It doesn't require a conceptual leap about how to do work. It is merely a tooling change, an upgrade, or a refresh of what has already been offered for some time.

Data from Survey 2012

Figure 8-9. Data from Survey 2012 for the Build It And They Will Come Strategy

Use of the Build It And They Will Come Strategy
Percentage of respondents using the strategy sometimes or frequently

Effectiveness of the Build It And They Will Come Strategy
Effectiveness rating by respondents using the strategy sometimes or frequently

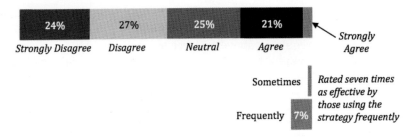

Highest Use in the Adoption Lifecycle
Use of the strategy correlated with length of time working on adoption

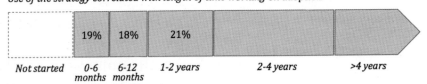

Complementary Strategies
*Other adoption strategies most commonly
used with Build It And They Will Come*

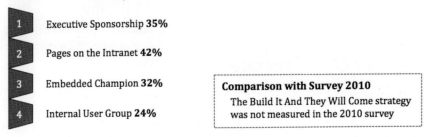

1 Executive Sponsorship **35%**

2 Pages on the Intranet **42%**

3 Embedded Champion **32%**

4 Internal User Group **24%**

> **Comparison with Survey 2010**
> The Build It And They Will Come strategy
> was not measured in the 2010 survey

While the Build It And They Will Come strategy is commonly used, over 75% of respondents were neutral or disagreed with its effectiveness as a user adoption strategy.

Examples and Case Studies

Here is an example of an organization that succeeded with the Build It And They Will Come approach:

- *Most of the time the best way has been to just let people know what's available. When we started using Google Apps for Business, most people didn't realize there was a feature called Sites they could use as a wiki. A few of us mentioned it to people when they wanted to share information, and eventually Sites started popping up and people starting using it.*

As might be expected, trying to use the Build It And They Will Come strategy without the required groundwork often leads to failure. Survey respondents commented on the pain they were experiencing in using the strategy:

- *We started with the "Build It And They Will Come" strategy for IBM Connections which didn't work with our business. The project was also run by the IT team. Based on our experience, we don't recommend that IT leads the project—it should be defined and run by the business to meet the business needs. We had to change track a year ago and started to define what we actually needed IBM Connections for. This involved an iterative process of gathering and refining requirements, and creating a plan for how we could measure the progress of adoption and performance improvements. We were then able to target areas of the business we knew would benefit and concentrate on them. In doing that we found the other areas of the business picked up their usage and are beginning to make progress in adoption.*

> Our approach is "build it and they will come," and too often there is no clear strategy behind development and implementation. It's no more than visions and ideas inside a few executives heads.

- *The User Adoption Strategy in our organization for SharePoint is really weak, or more like non-existent. Our approach is "build it and they will come," and too often there is no clear strategy behind development and implementation. It's no more than visions and ideas inside a few executives heads. I would love to start again and convince the decision makers of the importance of better user adoption strategies.*

Attendees at the User Adoption Strategies workshop often say how much they wish this strategy would work more often, but after we have talked through the nature of second wave people, the theory of change, and the user adoption model, they begin to see why it usually won't work. Thankfully there are many other strategies that can be used to help people make the transition to new ways of working.

Other Enlivening Strategies

The above sections have looked at six major Enlivening strategies for user adoption. In this section, we turn our attention to three smaller, supportive strategies which can be used towards the same end. Each strategy is dealt with in less depth, and no survey data is reported for these strategies.

Strategy 3.7 Give It, Remove It, and See Who Yells

One of the clear objectives of your work with the different user adoption strategies is to discover people in the business groups who are able to make the conceptual leap from how they work today to how they could work tomorrow and into the future with new collaboration technology. You can use audit logs from your collaboration technology to discover this, or you can use a different approach.

The "Give It, Withdraw It, and See Who Yells" strategy is one way of taking a different approach. Imagine this setting. You decide to implement a new technology for a particular process. You get some early adopters to talk about what they've done with it, and how it's helped them (Stage 1). You provide training via the classroom and the Web (Stage 2). You make the new technology available, and do some work with particular groups around how they could use it (Stage 3). Then you leave for a couple of weeks, and see what the groups do. And then you turn it off. They can't get to it. They can't see it anymore. And you wait to see who yells.

> The "yellers" are the people who are really passionate about the new collaboration technology and approach.

The "yellers" are the people who are really passionate about the new collaboration technology and approach.

- They will demand it back, saying "How dare you take this away when we were using it for our project!"

- They will show they have "got it." They understand what can be done and have embraced the new way of working, with an eye to future possibilities as well. You've hooked them; now don't let them get away!

- They will have seen the benefits that accrue from changing the way they work, and don't want to lose the benefits.

Clearly you'll have to use this strategy with care, because it can quickly make enemies. When you do give it back—and do so quickly—be sure to explain what you were doing. And promise never to do it again! In any case, you will need to make sure that the next time they want it, it is definitely accessible to them. Otherwise they may really lose faith in the system, and you will lose your greatest advocates.

During the discussion time after a recent User Adoption Strategies seminar, Greg, one of the attendees, relayed his experience with this strategy. His group had been talking long and hard about the value of discussion groups for knowledge sharing and collaboration, and had seen some minor interest, only to have it fizzle out and die away after a few open discussion groups had been set up by the Intranet manager. Greg said:

> So we turned discussion groups off, and would you believe it, sometime later we had the secretaries in our firm come and ask for a private discussion group. When they had a clear and immediate need for a discussion forum, along with an inkling about what COULD be done from someone in the group who had prior experience with such things, then they were prepared to find a different way to get together. Using technology we already had available, the new discussion group has come together excellently, quietly guided by two people in the group keen to see it succeed.

Strategy 3.8 Early Public Encouragement

Do you like doing things for no benefit? Whether the benefit is extrinsic (you get something for doing it) or intrinsic (you get an inner warm-fuzzy for doing it), the benefit is a helpful signal to keep going. The Early Public Encouragement strategy is a way of giving feedback about someone's involvement and use of the new collaboration technology, showing that people are listening and getting value. This encourages the person to keep going, rather than feeling as though they are speaking into a vacuum. For example, you could show early public encouragement in the following ways:

> The Early Public Encouragement strategy is a way of giving feedback about someone's involvement and use of the new collaboration technology, showing that people are listening and getting value.

- Leave a comment on someone's blog post. For example, a project leader could comment on a blog post in the collaboration space. Feedback and involvement needs to be actively practiced, or people will lose heart and give up.

- Make a blog post about a colleague's recent blog post, and link back to the original blog post. This shows that others are listening and taking an active part in exploring how the new technology could become part of daily life.

- Refer to blog posts or discussion contributions in meetings or during conference calls. Allow it to become part of the fabric of how the group works together.

The strategy works because it reinforces that others are listening and getting value, and that the new technology is real in the group or team context—because real people are seeing and responding to what's being said. This is part of the Enlivening Applicability stage because people start to see that it actually works.

What starts as a deliberate strategy should give way to "The way we work around here." Use the new technologies to facilitate interaction and conversation—leaving a comment on someone's blog, or repeating one of their statements on Yammer—goes a long way to showing the effectiveness of the medium. But while this starts as an explicit strategy in the short term, it eventually becomes just the standard way of doing things—the way to work, the way to communicate, the way to have conversations, the way to request and gain feedback.

Strategy 3.9 Social Pull Through Invitations

The final enlivening strategy is "Social Pull through Invitations." This strategy involves making a conscious effort to invite other people to view, check out, read or comment on something in the collaboration technology that's being used. It's about people reaching out to other people and pointing out discussions, blog posts, or happenings of potential value to them and their work.

The strategy helps with the enlivening stage because it demonstrates that real stuff is going on inside the new collaboration technology. Other people are working in there. Other people are sharing their thoughts, managing their projects, writing blog posts and getting feedback, joining and contributing to groups. Once people see what's going on, and how other people are getting value, there's a chance that they will want to come back again.

> The Social Pull strategy is about people reaching out to other people and pointing out discussions, blog posts, or happenings of potential value to them and their work—creating interest by showing that real life is taking place in the new system.

You may have to invite them a few times—pointing out stories of interest, news items of value, discussions of relevance, and so on. If they still aren't getting it, walk to their desk (if you can), have a chat to them, and show them how to subscribe for updates to particular items. Then you won't have to do it as such, but they'll be prompted for involvement based on what's going on inside the system.

Summary

In this chapter, we have looked at six major strategies for helping people embrace new collaboration technology, with a focus on exploring and enlivening the applicability of the new technology to their work. The strategies in this chapter emphasize the value and benefits that come to a group, team or organization as a result of embracing the new technology. This stage requires the foundational work of the two previous stages— Winning Attention and Cultivating Basic Concepts.

In the next chapter, we look at the final stage of the Four Stages Model of User Adoption: Making It Real. During the final stage of your work, the strategies are focused on doing things that make the new technology real in the context of work. It's not optional. It's not a nice-to-have. It has become the new standard approach—the "new" now.

Sidebar: Give People a Reason to Visit—by Lee Reed

People will only visit SharePoint and use it as a primary information source when the pain of accessing the information any other way is greater than accessing it through SharePoint. Giving people a reason to visit, then, may be as simple as providing up-to-date information, access to common forms, automated information routing and providing access to information that simply cannot be found elsewhere.

Keep Information Current, Remove Old Content

Deleting aged information is one of the most difficult things for information workers to do. We generally have the mentality that we should keep everything we create simply because we might need it 'someday.' This is a fine strategy for us to adopt when we store our files on a network share but it's not acceptable when we view 'old' information within our intranet. When we see out of date information on our Intranet or Internet site we begin to discount all of the information on the web site. Why is there this difference between what's available on the network share and what's available on the Intranet? I bet it has something to do with the fact that we've grown accustomed to old information being stored on our network drives. If we associate 'old' with 'network' then we're not surprised when we encounter old info on the network. The other side of this coin is that we associate browser-based web sites with 'new.' Therefore, when we see 'old' information on a platform that we expect to contain 'new' information, we are surprised. This makes it all the more important to remove aged content from SharePoint, such as old documents, aging budget information and previously important contact names and numbers. Information that is removed from SharePoint can be placed in an archive location that allows users access to it while not representing itself as 'current.' Keep all the information that is presented on your SharePoint sites as current as possible and remove old content with a vengeance. This will give people a reason to visit—to see the latest information that's available on a particular topic.

Create SharePoint-Only Information

When you are attempting to modify the behavior of your user community and have them adopt SharePoint, one way to get them to use the tool is to create SharePoint-only information. This information will only be found on SharePoint and will not be emailed, printed, distributed or communicated in any other fashion outside of SharePoint. Good examples of this are messages from the CEO about corporate performance, strategic focus for the fiscal year, a departmental budget submission process and sales figures. Any type of information that forces the user to go to SharePoint will contribute to increased adoption of your SharePoint solution. Consider providing content that probably hasn't ever been created and socialized within your organization previously, such as a Podcast with your corporate Vice President, a video showing an overview of the new corporate headquarters or a webcam that shows who is sitting in your lobby. Providing content only on your SharePoint sites make your SharePoint sites attractive to your users and they will repay you with increased use.

"SharePoint Will Support Our Existing Collaboration"

People are often led to believe, through even the most well-intentioned IT Department, that SharePoint is introducing collaboration into your organization. This mindset communicates that somehow the socialization and sharing of information magically begins shortly after SharePoint is installed and training on how to use it concludes. Truth is, collaboration is already occurring every day within your company. Each meeting, project status report, document review and hallway conversation defines the collaborative nature of your organization. Your mindset, therefore, should shift from "I will implement SharePoint to enable collaboration within my company" to "I will be implementing SharePoint in support of the collaboration that's already occurring in my company." As you work to implement SharePoint, seek out every opportunity to apply its capabilities to increase the efficiency of the collaboration that is already occurring rather than searching for new places to apply this technology.

Communication, Not Technology, Is The Success

Keep in mind that a successful implementation of SharePoint doesn't mean that the technology is implemented successfully. A successful SharePoint implementation is one in which communication amongst diverse areas of the business or geographic locations increases. It means that a department or project is now creating documents communally rather than individually. It means that people are beginning to see the benefits of sharing information and are contributing their knowledge for the common good of the company. With SharePoint it's very easy to focus on all the nuances of the technology and its implementation. What web part should you use? Do you need to purchase a third party web part to accommodate a particular need? How much storage do you need to plan for so you don't run into problems down the road? These are important issues, but they aren't the most important things to focus on in your user adoption efforts. SharePoint's greatest uplift for your organization comes from the demolition of the silos of information that have existed in your organization for some time and allow the information to be freely available for people to make real business decisions.

About Lee Reed

Lee is a SharePoint Consultant in Atlanta, GA and has held technology leadership positions in the healthcare, commercial real estate, multifamily, consulting and legal industries. He is laser focused on assisting companies to leverage their technology investments with a driving passion around demystifying technology to drive collaboration success.

www.linkedin.com/in/leereed

---

[1] Chris Yeh is the Vice President of Marketing at PBWorks (www.pbworks.com), a provider of hosted collaboration solutions for business and education customers. This quote is drawn from a comment Chris contributed to Lee Bryant's August 2009 blog post, *Behavioural transition strategies for E2.0*, at www.headshift.com/blog/2009/08/behavioural-transition-strateg.php.

[2] Think about it this way. The new technology has been approved for implementation within your organization based on a proposed vision of how it could improve the effectiveness or efficiency of the way work gets done. Depending on where the technology sits on a continuum between a broad-based platform for getting a variety of work done better, to a tightly-focused solution for a particular end result, will determine how much freedom you have in your Stage 3 activities. If the technology is a broad-based platform, you will have more freedom to explore how and where it can be tailored to improve the work of a particular group. If it is a tightly-focused solution, you will have less freedom.

It is unlikely you will be able to fundamentally revise what the technology is actually used for. If you discover, as part of your Stage 3 activities, that the Engagement or Scenario Development processes were fundamentally flawed, you can't fix these within the context of user adoption. You will need to step outside of your user adoption work and go back to the people who were involved in the earlier contextual work. If they are willing to listen and expand the scope, well and good. If not, document what you are learning and find a way of having input into the wider contextual process the next time it happens.

[3] A few years ago I heard about a Boeing study which found it could take upwards of 20 hours to schedule a meeting. Yes, you read that right—merely to schedule the meeting to take place! That's a pretty horrific statistic, and a colossal waste of time. For more, see my June 2006 blog post at currents.michaelsampson.net/2006/10/20-hours-to-set.html

[4] See my April 2011 blog post for more details, *Improving User Adoption of SharePoint By Streamlining Essential Tasks—the Harmon.ie Study Findings*, at currents.michaelsampson.net/2011/04/harmonie-sharepoint.html.

[5] See the discussion and link to Don's paper at *Benefit of Virtual Teams - the BP Experience (from mid-1990s)*, June 2011, at currents.michaelsampson.net/2011/06/bp1990s.html.

[6] See Jack Vinson's blog post, *You can't make me do it*, at blog.jackvinson.com/archives/2010/05/19/you_cant_make_me_do_it.html. To learn more about Patti Anklam and her work in the collaboration space, see www.pattianklam.com.

[7] For more on ISW Development and Kudos Badges, see www.isw.net.au/domino/isw/iswdevelopmentwebsite.nsf/vl-titles/Kudos+Badges and www.kudosbadges.com.

Chapter 9.
Making It Real

 The deployments I have seen succeed the fastest and become the most enduring are those that are built under the backdrop of a defined work process that is better conducted wiki or blog-style than in email, Notes, SharePoint or whatever the alternative. Patterns emerge within these deployments that change their nature and branch into new uses of the technology—but leveraging the core process (or processes) is vital to gaining high participation and sustained user attention. [1]

Jordan Frank, Traction Software

The final stage of the Four Stages Model of User Adoption is to make the new way of doing things real—make it the "new" now. Make it part of daily life. Make it a regular place where work gets done, and the normal thing to do. And most importantly, don't shoot yourself in the foot by failing to do such things as turning off older ways of accomplishing the same work.

In this chapter, you will:

- Explore the importance of making it real for the second wave people at your organization.

- Look into a number of key strategies that make the new technology and approach real.

- Evaluate the effectiveness of the different Making It Real strategies, based on data from the user adoption survey.

- Discover how Landcare Research used the Bulk Loading Party strategy to good effect, and how it turned a group around to become a lead champion for the new approach.

How Do I Know This Is Real?

Here's the question: How do people know that the new collaboration technology and approach is "real"? Sure, we have spent three distinct stages winning their attention, cultivating their understanding of the basic concepts, and enlivening applicability of the new technology, so perhaps the answer is that we want them to believe it is real based on the effort we have expended. But what makes it real to them? The answer: The new approach has become the "new standard" way of doing things. In practice, this means:

- *Business gets done in the new system.* Regular business processes are accomplished using the new collaboration technology and approach.

- *Alternative systems are removed.* Previous ways of accomplishing the same work are removed, either technically by preventing changes to documents and data in the old systems, or socially through the establishment of new group norms.

- *Other people expect you to use it.* Peers and colleagues are actively using the new technology and approach to get their work done, and they expect others will do the same. They also wonder why some people have not yet made the transition.

- *The new system becomes invisible.* The "new standard" way of doing work starts to become invisible to the people using it. That it was "recently new" starts to be forgotten. People have used it frequently enough that they know how to use it, and have internalized what they need to know to use it efficiently.

- *The new system is integrated with other systems.* For organizations subject to regulatory requirements, the new system is integrated with compliance management systems. If content archiving is a standard requirement, the new system integrates with the current archiving tools.

Strategies for Making It Real

Four major strategies can be implemented to make the new technology and approach real, and these are explored in this chapter:

1. Zero Other Options.

2. Stop Doing, Start Doing Patterns.

3. Bulk Loading Party.

4. Internal User Group.

The chapter finishes with a brief review of several supportive strategies.

Survey Snapshot

Figure 9-1. Snapshot of Survey Results for Stage 4

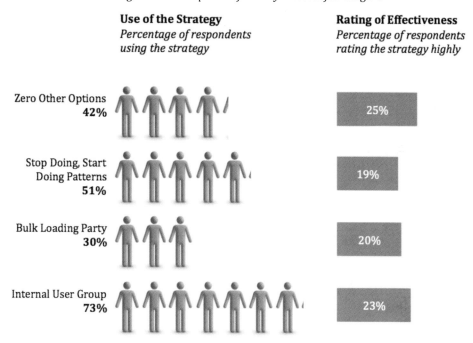

Use of the Strategy
Percentage of respondents using the strategy

Rating of Effectiveness
Percentage of respondents rating the strategy highly

Zero Other Options 42% — 25%

Stop Doing, Start Doing Patterns 51% — 19%

Bulk Loading Party 30% — 20%

Internal User Group 73% — 23%

Highest Use by Size of Organization
Most commonly used strategies by size of organization (number of employees)

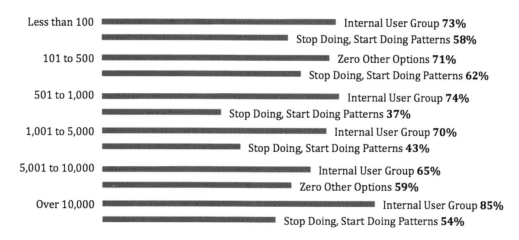

Less than 100 — Internal User Group **73%**
Stop Doing, Start Doing Patterns **58%**

101 to 500 — Zero Other Options **71%**
Stop Doing, Start Doing Patterns **62%**

501 to 1,000 — Internal User Group **74%**
Stop Doing, Start Doing Patterns **37%**

1,001 to 5,000 — Internal User Group **70%**
Stop Doing, Start Doing Patterns **43%**

5,001 to 10,000 — Internal User Group **65%**
Zero Other Options **59%**

Over 10,000 — Internal User Group **85%**
Stop Doing, Start Doing Patterns **54%**

The Internal User Group strategy was the highest used strategy, and second in effectiveness to the Zero Other Options strategy.

Strategy 4.1 Zero Other Options

One of the, if not the, biggest roadblocks to the adoption of a new way of doing things is the continued support for the old way of doing things. For managing a project, this could be having the old file server still available. For publishing updates to a blog, it could be the continued support of email distribution lists. The first strategy for Making It Real is called Zero Other Options.

Description

The Zero Other Options strategy requires the removal of other options for collaboration. It's SharePoint, or nothing. The plan is in Central Desktop, or it doesn't exist. Documents are reviewed via PleaseReview, or they don't get reviewed. This means that people have one of two choices regarding the new system—use it and get on with work, or don't and fall behind. It's not a matter of being unkind. It's about how we work now.

How to Use It

Use the Zero Other Options strategy by turning off, making inaccessible, or marking as read-only previous systems through which collaborative work was done. The expectation is set that all work is now to be done within the new system, and under no circumstances is the old system to be used for current work. Note how the technology decision and social expectations come together in the following examples:

> The expectation is set that all work is now to be done within the new system, and under no circumstances is the old system to be used for current work.

- Key discussion points and decisions from meetings are published on the Socialtext wiki, and people are expected to have an RSS alert set up to get them. When the project manager is asked to email the meeting minutes directly, they reply, "It's in the wiki; go and get them from there."

- Once a group has migrated their current documents off the file server into Lotus Quickr, their access rights to the file server are changed. They retain the right to read and delete documents off the file server, but they can't create or save new documents to the file server.

- Updates on projects that are broadcast by email receive replies from multiple people saying "Please post this to the team blog." And then they delete the message.

When to Use It

Don't use the Zero Other Options strategy at the start of the user adoption process! It's too heavy-handed, and will only earn you dislike, active efforts to undermine what you are doing, and an executive rebuff as well.

So how do you use the Zero Other Options strategy? Start with the other strategies outlined in this book—Web-based Training, One-to-One Coaching, and Facilitated Group Re-Imagining. At some point, however, the new system has to become the new place to work. I heard a good example of how to use the Zero Other Options strategy during a recent masterclass. The attendee said:

> *Our engagement approach is to work with a specific group within our organization for three months. We learn about their work, and explore ways of improving their work through the new collaboration technology. During the initial two months we develop a joint understanding of where and how improvements can be introduced, and we build a solution to address their requirements. It is agreed at the beginning of the process, however, that at the three-month mark, they will no longer be able to use their current file shares. We turn them off at the end of our engagement with them.*

Why It Works

The Zero Other Options strategy works because it makes the new system the place where work is done. Alternative, historical systems are no longer available for current work, nor are they treated as equally valid places to get work done. It's the new system, or nothing.

The Zero Other Options strategy works because it makes the new system the place where work is done.

While there is a technology element to this—the old systems are made inaccessible or read-only—there is a much greater social element to it. People see their work colleagues getting work done in the new system, and if they want to get their work done, they will need to as well. People receive requests to review a document that's in the new system, and have to go there to complete the review. Updates on the team project don't come out by email anymore, so if they want to see the original update and have an opportunity to comment on it, they need to visit the team blog.

Another reason for the Zero Other Options strategy is to reduce the number of systems people have to check into each day, or use as part of their work repertoire. Removing older systems and tools reduces the burden for the people in your organization. It provides clear signals about which tools have current and future value, and which ones were valuable in the past but have no future.

Data from Survey 2012

Figure 9-2. Data from Survey 2012 for the Zero Other Options Strategy

Use of the Zero Other Options Strategy
Percentage of respondents using the strategy sometimes or frequently

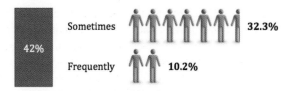

Effectiveness of the Zero Other Options Strategy
Effectiveness rating by respondents using the strategy sometimes or frequently

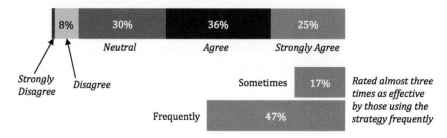

Highest Use in the Adoption Lifecycle
Use of the strategy correlated with length of time working on adoption

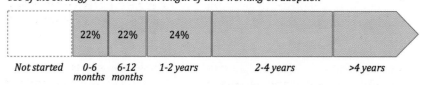

Complementary Strategies
Other adoption strategies most commonly used with Zero Other Options

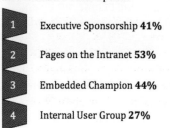

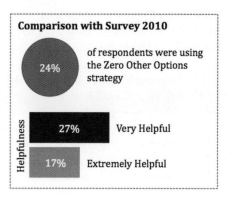

About 40% of the respondents were using the Zero Other Options strategy, and it is rated quite highly for effectiveness.

Examples and Case Studies

Using the Zero Other Options strategy in the right way is important. It's not a Stage 1 strategy—even though many of the people I talk to wish it was! Here's some examples of how different firms have successfully used the strategy:

- A firm in the United Kingdom uses the Zero Other Options strategy as part of its engagement and adoption approach. Specifically, the IT group works with a team of 10-25 people over a six week period. The aim of this time is to introduce them to the new system, provide training and support, give the target team the opportunity to learn where the new tools and approach will be valuable in their work, and to migrate documents and data from the old system to the new one. At the end of the six week period, the old system is turned off, although there is a three month grace period where any documents and data in the old system can be recovered if needed.

> At the end of the six week period, the old system is turned off, although there is a three month grace period where any documents and data in the old system can be recovered if needed.

- A chip manufacturer used the Zero Other Options strategy for driving wiki adoption.[2] Sameer Patel writes, *How did a leading chip manufacturer drive Wiki adoption? Simple: Delete all emails and attachments from the server after 45 days. Everyone flocked to the wiki for fear of losing access to valuable discussions and attachments in the future .... In the case of this un-named company, it worked like a charm for all of its 4000+ employees.*

- In the survey from 2010, one respondent wrote: *We removed the shared file that people were accustomed to using and put all the information into Central Desktop. Any work related to clients had to be entered there. Also, any documents that needed to be approved had to be sent via Central Desktop or we would ask them to resubmit the correct way.*

Finally, in looking at the survey results (Figure 9-2), it's discomforting to note how frequently the strategy is used in the early part of the user adoption process—in the zero to two years timeframe. It's not the best strategy to use at those times, because it comes across as too heavy-handed, and because employees may not have been given the opportunity to see the value of the new collaboration technology before being forced to use it. I would recommend organizations use this strategy less in the zero to two years timeframe and more after that.

Strategy 4.2 Stop Doing, Start Doing Patterns

The Stop Doing, Start Doing Patterns strategy embraces the social nature of collaborative work to encourage people to make the transition from the old way to the new way of doing things. Whether this strategy is used in conjunction with Zero Other Options or not, it provides clear social signaling and agreement about the way to get work done.

Description

Patterns are frequently repeated collaborative activities undertaken within a particular group or team. The pattern could be how projects are managed (assigning tasks on a whiteboard in a meeting room), how documents are collaboratively authored (a Word document sent around by email), or how people are kept up-to-date with what's going on (frequent email blasts).

The Stop Doing, Start Doing Patterns strategy involves discovering the nature of the collaborative patterns being used by an intact team or group, and defining what has to stop, and what has to start in the pattern. The intent is that instead of talking at an abstract level about "collaborating more" or "building better communities of practice," the language is broken down into specific activities that people perform today and an agreement is reached about how to perform these same activities in the new system.

> The strategy involves discovering the nature of the collaborative patterns being used by an intact team or group, and defining what has to stop, and what has to start.

How to Use It

The specific patterns developed with a group or team will depend largely on what they do today, and how and where the new collaboration technology can be used to improve the current patterns. The purpose of the strategy isn't normative—to force a team or group to use a particular pattern if they have no need for it—but rather to be directive if they are using the pattern.

Let's consider a team within an organization. They are in the product development department, and are working on an upcoming and as yet not disclosed new product. The organization is in the high-tech sector, so it's a physical product that will be shipped to multiple locations around the world on release, so it can be stocked in both company-owned and third party retail stores.

The product development team is geographically distributed, but not too widely spread, so they have 3-4 hours a day when everyone is in their respective office during the same slice of time. Until now they have been using a collaborative workspace service to coordinate their work, but are finding it too static and "dead" to enable them to keep up with what's going on. The decision is made to use Yammer (www.yammer.com) as the new cornerstone of working together.

In the language of the Four Stages Model of User Adoption, here's what happened:

- *Winning Attention.* Yammer came to their attention as a result of reading about it in a recent news article on the company Intranet. The IT department featured a couple of Real-to-Life Scenarios based on what other product development organizations are doing with Yammer. A few members of the team have experimented with Twitter, so were interested in learning more.

- *Cultivating Basic Concepts.* The team recently held an in-person intensive three-day "work fest." Everyone came, and a lot of work got done—and a lot of fun was had in spending time together outside of "work." There was a 30-minute classroom training session on Yammer.

- *Enlivening Applicability.* Once everyone was back in their respective offices, the Over-the-Shoulder Watching strategy was used to gain an appreciation of the common collaborative patterns within the group. A business analyst spent half a day with 10 different people, observing the work they did and looking for common patterns. These were discussed and agreed during a recent conference call.

- *Making It Real.* To make Yammer real within the group, it was decided to use the Stop Doing, Start Doing Patterns strategy. With the help of the business analyst, the group has come to an agreement about the key collaborative patterns it embraces today, and how these patterns will be done using Yammer. The analysis and decisions are shown in Figure 9-3.

Figure 9-3. Stop Doing, Start Doing Patterns in Yammer

Pattern	Stop Doing	Start Doing
Finding Expertise	Search profiles in the team workspace	Search Yammer for key phrases.
Advising About New Content	Post into team workspace, leave people to find via alerts	Quick post on Yammer, with link to document or content
Requesting Feedback on Ideas	New discussion thread in workspace	New discussion with a particular hashtag
Sharing Web Links	Link and classification in team workspace	Link and hashtag shared via Yammer
Brainstorming Solutions	Discussion thread in workspace	Brainstorm using a particular hashtag

After defining the key patterns used for collaborating with others today, the product development team decided how they were going to transition those patterns into Yammer.

To support the team in using the new patterns, five two-minute videos were recorded and published on the intranet. Each video featured a team member starting down the path of the Stop Doing pattern, and then had them switching across to the Start Doing pattern. To give everyone access to the videos, each was the subject of a Yammer post, with the hashtag #newpatterns. Everyone in the group was encouraged to subscribe to the #newpatterns hashtag, so they could easily find the videos whenever they needed a reminder about how to enact their team's common patterns in Yammer.

When to Use It

As part of your work in Stage 4, use the Stop Doing, Start Doing Patterns strategy when:

- There are many possible ways of using the new collaboration technology, but you want to help a particular team or group focus on how they can use it best within their current work. The strategy is therefore used to reduce the number of available options.

- It's important for business reasons to incorporate the new technology into the standard way of doing things as quickly as possible. By defining the patterns with the group, they can more rapidly translate the possibilities of the technology into something they will actually do.

- Peer accountability will keep people on track with the new system. For this to work, there will need to be at least a couple of people in the group or team who will set the pace for using the new technology, and who are willing to encourage others to do their work through it too.

Why It Works

When Stop Doing, Start Doing Patterns are done with a particular group or team, the strategy works because it helps with resetting everyone's expectations about how the group's work will get done. Since everyone has had involvement in setting the new ways to perform tasks, tentative starts turn into better ways of collaborating using the new tools. More than that, it gives everyone a new level at which to hold others accountable—in a nice way of course! For example, when Justin sees Lauren start a new discussion in the team workspace, he can remind her that new discussions are now being started in Yammer. Perhaps he even suggests a hashtag for it. Justin's polite pushback and coaching reminds Lauren of the stop doing, start doing pattern.

The main point here is not to "do" the Stop Doing, Start Doing Patterns strategy to a group or team, but to facilitate the process of helping them see the patterns they are using today, and guiding them to understand the options they have for doing things differently with the new tools.

Data from Survey 2012

Figure 9-4. Data from Survey 2012 for Stop Doing, Start Doing Patterns

Use of the Stop Doing, Start Doing Patterns Strategy
Percentage of respondents using the strategy sometimes or frequently

Effectiveness of the Stop Doing, Start Doing Patterns Strategy
Effectiveness rating by respondents using the strategy sometimes or frequently

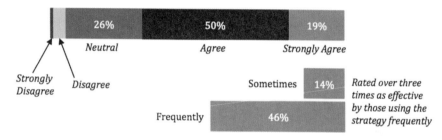

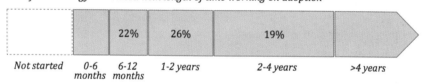

Highest Use in the Adoption Lifecycle
Use of the strategy correlated with length of time working on adoption

Not started	0-6 months	6-12 months	1-2 years	2-4 years	>4 years
	22%	26%	19%		

Complementary Strategies
Other adoption strategies most commonly used with Stop Doing, Start Doing Patterns

1 Executive Sponsorship **44%**

2 Pages on the Intranet **47%**

3 One-to-One Coaching **38%**

4 Internal User Group **32%**

Comparison with Survey 2010

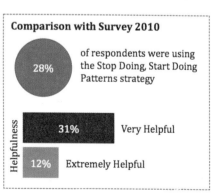

28% of respondents were using the Stop Doing, Start Doing Patterns strategy

Helpfulness

31% Very Helpful

12% Extremely Helpful

Respondents made some use of the Stop Doing, Start Doing Patterns strategy. Those using it frequently, ranked it as highly effective.

Examples and Case Studies

During a recent consulting engagement, Susan Hanley helped a project team to develop a team compact. In essence, the team compact specifies how the team was going to use the various tools in SharePoint for working together. Here's an extract from the team compact outlined in Susan's article for a particular project team:[3]

> We will use the team site template that's been used on other projects—the one that we are either already used to using or will start seeing on everything that we are working on.
>
> We won't email documents to one another—we will just send links to documents in our team site.
>
> We will make sure that all of the work for the project, even documents that are not finished, are stored in the team site.
>
> We will all make sure to use the Status attribute when we share documents, indicating whether a document is a Draft, Ready for Review, or Final.
>
> We will use Ratings to indicate whether a document is potentially reusable or a candidate for a best practice example. (In other words, this is the framework we will use to apply document ratings—this is what ratings mean for our team.)
>
> When we are assigned a task to review a document for a colleague, we will review the document and update the assigned task.

Ruven Gotz tells how the CEO of his company made a pattern real:[4]

> Very early in my career I learned about the power of leadership when it comes to SharePoint. I was working for a consulting firm that had a strategic planning meeting every Monday morning. The CEO would sit at the head of the table with a keyboard and mouse, and his computer would be projected onto the screen at the front of the room. All meeting notes were kept in SharePoint, along with links to key documents, which were also housed in SharePoint.
>
> At one point in the meeting, the CEO asked me about how I was coming along with a particular proposal. I said it was 90 percent done. He wanted to see it and asked me where it was in SharePoint. I said, "Sorry, I have it saved to my desktop, I'll upload it after the meeting." He said, "No, we'll wait while you go and upload it now." From then on, everyone knew: Documents must be saved into SharePoint. I was held accountable for not following the company policy on documents: I never made that mistake again.

Strategy 4.3 Bulk Loading Party

How do you get the team or group to actually make the transition from the old way of doing work to the new way? One gravitational pull to overcome is the existence of their current documentation and project plans in the "old system." If it stays there, it will keep pulling them back into the "old system." Thus the challenge is how to get enough material into the system to make it valuable.

Description

A bulk loading party brings together a group of users for 3-4 days to transfer and migrate as much information as possible from the old system (and old way of doing things) into the new system (and new way of doing things). The benefit of this strategy is that people don't have to straddle two systems, and they gain an in-depth understanding of how to use the new system during the process. For example:

> A bulk loading party means that people don't have to straddle two systems, and they gain an in-depth understanding of how to use the new system during the party.

- Team projects previously managed using a mishmash of tools are giving way to Central Desktop. Documents, project plans, team members, data tracking spreadsheets, and other data is transferred from their current locations into Central Desktop, and put into the correct form.

- Organizational updates will now be done on a new blog, thereby replacing distribution by email. The last 12 months worth of email updates are posted into the blog, denoting the original date of distribution, so the new blog isn't blank and empty. The sense of history is maintained.

- Documents will be authored collaboratively using Atlassian Confluence. People in various groups hold bulk loading parties to transfer the contents of current in-progress Word documents into Confluence, and then include a comment in the original Word document that the new master is now in Confluence, and a link to its new location.

A bulk loading party is only one of the various ways to transfer information into the new system, and has definite appeal due to the social nature of learning that takes place as people work together. Other options minimize the social learning, but still get the information across, such as:

- *Data migration by the IT department.* The IT folks purchase special migration software to transfer the data from the old system into the new, and make any translations in form and structure required. In collaboration technology terms, this happens when a file share is migrated into a SharePoint document library or a Lotus Quickr place. While data migration of this nature can speed the process, there are two drawbacks. First, an opportunity to learn about the new technology within the context of an actual project is lost. And second, the lack of involvement by the actual team can breed contempt for the new system and feelings that it was foisted on them.

- *Old data is marked read-only.* All data in the "old system" is marked read-only, thus putting a clear stake in the ground between "what was" and "what will be." Nothing new can be created in the old system, but old content can be referenced from the new system.

- *Only current data is migrated as needed.* Rather than a one-shot-wonder approach to migrating the data, team members are told to refer to the old space for read-only documents and plans, and if something has to be updated, then they must create a new edition of it in the new collaboration space.

How to Use It

A bulk loading party can be applied broadly for the entire system, or on a project-by-project basis. For example, when a project group is shifting from the old way of working to the new way of working, a party provides the initial impetus to get all current documents and artifacts into the new system.

> A bulk loading party can be applied broadly for the entire system, or on a project-by-project basis.

Here's how to use the Bulk Loading Party strategy:

- *Choose a particular group for the party.* Given the activities you have previously undertaken in Stages 1-3 of the User Adoption Model, you should know of some candidate groups. Choose one group.

- *Set a date and confirm a location.* In negotiation with the group, set a date for the bulk loading party and select an appropriate location. You'll need a room big enough to hold everyone in the group, and ideally one or two projectors at the front of the room. If you can use an existing training room, people won't have to bring their own laptops. On the other hand, some people may want to bring and use their own laptops.

- *Support distributed group members.* If the group includes remote group members, provide a way for them to be involved. You could do this by having an open audio channel during the party, or project remote members on the big screens at the front of the room. If there is food for people at the central location, make sure the remote people can get food too.

- *Set the vision for the day or days.* Start with a 5-10 minute overview of the task for the "party"—a short speech that sets the vision for what the group needs to accomplish. For example, it could be the migration of all documents and discussion threads from the old system into the new system.

- *Review the key steps involved.* The steps involved in moving documents and data from the old system to the new one shouldn't be complex; it's just that they'll have to be done frequently throughout the party. If the Stage 2 Cultivating Basic Concepts work took place more than a week prior to the party, re-establish the basic concepts through a quick demonstration.

- *Provide shortcuts.* If there are ways of streamlining the actions people have to undertake when migrating documents and data, be on hand to suggest those and make them available. Perhaps it's being able to migrate multiple documents at the same time. Perhaps it's a quick script for copying and pasting from one screen to the next.

- *Be available for coaching throughout the day.* As people work through the migration of their data into the new system, they will have questions about the most effective way to do something. Or how to perform a particular action. Or how to create a special link between a couple of items. Be on hand—in the room is ideal—to help out.

- *Do fun stuff.* Have food available—nibbles, chocolate fish, muffins, carrot sticks— whatever would be appropriate. Set up friendly competitions to see who can migrate the most files within a set period of time. Have lunch sitting on the floor. Make the day memorable by doing out-of-the-ordinary activities.

When to Use It

The Bulk Loading Party strategy works best just before a particular group or team starts using the new system. It offers a way for people to learn to use the system through in-depth hands-on experience over a short period of time.

For example, a group is going to switch from using email and file shares to using Lotus Quickr. The group has been working together for a couple of months, so has numerous documents, files and email discussion threads. The group leader calls for a half-day "all-hands-on-deck" bulk loading party, whereby all of the current material still relevant will be shifted into a new Lotus Quickr space. The group meets, they have 15 minutes of just-in-time training, and then are set to work—putting the current material into Quickr. At the end of the four hours, everything of relevance is transferred across, and the session ends with food and drinks to celebrate the transition. Effective immediately, everything in the file share is marked as read-only.

Why It Works

Why does the Bulk Loading Party strategy work? There are seven reasons:

- *It's for a short duration of time.* A bulk loading party creates a defined time and space to get the work done, and get it done swiftly. The migration isn't stretched out over weeks or months, which if it is, makes it easier for people not to take the new approach seriously and fall back into older ways of working.

- *People don't have to straddle two systems.* People are able to make an immediate change from the old to the new, because everything they need is in the new tool. They don't have to straddle two systems.

- *Peer learning at its best.* It's highly social, because everyone is working on the bulk load at the same time, in the same place. When someone has a question, they can ask the colleague sitting next to them.

- *Reinforces basic concepts.* Particular sequences of using the new collaboration technology—uploading and tagging a file, creating a discussion thread—are carried out multiple times in the space of the bulk loading party. This helps with habit formation.

- *Provides in-depth involvement.* It breaks down the new tool into a set of simple things. Rather than being viewed as a single complex system, people can distinguish the different capabilities in the system that perform various functions.

> When the team transfers their information into the new place themselves, it cultivating a sense of ownership and pride in their new system.

- *Cultivates ownership of the new system.* The team transfers their information into the new place themselves, thus cultivating a sense of ownership and pride in their new system. This is much better when compared with the IT team "doing the transition to the team" through automated data migration, and thus losing the opportunity to cultivate ownership.

- *The data gets reviewed by human eyes.* The party provides people on the team with the opportunity to review, check and confirm the data is still valid and useful. Human judgment can be brought to bear on the current importance of particular documents and data, rather than a accumulation of junk being automatically dumped into the new system.

Data from Survey 2012

Figure 9-5. Data from Survey 2012 for the Bulk Loading Party Strategy

Use of the Bulk Loading Party Strategy
Percentage of respondents using the strategy sometimes or frequently

Effectiveness of the Bulk Loading Party Strategy
Effectiveness rating by respondents using the strategy sometimes or frequently

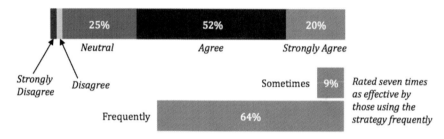

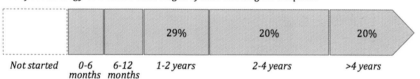

Highest Use in the Adoption Lifecycle
Use of the strategy correlated with length of time working on adoption

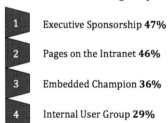

Complementary Strategies
*Other adoption strategies most commonly
used with the Bulk Loading Party strategy*

1. Executive Sponsorship **47%**
2. Pages on the Intranet **46%**
3. Embedded Champion **36%**
4. Internal User Group **29%**

Comparison with Survey 2010

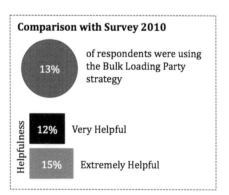

13% of respondents were using the Bulk Loading Party strategy

12% Very Helpful

15% Extremely Helpful

The Bulk Loading Party strategy is not frequently used, but the small number of respondents who do use it frequently say that it is highly effective.

Examples and Case Studies

While holding a bulk loading party is not a commonly used strategy, there are some examples of it being used. Here are two examples:

- A research firm had been using SharePoint for a number of years, and had good usage across many teams and groups. One team, however, was very reluctant to get involved, but this changed quickly when a new team leader was introduced. To help the team rapidly embrace the new system, a bulk loading party was held over a one-day period. The team members got together in a training room and migrated the current documents off their file share into a new SharePoint site—there was some coaching provided at the beginning of the day, and a fun atmosphere was maintained through food, drink, and a light competitive spirit. By the end of the day they had migrated almost everything they needed to start using the new system, and what hadn't been migrated during the day was shifted across pretty quickly in the days that followed. As a consequence of the bulk loading party and subsequent usage of the system, the team transformed from being one of the most reticent to being on the vanguard of wider applicability across the firm. For more on this example, see the sidebar at the end of this chapter.

  > As a consequence of the bulk loading party and subsequent usage of the system, the team transformed from being one of the most reticent to being on the vanguard of wider applicability across the firm.

- A second example comes from a law firm in the United Kingdom. With the introduction of a new document management system, documents from the old system had to be moved into the new one. The lawyers, however, didn't want to play any role in the movement of these documents, and ordered that temps be hired to perform the migration. This duly happened, but the lawyers did not take to what the temps had done. Work and legal meaning is tied up in the documents and items in such a system, and actually a lawyer's interpretation was vital. This signals the importance of having the people in the group involved in the migration of documents and data to the new system.

Getting the dynamics right in a bulk loading party is important, as well as giving people an achievable task. If the team or group has tens of thousands of documents to migrate, the sole reliance on the bulk loading party strategy will backfire. You will need to complement a short-term bulk loading party for some documents with an automated process for migrating most of the documents.

Strategy 4.4 Internal User Group

If you have a good number of people at your organization, say over 100, you can use an Internal User Group as a strategy for Making It Real.

Description

A "user group" is a self-organizing or lightly-organized collection of individuals who share a common usage of a particular thing. It is often used in the context of computer software —for example, the local Atlassian Confluence User Group, the SharePoint User Group, or the Yammer User Group. Such user groups provide ongoing education in the use of the particular technology, with a special focus on its application to business processes and challenges.

An internal user group builds off the same idea and results in the creation of such a group inside your organization. Participation is voluntary, and the group has a focus on continuing education.

How to Use It

Use the Internal User Group strategy to spread good ideas on how the new collaboration technology could be used within your organization. In your travels between different groups and teams, you will come across people doing interesting things. They have applied the collaboration technology in a special way. They have explored some advanced concepts and found a particular benefit from doing so. They faced a difficult challenge, and used the new technology in a certain way to resolve it. Topics of this nature should be shared more broadly across the organization, so other people learn from what their peers and colleagues are doing.

There are two general ways of establishing an internal user group:

> Use the Internal User Group strategy to spread good ideas on how the new collaboration technology could be used within your organization.

1. *Center it on events.* In an event-centric approach, a user group meeting of an hour or so is held once a month at which someone talks about what they are doing. The discussion after the presentation is usually limited to the people who attended the meeting.

2. *Center it on sharing.* In a sharing-centric approach, point-in-time events are deemphasized in favor of continuous sharing and interaction. Someone has a story to tell—and they tell it. Others can read or listen to the story, comment on it, and discuss their reaction and further ideas.

The event-centric approach is best when people are co-located and about 80% of attendees are able to come each month. This builds rapport, and will help other members of the user group to be willing to share what they are doing.

The sharing-centric approach is best when people are geographically distributed, and getting together in person is an infrequent event. You will need collaboration technology to provide a place for the user group to "meet"—including screen-sharing tools for event-style presentations, combined with community forum or discussion board type technology to store those presentations and give people a way to interact around the topics.

Finally, user groups need a moderator. Somebody has to take responsibility in the early days for inviting people to talk about what they're doing, organizing the events, taking an active part in the discussions, reaching out to others and asking them to share their feedback on ideas, and so on. The moderator's work is all part of making the internal user group real.

> User groups need a moderator. Somebody has to take responsibility for inviting people to talk about what they're doing, organizing the events, taking an active part in the discussions, reaching out to others and asking them to share their feedback.

When to Use It

The Internal User Group strategy can be used when you have a sufficient number of people in your organization. You need enough people to provide a diversity of experiences and new ideas to stimulate creative thinking and a willingness to push the boundaries.

The strategy can be used when you want to clearly transition ownership for the use of the new technology and approach to the business. Having people from different business groups explain what they are doing and how they are using the technology in their work, makes it a business-focused community. Finally, when support and encouragement to keep going and explore new ways of using the new technology comes from business peers and colleagues, it is seen as being grounded in the real work of the organization.

Why It Works

Internal User Groups work for a number of reasons.

- *They connect people across the organization*. People working in particular groups and teams can see that others are using the same technologies as part of their work. The technology is real because others are actively using it.

- *They demonstrate real stories*. People hear about what others are doing, and how their work has improved and benefitted from the new technology. It's not just IT spinning a fantasy. For example, when Judith hears how Sarah is using Yammer to ask questions from others inside the firm, she gets an idea of how she too could use Yammer in her work.

- *They spread learning.* The lessons people learn about using the technology as part of their work are spread throughout the organization. This means that other people don't have to do the hard work themselves of discovering the basic steps to success.

- *They offer encouragement to start.* Learning how a group is using the technology in their work will give other people the encouragement to start using the technology. For example, seeing the layout of an online community and a list of current discussions will provide encouragement to another group to try this approach in their own work.

- *They offer encouragement to keep going.* Existing groups and teams can learn about what others are doing with the new technology, and be encouraged to keep going in their own efforts. Yes, there will be speed bumps on the way to mastery, but it's worth it in the end.

- *They give people ownership.* "Real people" from the organization are showing what they are doing in applying the technology to their work. Ownership has transitioned to the business, and people have a voice.

> The user group focuses on doing the work of the organization better, not on the technology itself. Business users talk about how the technology is enabling new ways of working.

- *They promote a business focus.* The user group focuses on doing the work of the organization better, not on the technology itself. Business users talk about how the technology is enabling new ways of working, not that the technology has a particular feature or shiny button.

- *They push the boundaries.* User groups provide a way of introducing advanced concepts and providing a learning pathway for people wanting to do more with the technology. Seeing what one group has done will lay the foundation for people in another group to think how they could apply and extend the idea in their own work.

Given this long list of benefits, it should come as no surprise that the internal user group strategy is widely used as organizations gain greater experience with new collaboration technologies and approaches.

Data from Survey 2012

Figure 9-6. Data from Survey 2012 for the Internal User Group Strategy

Use of the Internal User Group Strategy
Percentage of respondents using the strategy sometimes or frequently

Effectiveness of the Internal User Group Strategy
Effectiveness rating by respondents using the strategy sometimes or frequently

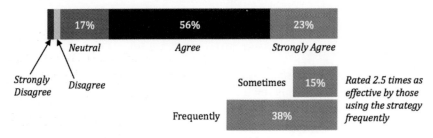

Highest Use in the Adoption Lifecycle
Use of the strategy correlated with length of time working on adoption

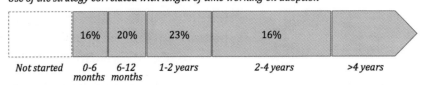

Complementary Strategies
Other adoption strategies most commonly used with Internal User Group

1   Executive Sponsorship **43%**

2   Pages on the Intranet **46%**

3   Embedded Champion **40%**

4   Zero Other Options **10%**
    Stop Doing, Start Doing **10%**

> **Comparison with Survey 2010**
> The Internal User Group strategy was not measured in the 2010 survey

The Internal User Group strategy is the most commonly used strategy for Stage 4. Over 75% of respondents agree or strongly agree that the strategy is effective for user adoption.

Examples and Case Studies

Here are some examples of how organizations have used the internal user group strategy:

- A global software firm had been using a particular collaboration technology for a number of years. The early approaches to adoption centered on exemplar stories and real-to-life scenarios, followed by a few years focused on various training efforts and the development of local champions. As the technology became more and more ingrained in the way the firm worked, an internal user group was established to provide a forum for business users to discuss how they were using the technology to achieve their goals.

- A global insurance firm developed an internal user group to provide a forum for business users to talk about what they were doing with SharePoint, as well as for the collaboration team to talk about upcoming capabilities. The user group met once a month using WebEx, due to the geographical distribution of its staff, and business users were invited to bring a 10-minute live demonstration of how they were using SharePoint in their work. Business users were asked to talk about the challenges they faced, as well as the successes they were achieving.

> The user group helped spread good ideas on how to make effective use of SharePoint to other teams that were just learning or hadn't started on their SharePoint journey.

  The user group was good for people's exposure inside the firm, and it helped spread good ideas on how to make effective use of SharePoint to other teams that were just learning or hadn't started on their SharePoint journey.

- A government agency in the United Kingdom formed an expert group around its new collaboration technology. The experts were drawn from business groups using the technology in their work, and met in person a couple of times a year. The intent was to build communities in the agency around the use of the technology, and to help staff understand the areas of expertise available to them from their peers and colleagues. While there were only a couple of formal meetings of the expert group each year, individuals were encouraged to network with each other and keep the discussions going between meetings.

Other Making It Real Strategies

The above sections have looked at four major strategies for Making It Real. In this section, we look at three smaller, supportive strategies that complement these major strategies. Each supportive strategy is dealt with in less depth, and no survey data is reported.

Strategy 4.5 User Support

In the process of adopting the new way of working, people will have questions. They'll want to know how to do something. They will have forgotten how to link to a particular item. They won't be able to find the command for something they do only infrequently. How you offer support to people at times like this will affect adoption, and the perception of whether the new system is real or not. If there is good and responsive support on offer, they will see the system as being real. If it isn't, they'll quickly come to the conclusion that it's a waste of time.

There are many established ways of offering user support:

- Pages on the Intranet that explain particular functions and how to get particular work tasks done.

- A local champion who is available to give guidance and coaching. It works best if this is part of their job.

- Help lines that connect people to knowledgeable people who can provide real assistance.

User support is important!

Strategy 4.6 Social Recognition of Contributions

A new system becomes real when people start using it to facilitate conversation and interaction. Email works, or at least used to work, because people responded. Yammer works when other people reply to a question you asked, or use a hashtag you just created to give additional context. Blogs work when senior members of the organization leave comments and ask questions. Anything works when people refer to the contributions you have made in real speech—while on the phone, during a meeting, or at the airport.

> A new system becomes real when people start using it to facilitate conversation and interaction. Email works, or at least used to work, because people responded.

Make use of this strategy by encouraging people to recognize the work that others are doing in the new system. Respond to questions. Comment on blog posts. Mention a recent discussion and that person's contributions in the new system at coffee break. The system thus becomes real because it is integrated into the social fabric of organizational life.

Strategy 4.7 Data Pull

As the new system gets used for more and more business activities, there will be an increase in the volume of data held within the system. The Data Pull strategy involves getting people set up with "Saved Searches" or particular queries so that whenever something of interest to them is published in the new system, they are alerted. This could be through a hashtag search in Yammer, an email alert in SharePoint, or an RSS search feed.

The strategy helps with adoption and making it real because it provides a constant reminder of the data that's being added to the system, along with potentially new connections to people who are actively working in areas of interest in other parts of the organization.

> The Data Pull strategy involves getting people set up with "Saved Searches" or particular queries so that whenever something of interest to them is published in the new system, they are alerted.

And You're Done?

Given that we're at the end of Stage 4, does this means we are finished? Unfortunately, no!

You have worked with one or two groups, and now it's time to keep going. As we'll talk about in the next chapter, working through the Four Stages takes time—18-36 months for a large organization.

Before looking at this in more detail, a couple of points of note:

- *Look out for new Exemplar Stories*. Real stories from your organization about how other groups and teams are getting value from the new collaboration technology are very effective in getting new teams onboard. Capture the stories while you can! In addition, tell your executive supporters about what's happening, so they feel comfortable about the active role they are taking in advocating for the continued use of the new system.

- *Work with new teams*. When new teams are formed to take on new projects or as part of an organizational restructuring, work with them to explore how the new collaboration technology can be made real for them. Perhaps there are some

people in the new team who have had previous experience in using the new
technology. If they have had a positive experience, use their experience to the
benefit of the new team.

- *Induct new staff.* When new staff join your organization, provide induction
  training on the new collaboration technology. Since they are coming into an
  established way of doing things, your efforts should focus on helping them
  understand how your organization gets work done.

Summary

This chapter has reviewed four major strategies that can be used for making the new
collaboration technology real within a group or team. The strategies—Zero Other Options,
Stop Doing, Start Doing Patterns, Bulk Loading Party, and Internal User Group—are
focused on translating the potential capabilities of the new collaboration technology into a
set of meaningful things that people do. There is also a high emphasis on leveraging the
power of social factors to transition the new system into the new standard way of carrying
out day-to-day work.

This chapter marks the end of our discussion of the Four Stages Model of User Adoption.
The five previous chapters have introduced the model, and highlighted various strategies
in each stage that can be used to encourage adoption. In the next chapter the attention of
this book shifts to you, and how you can apply these ideas within your work. Chapter 10,
then, is about creating a User Adoption Approach for your organization.

Sidebar: Our Bulk Loading Party—by Mandy Spearing

Landcare Research is New Zealand's foremost environmental research organization, specialising in the sustainable management of land resources, the protection and restoration of biodiversity, the effective management of weeds, pests and diseases, climate change mitigation and adaptation, and more sustainable businesses and communities. Landcare Research has introduced an off-the-shelf collaborative tool that we brand as InfoFile. My role as Information Support Specialist is to train and support InfoFile users, encourage its use as a collaborative tool and to 'champion' collaborative ways of working.

InfoFile is used as a collaborative workspace for science research projects—both as a document repository available for both onsite and remote researchers, and as a collaborative environment for the various teams within the organisation. Recently we have been trying to encourage the use of InfoFile by business teams to enable them to share documents and to develop the use of wikis, discussion boards and shared tasks. Those groups who have started to use InfoFile are now beginning to reap the benefits, but there are still some groups who have not engaged with it at all.

The HR Team and Our Party

Our HR team had some training at the start of this initiative covering the concepts of InfoFile and some of the potential benefits. At that stage they didn't have the time to do any more and were concerned about the confidentiality of their documents.

However, two things happened to change this. Firstly, there have been some changes in staff in our HR team, and secondly, one member of the team became involved in the setting up of another group's site, which has proved to be very active.

They asked me to restart their InfoFile sites and support them in moving their documents from their shared network drives. We had an initial meeting to tease out issues like security, the use of a wiki for their weekly team meetings, etc. I always ask teams what their strategy is going to be for moving their documents into

> I generally recommend that a team starts with new things in InfoFile, copy over anything used on a daily basis and leave the rest as 'read-only.' Otherwise I find that files just get copied across along with all the issues that shared drives bring.

InfoFile and generally I recommend that they start with new things in InfoFile, copy over anything used on a daily basis and leave the rest as 'read-only.' Otherwise I tend to find that files just get copied across along with all the issues that shared drives bring—no version control, folder structures with multi-layers and no regular housekeeping. However, in this case, the HR team wanted to move all their personnel files in one go and start using InfoFile entirely. They also wanted to 'housekeep' their files as they copied them across.

So it seemed sensible to do this as a team event with me supporting them. In essence, we organised a bulk loading party. The key things that worked for us in organising this event were:

- It happened very soon after our initial meeting, before enthusiasm had waned.

- We used a training room with enough computers for everyone to log in and work on loading the documents. I used the computer attached to the overhead projector so my view was on the big screen at the front of the room.

- We organised food—lots of nibbles and treats and cold drinks. It was a long day so it was well worth giving people some treats.

- I had created the site beforehand so everything was ready to go.

- I started by showing the team how to upload documents in bulk, how to use good metadata, and how to apply metadata to multiple documents at the same time.

- We planned for everyone to be there for at least part of the day. In fact not everyone came.

- I stayed for the whole day to field enquiries, make changes, and provide support.

Apart from some initial training in bulk uploading and attaching metadata to groups of documents I really didn't have to do much training before the team were loading things. They decided amongst themselves who would do what and agreed as a group to move the files into a temporary folder after they had copied them into InfoFile. They weren't quite brave enough to delete this copy, but needed to move it so they could see where they had got to. They worked out for themselves how they could filter things to see their own documents and, particularly because some of the team members were fairly new staff, they helped each other with unfamiliar filenames.

My role was to encourage them to use sensible metadata, build views and filters, and to support them generally. This involved some quick thinking and the ability to react to issues as they occurred.

My role was to encourage them to use sensible metadata, build views and filters, and to support them generally. This involved some quick thinking and the ability to react to issues as they occurred. One of these was the general deterioration of speed as more documents were added. So I quickly built some new views that filtered by surnames, for example, Surnames A-E. I have a feeling this would have been a real stumbling block if they had hit this problem back in their office.

To add a bit of light-hearted competitiveness we also had a view on the big screen of the number of documents each person created. At the end of the day we had loaded about 1600 documents and they have continued to add things since then.

Although the day was a great success it was very important to follow up with the team. This has been really easy because the rapport we built up on the day means they are happy to contact me and involve me when they want to change something or when they get stuck. In fact, in only a few weeks, the team has gone from a group who had minimal engagement with InfoFile to one of my best teams of users and I use them as an example to others. I am going to use the same strategy for some other groups where the sticking point seems to be the overwhelming array of documents to be transferred.

> In only a few weeks, the team has gone from a group who had minimal engagement with InfoFile to one of my best teams of users and I use them as an example to others.

Reflections on the Party

In summary, the key benefits were:

1. A good rapport built up between the team and me.

2. A huge number of documents transferred at once.

3. A chance for me to encourage the team to develop some good habits in metadata.

4. A great way to train people where they use what they have learned straight away.

5. A good way for me to learn more about a team's work which helps me to support them better.

On the down side, I would not under-estimate the workload to make this effective. You need to:

*   Prepare things well.

*   Be ready to plan the party very quickly (I had to pull it together in three days).

*   React to things quickly on the day.

*   Know enough to change things quickly as they come up.

*   Follow up with the team very soon afterwards.

I will not use the Bulk Loading Party strategy as my only strategy for engaging groups with InfoFile, but as far as I'm concerned, it's great to have another tool in the armory!

But don't just take my word for it—here's some feedback from one of the team members:

> *From a user's point of view the reason I feel it worked so well was that the team decided this was something we needed to do and we wanted to get on board quickly. The suggestion to make a day session out of it with nibbles to keep it fun, and a day away from our current workload would ensure we got right into it. It was daunting setting things up and we were worried if it wasn't set up correctly before we got started we would hit dead ends when trying to upload the information. This did happen, but having an administrator there ready to change things behind the scenes immediately made a HUGE difference with getting this up and running. We had a great day of fun and left the end of the session confident in our abilities to use the system, thanks to Mandy.*

About Mandy Spearing

Mandy has worked in Information Management roles for over 30 years, in various colleges and universities in the United Kingdom, and at Landcare Research from 2008 to 2011. She is passionate about making systems work for the people who use them, and enjoys supporting end-users in embracing technologies that make their working lives simpler and more effective.

[1] Jordan Frank is the Vice President of Sales and Business Development at Traction Software (www.tractionsoftware.com), an Enterprise Social Software vendor. Jordan has many, many insightful things to say about effective collaboration, and he has been a friend for at least half a decade. This quote is a slightly modified version of a comment he made on Sameer Patel's blog post from May 2009. See *2009 is the year of Enterprise 2.0? Hold your horses...* at www.pretzellogic.org/ 2009/05/19/2009-is-the-year-of-enterprise-20-hold-your-horses/.

[2] Sameer Patel, *How did a leading chip manufacturer drive Wiki adoption?*, Pretzel Logic, July 2009. See www.pretzellogic.org/blog/2009/07/06/how-did-a-leading-chip-manufacturer-drive-wiki-adoption/

[3] Susan Hanley, *SharePoint User Adoption Strategy: Team Member 'Service Level Agreement'*, NetworkWorld, November 2011. See www.networkworld.com/community/blog/sharepoint-user-adoption-strategy-team-member.

[4] Ruven Gotz, *Practical SharePoint 2010 Information Architecture: Proven Tools and Techniques for Architecting Successful SharePoint 2010 Deployments*, Apress, 2012. This wonderful story is from page 198 in Chapter 10 (Governance, Adoption, and Training). If don't use SharePoint, don't let the title put you off—it's a great book for anyone involved in helping people be successful with collaboration tools. See currents.michaelsampson.net/2012/06/ruveng-book-review.html.

Chapter 10.
Crafting Your User Adoption Approach

 Many big organizations have failed with collaboration tools because they focus on the technology, not the human and business stuff. [1]

Andrew Mitchell

We have covered many topics in this book—the organizational context for user adoption, various strategies to encourage user adoption, and survey data on the use and effectiveness of particular strategies. Now it's your turn to pull together the User Adoption Approach for your organization. Providing simple but effective tools for you to do so is the focus of this chapter.

In this chapter, we will:

- Discover the user adoption jigsaw, and how to use it when planning your User Adoption Approach.

- Find out why having a written plan for user adoption is important.

- Be warned about dropping the ball, and how a User Adoption Analyst can help prevent that from happening.

- Learn about the User Adoption Approach taken at Novozymes, and what Frederik would do differently if he could start over.

- Think through some other factors you will need to consider when crafting your User Adoption Approach.

Tools for Your User Adoption Approach

Armed with the theory, strategies, and practical advice in this book, it's now time for you to develop the user adoption approach for your organization. In this section I profile three tools to help you with this task:

- Using the user adoption jigsaw—for planning your approach.

- Having a written plan—for communicating your approach.

- Appointing a user adoption analyst—for keeping your approach on track.

Let's consider each in turn.

Tool 1. The User Adoption Jigsaw

I want you to visualize a jigsaw. It's not a complex jigsaw—it's actually a very basic jigsaw with just four pieces laid out in a row. The four pieces correspond to the four stages in the user adoption model.

Figure 10-1. User Adoption Jigsaw

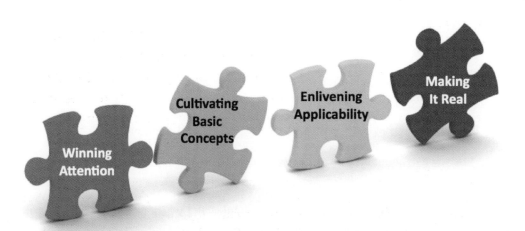

The User Adoption Jigsaw provides an intuitive way to plan your User Adoption Approach. Each piece corresponds with one stage in the User Adoption model.

Here's the big idea. For each stage of the model, make one main strategy your heavyweight. For example, you might choose the following strategies for each of the four stages of the model:

- *Stage 1 (Winning Attention), Exemplar Stories.* Some people in your organization have already been using the new collaboration technology, and have some great success stories to share. Exemplar Stories becomes your Stage 1 heavyweight strategy.

- *Stage 2 (Cultivating Basic Concepts), Web-Based Training.* You work in a large organization, and are blessed to have great content creators on staff who can write excellent content and prepare screen movies about the new collaboration technology for delivery over the web. Also, you want to keep your budget for face-to-face engagements in the third stage.

- *Stage 3 (Enlivening Applicability), Facilitated Group Re-imagining.* You have a pretty good relationship with various groups in the business, and have already fielded some enquiries about group discussions and planning.

- *Stage 4 (Making It Real), Zero Other Options.* Once you have worked through how a particular group can revamp its way of working, you will move to restrict access to previous tools that enabled the previous way of working.

What you have before you is now a draft first edition of your user adoption approach. You have selected a main strategy for each stage of the model, taking into consideration the wider factors in your organization (for example, culture, budget, and geography), the directions in this book about the relative effectiveness of each strategy, and financial considerations for implementation. Different strategies have different cost profiles—that should be very clear.

The reason for taking the "one main strategy for each stage" approach is to give you a focusing device. You don't want to become a headless chicken running here and there with no forethought. Make a deliberate choice about a main strategy for each stage, and then run with it. If it isn't working, by all means go back and re-evaluate why you chose the strategy you did. Perhaps the Web-Based Training in Stage 2 isn't as effective as you thought it would be. Take the feedback from your early attempts, and see if the strategy can be saved. Perhaps it's a matter of wording the text differently. Perhaps it's about using better screen recordings.

Adding More Pieces to the Jigsaw

It's the user adoption "jigsaw" for another reason—it can be extended. For example, you may discover that one strategy is insufficient to achieve the intent of a particular stage—some classroom training is actually required in Stage 2, and Stop Doing, Start Doing Patterns need to be added to Stage 4. You can do it—there is no problem with adding more! The jigsaw allows you to build up or down on a particular main strategy. Just don't do too many strategies and thus lose your ability to focus resources and effort on the heavyweights.

Let's take an example. Gillian is in charge of user adoption for IBM Connections at her firm —all of the pre-work has been done to develop a business vision for where and how IBM Connections will add value to the firm. It has been installed by the IT department, and some early Exemplar Stories have been captured. In planning her approach, though, Gillian is concerned that the Facilitated Group Re-Imagining strategy won't be sufficient in Stage 3 to bring the changes she is hoping for. So Gillian adds two strategies to her jigsaw. The One-to-One Coaching strategy is added so she can gain a better sense of the type of work people do, in advance of the workshops. By doing this, Gillian is hoping that during her one-to-one coaching sessions, she will be able to ask pertinent questions about the way work is done today, and explore the openness of specific team members to using IBM Connections as part of the new way of doing things.

Figure 10-2. Extending Stage 3 of the Jigsaw

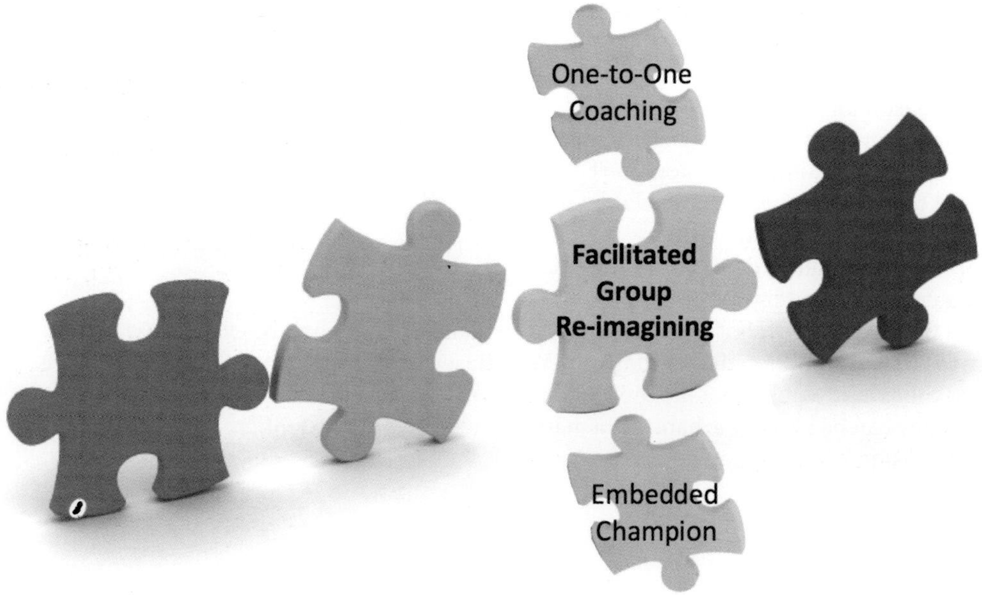

The User Adoption jigsaw can be extended up or down to add complementary strategies to the main strategy for an appropriate stage. Just don't try and add everything!

Gillian also adds the Embedded Champion strategy. She knows that her group does not have sufficient resources to be all things to all people, so part of her challenge is to cultivate a network of supportive people across the organization. The embedded champion strategy works well for this, and Gillian makes a note to look out for key people in each group to approach about receiving special training and joining the champions community she has set up in IBM Connections. If she can't find anyone in a particular group, her back up plan is to ask for a volunteer.

It Takes Time to Complete the Jigsaw

Selecting the jigsaw pieces for your User Adoption Approach may take days or weeks to finalize, but putting the jigsaw into practice across your organization may take months or years. The timeframe hinges on two main factors: the magnitude of the change that's being introduced, and the size of your organization. Let's unpack these thoughts.

> Selecting the jigsaw pieces for your User Adoption Approach may take days or weeks to finalize, but putting the jigsaw into practice across your organization may take months or years.

Selecting the pieces—the act of selection—could be done within a minute if you were so inclined. Draw a circle on your desk, throw all the jigsaw pieces into the air, and whatever lands inside the circle is your Approach. It definitely has the benefit of speed, but is unlikely to be effective.

Therefore, in light of a greater need for effectiveness, take your time in selecting the jigsaw pieces for each stage. Don't take forever, but equally don't do it using the "circle-throw-and-drop" approach. Expect the process of working out your approach to take days or weeks—reading, thinking, discussing with others, and so on.

The bigger timeframe—the months and years—is what's involved in implementing your User Adoption Approach across your entire organization. While you will start with a first edition, there will be mid-course corrections and feedback that can be embraced to enhance the effectiveness of your work—as a suggestion, go back and read the discussion in Chapter 5 ("Is the Process Linear?"). Thus for a new technology that fundamentally re-wires the way thousands of people work together, plan for upwards of 18-36 months work. For new technology requiring a smaller degree of change, or fewer people, plan for a 6-18 month timeframe.

Tool 2. Have a Written Plan

Not all organizations have a written user adoption document or plan. Among respondents to the 2010 survey, only 12% had a written user adoption plan. Among respondents to the 2012 survey, this number had grown to just over 30%—probably reflective of the larger organizations represented among the respondents. Regardless, such low numbers are quite startling given the financial investment in a new collaboration technology. When the respondents were asked about what they wished they had done differently, having a clearer strategy or plan was the number one reaction.

For example, survey respondents said:

> *I wish we had started out with a strategy—what we have done has worked fairly well having just evolved naturally, but we are in a position now where managing the demand for new features and functionality is becoming a challenge. We are the victims of our own success I suppose!*

> *Create a formal user adoption plan; offer more options for learning about SharePoint; most importantly, create an internal SharePoint users' group at the beginning of the rollout.*

> *I would have got more support from executives and planned a strategy. I still have time to work this out, but we need more resources both in staff and financial backing.*

> *If we started again, I would double the funding and effort, rather than the training and communications coming haphazardly or informally. This would be about creating a more coherent message with a running theme that users could relate to and latch on to and follow. Try not to do too much at once, but keep the frequency and relevance of messages high.*

Building on what the respondents said, there are three main benefits to having a written plan:

> **Having a written user adoption document or plan gives you something to show to others, as a communication device, and as a tool to encourage shared thinking and dialogue.**

- *It Makes You Think.* The process of writing down your thoughts shows you have thought through the user adoption challenge, and have developed an approach to dealing with user adoption. Deliberate intent is required to write a plan.

- *It Gives You Something to Share.* You have something to show to others, as a communication device, and as a tool to encourage shared thinking and dialogue. Given the many situations in which new collaboration technologies can be applied, this would be a good thing.

- *It Involves Other People.* It demonstrates that more than one person is involved; it's not a lone ranger approach. As we explore shortly the dynamic around the role of influential people in the user adoption process, having more people involved upfront is a good thing.

By advocating that you write down your user adoption approach, I am not suggesting a long and wordy document that merely takes up shelf space. One page will do, especially for smaller organizations. The one page strategy should contain the written summary of what will happen during the user adoption process—the various strategies you will follow. Use the document to show your completed jigsaw. If required, include more information about why you chose specific strategies for each stage. You can use material in this book for that, complemented by your own experience and perspective from applying the material to your work.

> By advocating that you write down your user adoption approach, I am not suggesting a long and wordy document that merely takes up shelf space. One page will do, especially for smaller organizations.

Tool 3. Appoint a User Adoption Analyst

The biggest danger on starting to implement your User Adoption Approach is to get all excited during Stage 1—signing up executives to support the initiative through words and actions, diligently searching out the Exemplar Stories from people across your organization, and crafting a few Real-to-Life Scenarios to help particular groups expand their thinking about "what's possible." You blow your trumpet loud and long over everything the new approach and technology will bring to your organization. Much appears to be happening. And then you get busy.

- People start calling for more information, and asking how they can get involved.

- Groups want facilitated workshops to help them understand the possibilities.

- Executives start demanding more evidence about the effectiveness of what's being proposed.

And you drop the ball. The momentum peters out. The jigsaw is put to one side, so you can focus on immediate concerns. While some things happen with a few groups, the wider impetus is lost and the benefits of the new technology and approach are limited to a few in the organization. While there is no silver bullet to prevent this from happening, one answer is to appoint a User Adoption Analyst to the project team.

Figure 10-3. The User Adoption Analyst

The User Adoption Analyst has formal responsibility on the Project Team to plan the User Adoption Approach, and ensure it is adequately implemented.

The person in this role could be full-time for large projects, or user adoption responsibilities could complement their other activities. In order for the User Adoption Analyst's work to be effective, though, it is vital that they have some clout within the project to ensure user adoption challenges have been adequately planned and addressed.

Let's explore the job description for the User Adoption Analyst.

- *Plan the Approach.* A User Adoption Analyst has lead responsibility for crafting the User Adoption Approach for the project. This book—and others that deal more deeply with change—will become well-read resources!

- *Own the User Adoption Approach.* The resulting approach is ultimately their responsibility to implement, in line with the work of the wider project team.

- *Advocate for the User.* It's the analyst's role to speak up for the user in project meetings, and constantly remind other members of the team that the project's success is predicated on achieving good adoption. Driving home the message that "adoption is a process, not an event" will be a key mantra for the User Adoption Analyst.

- *Watch Out for Adoption Pitfalls.* When new ideas proposed during project team meetings will have negative consequences for user adoption—new features that will be complex to use, late-course technology changes, or even dropping the user adoption piece all together—it's their formal responsibility to speak up and warn project team members of the dangers.

> When ideas proposed during project team meetings will have negative consequences for user adoption, the User Adoption Analyst has the responsibility to speak up and warn project team members of the dangers.

- *Keep In Touch with Other User Adoption Analysts*. Organizations with many change programs under way will need multiple User Adoption Analysts—at least one on each major project. The people working in these roles will want to get together in-person or through collaboration technology to compare notes and share good ideas. Improving the adoption of new technology and ways of working across the organization can become an aspect of competitive advantage.

The role of User Adoption Analyst is a very clear way to make the user adoption challenge real to the organization. Having someone take responsibility for user adoption in major programs is a critical step forward to finally addressing the lack of adoption for collaboration technologies.

Case Study: User Adoption at Novozymes

Novozymes (www.novozymes.com), a global biotechnology company, introduced SharePoint 2007 for its knowledge sharing and collaboration processes. In this case study, I interviewed Frederik Zebitz[2] about their User Adoption Approach. Frederik also discusses some of the follow-on thinking about what worked well and what they would do differently if they were to start over with SharePoint.

Michael: *Tell us a bit about Novozymes.*

Frederik: Novozymes is the world leader in bio-innovations, and we work with customers across a broad array of industries. We offer biotechnology products for detergents, biofuel, food production, and more. Novozymes is a global company with more than 5,000 employees working in research, production and sales around the world.

Michael: *Why the focus on user adoption?*

Frederik: There were three reasons. Our primary goal is to raise the user's capability with SharePoint so we can maximize the benefits Novozymes receives as a result of its usage. This will perhaps be extended with a focus on raising our users' general IT capability. The second (and longer term) reason is to lower email storage costs, as users really start to link to SharePoint items instead of mailing documents to each other. Third, we hope to reduce search time by using metadata, findability techniques, and improved search technology.

Michael: *What user adoption strategies have you followed?*

Frederik: At Novozymes, we distinguish between four types of SharePoint users—Experts, Site Owners, Members and Bystanders. We primarily focus on the Site Owners group, because we believe that by focusing on the skills of this group we will see more sophisticated SharePoint sites, and that this will encourage other users to participate and eventually to have their own SharePoint site. We hope to see a general movement from Bystanders to Members, and from Members to Site Owners. At the moment we do not address the Experts.

In order to reach our goal, we take the following approach:

- Provide in-house training of Site Owners. This is the "train the trainer" concept, and we offer training materials as well as various exercises available online.

- Provide training packets targeted at departments and project teams, aimed at improving the general user level (for users with the "Contribute" permission in SharePoint). By targeting a department or team as a whole we hope to improve the anchoring of knowledge.

- Provide two levels of support. For level one, it's a wiki with text and screen casts aimed at displaying better ways of doing common work practices. For level two support, there is an IT help system to request one-to-one assistance and specialized training.

- Provide consultancy on the technology, including general team site development, and the Nintex workflow software.

- Keep constantly on the look out for new capabilities that add value to team sites. These often come in the form of third-party products.

- Provide a sandbox, where all employees have been given "Full Control."

- On a larger scale, we run "Town Hall Meetings" on the benefits of SharePoint as seen from a user's perspective.

Michael: *Why did you choose this approach?*

Frederik: It was part of a wider strategy to increase the usability of our corporate IT systems, and explore how Web 2.0 tools could be used at Novozymes. As a Danish company with affiliates around the world, we wanted an approach that could support all of our users, but equally, we didn't have unlimited funding. We feel that the approach we took gives us maximum reach, and has helped to empower the users.

Michael: *What has worked well for you?*

Frederik: The in-house training worked very well, along with the "train the trainer" concept. We also found value from an internal Novozymes SharePoint user community, and the users and departments have responded really well to our consultancy services.

In terms of training, we found that by providing it internally, we could target the training to specific user needs. In that sense we have focused more on how SharePoint can support the way we work at Novozymes, as opposed to sending our employees to external training, where the focus would be on the capabilities of SharePoint. It also means that our team has gained valuable information about how SharePoint is being used internally, and that's been really helpful for us.

Michael: *What has not worked so well?*

Frederik: End user training is more effective and better integrated into a "new way of working" if a whole team or department have been trained together. By focusing on Site Owners, we were often only training one or two people from a department, and then had to leave it up to them to integrate the changes when they returned to their department. This is a hard job! One approach we have been following is to train groups of people with somewhat similar job functions, and who work together in informal networks.

> End user training is more effective and better integrated into a "new way of working" if a whole team or department have been trained together.

Michael: *What would you do differently if you were starting again?*

Frederik: We are really happy with the approach we took, and have found it effective. We have been learning along the way, just like our users have been. If we could start again, there are two things we would change:

- Technical decisions about SharePoint farms! We have our team sites stored on two different farms, and only one of them is integrated with our intranet. We are now facing a migration of the other farm. By having team sites and the intranet on the same farm the users experience benefits from a better search, a single "My Profile," and more. If we were to do it again, I would start with only one farm.

- We started off with just giving people their sites and no support or training. This was a calculated risk in order to get a feel for the users' capabilities. Going forward I still find this to be okay as a measuring tool, but I think I would have started our real user adoption approach sooner.

Other Aspects to Consider

When putting together your User Adoption Approach (and using the jigsaw), there are a variety of specific "other things" you should know about, or be aware of. If you don't, these could cause problems for your work. The top aspects to consider are:

- Is your organizational culture collaborative?

- What is the current state of the second wave people in your organization?

- Why should they listen to you?

- What do you want them to do?

- What else is changing in their work and work practice?

- How can you reach them?

- Are your strong champions ready?

This section provides a quick "heads-up" on each of these topics.

Question 1. Is Your Organizational Culture "Collaborative"?

Generally speaking, what is the organizational culture at your organization? Is it "collaborative" or not? For example:

- Are people willing to help other people? Can you ask for help, knowing that it will be forthcoming in a friendly and collegial manner?

- Are people willing to offer an idea or suggestion without having to get it perfect first? Are they willing to share half-formed ideas in the spirit of joint discovery?

If the culture at your organization is not collaborative, then you will have little success with collaboration technologies. No amount of collaboration technology will overcome a non-collaborative culture.

- Are work outputs viewed as joint deliverables, or as something that is individually owned (and don't you dare touch or modify it)?

- Are people open to constructive feedback focused on improving the way work is done?

If the culture at your organization is not collaborative, then you will have little success with collaboration technologies. No amount of collaboration technology will overcome a non-collaborative culture. If the culture is "anti-collaborative," then you will need to deploy "big levers" to change the culture. Strong executive sponsorship, linked with strong executive modeling of the collaborative culture—will be critical. Working in partnership with the corporate change management people from Human Resources will also be essential. Don't try and do it yourself.

Another comment on culture. Often a "bad culture" is blamed when collaboration technologies don't work, or are rejected by the people they are designed to help. Sometimes this is absolutely true—the culture is the problem.

But in other cases it is not true at all, but the "bad culture" still takes the blame. The real cause is that the people who are charged with "rolling out" the new collaboration technology see it merely as an IT deployment, and haven't give any thought to the impact it will have on the people doing the work. The new tool is rejected, not because it lacked the possibility of adding great value to people, teams and the organization, but rather because the user adoption approach was non-existent.

Question 2. Where Are They Today?

What is the current state of the second wave people you will be working with? How are things with them, and what is going on? For example:

- *Time.* Do they have time to listen to you and try out new things, or is their work so stressful that they are running mad 24/7? "Exploring" new ways of working signals that the process isn't perfect nor totally efficient, but without some white space in which to try out ideas and see what happens and what resonates, you will find it very difficult to engage with people.

> "Exploring" new ways of working signals that the process isn't perfect nor totally efficient, but without some white space in which to try out ideas and see what happens and what resonates, you will find it very difficult to engage with people.

- *Prior Experience.* Has what you are doing been done or attempted before in your organization? Are you merely the latest starry-eyed individual to take on the job of rolling out the new collaboration technology, but something similar has already been tried before and people didn't like it. Prior experiences like this can put people against you from the beginning, so if this isn't the first time, do you know how you will avoid the previous mistakes?

- *IT capability*. The general degree of IT capability is an important factor, as many of the new collaboration technologies expect people to do things in newer and less understood ways. Free-form tagging in Yammer or IBM Connections, for example, are less understood than formally constructed taxonomies. If you are working with people who have a very low level of basic computer knowledge, then your challenge will be even greater. Either you need the resources to mitigate this lack of basic knowledge, or you will need to drastically scale back the demands the new system will place on people. How simple can you make it, without eliminating the benefits sought?

Question 3. Why Should They Listen to You?

Have you earned the right to talk about new ways of working with new collaboration technology? Is the work you are doing viewed in a generally positive or negative light? Or are people sitting on the fence—neither committing nor rejecting the concepts. You do need to earn the right to be heard. For example:

- Have you sought their input on how things happen today, and how things could be made better? The people who do any particular work activity often know the shortcomings of what they are doing, and long for a better way of doing them.

- Are you sufficiently conversant with their current way of working? Can you compare and contrast the new way with the old? You will be taken much more seriously if you can do this, compared to turning up with a grandiose vision that has no grounding in current practice.

Question 4. What Do You Want Them To Do?

Saying you want people to "use SharePoint to share documents" or "use Confluence to wiki" or "Yammer to say what you're doing" is not enough. If that's the beginning statement to a more detailed explanation, then all well and good, but if that's the totality of what you are able to say, then even you won't make any progress.

In other words, you have to overcome the natural resistance to change, and one of the ways you can do this is to decrease the resistance mechanism by being very clear about what is involved. As we discussed in Chapter 3, sometimes resistance is a fear of the unknown, and you of all people should be able to make the unknown more known. You won't be able to elaborate perfectly on all of the consequences and implications, but you need to some ideas you can explain clearly.

> You have to overcome the natural resistance to change, and one of the ways you can do this is to decrease the resistance mechanism by being very clear about what is involved.

Question 5. What Else is Changing?

How much stuff is changing in people's work lives today, in addition to the new collaboration technology? If too much is changing, then no matter how beneficial the new way of working actually is, they will resist it. They simply can't handle any more.

I face this in my work. I frequently receive interview requests or beta offers for new collaboration products and services. The analyst relations firm reaches out to me and requests an analyst briefing, or the founder of a collaboration technology startup offers me a free license to use their tool. But I say no, not because it isn't good or potentially revolutionary stuff, it's just that I have too much else on the go and can't give them the thought they need.

> If too much is changing, then no matter how beneficial the new way of working actually is, they will resist it. They simply can't handle any more.

Question 6. How Can You Reach Them?

What forms of communication and interaction can you use to engage with the people you are trying to help? If they are in the same building, you can walk by and see them. If they aren't, you'll have to do some form of travel or use some form of technology-mediated interaction—email, instant messaging, a web meeting, or something else.

Frederik from Novozymes had to help numerous collaboration site owners in many countries around the world understand the new way of working. To do this, he presented a business case for onsite training workshops to provide face-to-face engagement and in-depth knowledge transfer. This was approved, and he spent six weeks traveling the globe to work with people.

But how do you sustain interaction after the initial burst of activity? In Frederik's case, he'd met the Site Owners once, but fiscal realities—not to mention family disruption—meant that continuous travel was out of the question. Instead, he planned to use an in-house web meeting service to provide the needed follow-on.

Question 7. Have You Got Your Strong Champions?

In Chapter 5, we talked about the role of Executive Support in the user adoption process, and in Chapter 7, about the Embedded Champion strategy. Have you lined up these people in your organization?

In my Lotus Roadmap[3] report from early 2010, I conclude with this paragraph:

> *... perhaps the greatest need that any organization using Lotus Notes requires going forward is a strong internal leader to champion the effective use of the technology*

throughout business operations. Most people don't care what they use, but a vocal minority will argue against whatever is put in place. For this reason, a strong leader to counteract this undercurrent is essential if the technology is going to be used effectively. If such a leader cannot be found within your organization, then regardless of the historical prowess of the technology and the future plans from IBM, Lotus Notes will be left to die a slow and painful death.

This requirement is not just limited to Lotus Notes. Any new way of working will have its detractors, and the strongest counteraction against detractors is internal people who will speak and actively champion the positive.

It's Important to Start

My original plan with this book was to write 120 pages and then publish. But as you can see from what you are holding in your hands, it ended up being more than twice as long! There's a lesson here: although you won't know the final state of your User Adoption Approach, you have to start. Please don't get stuck in the "just-one-more-thing-then-I'll-be-ready" trap.

Go! Learn! Adjust! And then Go some more!

What To Do When Nothing Works

Perhaps you have started on your user adoption approach, and it's not going all that great! Consider the following comments.

One respondent to the User Adoption Survey wrote:

> *Very little is working. The tool got in the way and people were reluctant to participate.*

If this happens to you, it's time to shift into detective mode. Why did the tool "get in the way?" Interview the people who were involved, and explore the reasons why the tool was less than effective. Ask why they were reluctant to participate, and what would need to change for them to do so in the future. Don't leave it as a failure. Find out what was going on, and make plans for overcoming these problems in the next round.

Another respondent to the survey wrote:

> *Nothing has yet worked well—we've tried classroom training and Pages on the Intranet so far.*

Classroom training and Pages on the Intranet are both from Stage 2 of the model, so in the situation of this respondent, perhaps nothing had been done to win people's attention first. Or, from the sound of it, nothing had been done afterwards to Enliven Applicability and Make It Real. There are strategies for both of these stages in this book—go back and work on your user adoption jigsaw!

Finally, a common observation is that younger people are more willing to embrace new ways of working than older people. That may be true in your particular context, but it's no excuse for writing off the older generation. Perhaps their pushback and lack of support has more to do with their reaction against the arrogant and rude younger people who have called them "out-of-date" and "so-last-year" whenever new approaches have been advocated. Or they haven't been treated with respect. Or they haven't had their learning and change needs adequately taken into consideration.

> Don't write off older people just because they are less inclined to jump quickly into the action with their full support. You'll need to win their attention and support—it may just take longer than younger people in the second wave.

So, don't write off older people just because they are less inclined to jump quickly into the action with their full support. You'll need to win their attention and support—it may just take longer than younger people in the second wave. Note that there are some cases where the most active participants in new approaches to work are among the older generation—they see the value, they see a path for them to make a contribution, and they know how to use the technology. Due to their greater years of experience and their ability to coach and inspire, they make a far greater contribution than many of the "younger" people in the same organization.

Summary

This chapter has given you permission to play with a jigsaw at work! It's the user adoption jigsaw, and it provides a simple but effective way to get going with your User Adoption Approach. The basic idea is to choose one main strategy as the heavyweight for each stage of the User Adoption model, but to feel free to complement the main strategy with one or two additional strategies if that is required.

Thanks to Frederik at Novozymes in Denmark, we took an inside tour of the User Adoption Approach they put in place for collaboration team site owners. In light of their situation and culture, Frederik designed an approach to maximize their ability to spread good practice around the organization.

Finally, we looked into various factors to be considered when crafting your User Adoption Approach, and what to do about them. These included culture, current state, credibility, and more.

In the next chapter we tackle the issue of measuring user adoption.

---

[1] I presented an evening seminar on User Adoption Strategies in Melbourne (Australia) on February 14, 2010, and Andrew attended. During the discussion time, my notes state that Andrew said this. You can follow Andrew on Twitter, at twitter.com/awmitchell.

[2] Frederik Zebitz is the Web Coordinator at Novozymes in Denmark, and has taken an active role in the user adoption approach for SharePoint at Novozymes. I "met" Frederik via online tools after he read *Seamless Teamwork* and *SharePoint Roadmap for Collaboration*. And in March 2010, I met him in person in Denmark, when he attended the User Adoption workshop I ran at IntraTeam 2010. See dk.linkedin.com/in/frederikzebitz. Since then, Frederik left Novozymes in 2011. He now works as the Collaboration Manager at Lundbeck in Denmark.

[3] The *Lotus Roadmap: Enhancing Business Collaboration with Lotus Software* report analyzes the future strategic role of Lotus Notes and other Lotus software within client organizations, and argues for a much broader definition of the term roadmap. For more information, see www.michaelsampson.net/2010/01/lotus-roadmap.html.

Chapter 11.
Measuring and Evaluating User Adoption

 The potential value of a new technology lies in the new and improved behaviors and practices that might emerge when the technology is introduced to, and adopted by staff. It's when people change the way they behave—for the better—and find better ways do their work. That is when operational performance can be improved, when the organization's ability to innovate can increase, when people can collaborate more efficiently and effectively, and when decision making can improve.[1]

Oscar Berg

Embracing the approaches and strategies outlined in this book will cost money, time, and effort. I argued earlier in the book that user adoption was a necessary part of achieving collaboration success, and have outlined a series of pragmatic steps to get there. Before closing this book, however, we should talk about measuring and evaluating user adoption —how to go about it, what that would look like, and the measures and metrics that make most sense. For those in the thick of developing new collaboration approaches, talk of measurement and evaluation can be an unwelcome thought. For the managers and executives funding the work, however, it is a way of assessing value. And therefore it's a critical topic.

In this chapter, we will:

- Look at three principles for measuring and evaluating user adoption.

- Consider four approaches to measuring and evaluating user adoption. These approaches are complementary, rather than either/or.

- Develop your own plan for measuring and evaluating user adoption, in line with the success you are seeking at your organization.

Principles for Measuring and Evaluating User Adoption

Peter Drucker is quoted for many topics, but his measurement quote rings true for this discussion—*You cannot manage what you cannot measure.* Measurement is a means to an end, and that end is better management. To contextualize our discussion of measuring and evaluating user adoption within a management framework, let's consider three principles of measurement and evaluation:

1. Know what success looks like, and design appropriate measures to bring that out.

2. Use measurement to inform management.

3. Make measurement a way of life, not a one-off event.

Let's talk about each principle in turn.

Principle 1. Have a Clear Picture of What Success Looks Like

The first principle of measuring and evaluating user adoption is that we need to know what success looks like for our organization at a particular time in the future, and then design appropriate measures to bring this out. For example, consider the following visions of success and the associated measures (see the summary in Figure 11-1):

> We need to know what success looks like for our organization at a particular time in the future, and then design appropriate measures to bring this out.

1. If success for the organization means broader participation by its employees in discussions, then the average number of comments per discussion topic is an appropriate measure. You would want to add a second measure that brings out the spread of contributions as well—to show the distinction between broad input from many employees compared to concentrated input from a few employees. Input from many employees is better correlated with broader participation than frequent comments from a select few.

2. When introducing an additional way of collaborating, success means that people transition appropriate activities to the new approach and technology, so that the value being sought is gained by the organization. For example, consider an organization that is introducing the option of new document collaboration approaches through Office Web Apps, which means that employees can work on documents together without having to use attachments sent by email. In this case, the right measure is the ratio of documents (or spreadsheets, etc.) that are developed using Office Web Apps compared to those that should be developed using Office Web Apps but are still developed using email and attachments.

3. Extending example 2 above, another way of introducing new document collaboration approaches is that it replaces the current way of working together. In this instance, success means that people transition all their activities to the new approach and technology, and stop using the older approach. The appropriate measure, therefore, is the percentage of documents developed using Office Web Apps compared to those developed using email and attachments.

4. Perhaps success means greater transparency of work-in-progress, and this is enabled by using collaborative project spaces rather than hidden email conversations. One measure of this will be the number of active projects that have an associated project space that is being actively used for the project.

For each of these examples, management is possible based on what the numbers are showing over time. If the number and spread of comments in a discussion are insufficient, strategies to encourage greater participation can be introduced. If the transition to new ways of working together on documents is not taking hold, it signals that more work is required to show the value and benefit of doing so. If the percentage of projects without an active collaborative team space is low, corrective action will be required.

Figure 11-1. Measuring User Adoption in the Context of Success

If Success Means ...	Then Appropriate Measures Include ...
Broader participation by employees in discussions	The average number of comments per discussion topic
	The spread of contributions across employees
Employees transition some activities to the new approach and technology. E.g., document collaboration with Office Web Apps	The ratio of documents developed using Office Web Apps compared to those developed using email and attachments that should have been developed using Office Web Apps.
Employees transition all activities to the new approach and technology. E.g., document collaboration with Office Web Apps	The ratio of documents developed using Office Web Apps compared to those developed using email and attachments.
Greater transparency of work-in-progress, by using project spaces	The number of active projects that have an associated project space that's being used

Ways of measuring and evaluating user adoption must be stated within the business context. Develop a picture of what success looks like, and then design appropriate measures.

One implication of this principle is that achieving high levels of sustained adoption of a technology or approach is not always good news—in fact, it can signal a huge problem. Consider the high levels of adoption of email and meetings:

- *High Adoption of Email.* It's not uncommon for people to send and receive 50-100 email messages each day, and in some occupations and email-intensive corporate cultures, the numbers can reach upwards of 150-300 messages. The reality is that doing justice to so many messages requires three-to-four hours a day of reading, thinking, and replying to the incoming flood of email. Do we have high and sustained user adoption with email? Absolutely. Is it an effective way to communicate and collaborate with others? Many are saying no.

> Do we have high and sustained user adoption with email? Absolutely. Is email an effective way to communicate and collaborate with others? Many are saying no.

- *High Adoption of Meetings.* People who spend three-to-four hours a day in email then spend the other half in a meeting room. If you are going from meeting-to-meeting—you "live in meetings"—then you have high levels of sustained adoption. Are these meetings effective? Some are, but many if not most are not. Again, we have high adoption of meetings as the way to work, but these are usually seen as an ineffective way of working.

In summary, high user adoption of a particular technology or approach to working together does not mean that it is effective or optimal. The general principle is to understand the band of optimal usage, and to initiate corrective actions if usage falls below or above this band. Thus adoption could be:

- *Too High.* There is too much usage of a particular technology or approach, and users are complaining about the volume of irrelevant activity. The task is to decrease usage.

- *Just Right.* The level of usage is optimal for the conditions. The technology or approach is generally being used for the right purposes, in the right volume, and is delivering appropriate outcomes. The task is to celebrate what's happening, and to sustain optimal usage.

- *Too Low.* There is insufficient adoption of a particular technology or approach. People are continuing to use older ways of working together, and this is costing the organization in time, money, and effort. The task is to explore why adoption is so low, and to use various strategies to increase adoption.

For email and meetings, the strategies for dealing with these three bands of adoption are shown in the following figure—and clearly this approach can be used with other technologies and approaches too.

Figure 11-2. Strategies for Dealing with Three Bands of Adoption

Current Status	Strategies for Email	Strategies for Meetings
Too High *Need to reduce levels of adoption*	Explore alternatives to using email, such as discussion systems, real-time document editing (to replace document reviews by email), instant messaging (for quick questions), phone calls, and meetings.	Analyze the types of ineffective meetings being held, and interview people to understand why they are ineffective. Introduce different ways of sharing information and keeping people up-to-date. Introduce the principles of effective meetings.
Just Right *Need to sustain current levels of adoption*	Remind everyone about the principles of effectively using email. Celebrate an effective email culture.	Celebrate an effective meeting culture. Encourage people to keep following the principles of effective meetings.
Too Low *Need to increase levels of adoption*	Interview people to understand why they are not using email when they could be. Have they shifted to new ways of interacting? If so, no change may be required. Are they relying on paper-based processes ideally suited to email? Help them make the transition to email. Are they holding a meeting when an email message would be sufficient? Encourage them to make the change.	People are avoiding meetings and using never-ending email discussions instead. The organization is paralyzed by a lack of decision-making and action. Institute the need for a meeting when an email discussion is not leading to closure. Train on the principles of effective meetings, and offer coaching and facilitation services to help the new meeting culture take root.

Adoption can be too high, just right, or too low. Depending on the current status, different strategies will be required to shift adoption back to the "Just Right" band.

Figure 11-2 shows an important nuance in the adoption discussion. There are various ways of achieving particular collaborative outcomes, and new technologies only add to range of approaches. Guiding people to ways of working together effectively involves a balancing act across current and new ways of working. Some approaches will increase, while others need to decrease.

Principle 2. Use Measurement to Inform Management

The purpose of measurement is informed management. We measure so we can manage better. Any measurements we make should fit within the ethos of improving, enhancing, and correcting what's happening. It's very common for easy measures to overwhelm the measurement and evaluation discussion, particularly quantitative numbers that describe the current state of the system itself. It gets even worse when these numbers are averaged per employee, and presented to three decimal points. For example, for a firm with IBM Connections—although this applies regardless of the specific technology—those easy measures would be things like:

- The number of communities.

- The number of blog posts.

- The number of bookmarks.

The problem is these measures lack any context around the specific vision for the use of IBM Connections at the firm, and do not address how the technology is supposed to improve the way the firm operates. Do the communities in IBM Connections add value to the vision? A count of communities will not answer that question. Are the blog posts creating value or merely contributing digital noise? Again, a count measure won't help with answering that. Broadly speaking, quantitative numbers that count items or artifacts in a system are unable to provide information for better management. They are easy to gather, but useless for management.

> Do the communities in IBM Connections add value to the vision? A count of communities will not answer that question.

Better measurements are possible, and will do more to inform the management function than any of these easy count measures. They are, however, less easy to gather by clicking a few buttons on a keyboard. It usually requires more time to capture these measures, more time to reflect on what they mean, and more tolerance for broad strokes in place of precise (but meaningless) numbers.

Let's go back to the firm using IBM Connections. In the language of *Collaboration Roadmap*, we will assume the vision is to increase organizational effectiveness by reducing duplication of effort and deepening learning.[2] The firm has employees in multiple countries, and these employees have usually worked on their own office-aligned projects, even though it was found that similar projects were happening all around the world. Measures that could be used to gauge the adoption and usefulness of IBM Connections include:

1. The percentage of communities that have active representation by employees who come from different offices.

2. The number of communities that have been merged with another community due to the discovery of overlapping interests and focal areas.

3. The percentage of blog posts that receive comments from employees in other offices, where the employees did not previously know about the existence of the blog nor the other employee.

4. The percentage of new projects that are set up in IBM Connections where employees from multiple offices are included in the initial invitation to participate in the project.

These are more difficult measurements to make, but they hold the promise of informed management. If the percentages or numbers for any of the above measurements are not where they should be (or where they should be trending in absolute terms or as a rolling average), management can initiate corrective actions to bring the reality in line with the vision. See Figure 11-3 for examples of possible corrective actions for measures 1 and 4.

Figure 11-3. Using Measurement to Inform Management and Corrective Action

Historical Situation	Desired Situation (Vision)	Current Status (What's Happening)	Corrective Action
Communities are formed along office lines. Only 3% of communities have employees from different offices as members.	*From Measure 1.* Increase the percentage of communities with active membership by employees from different offices to 60% within 2 years.	The percentage grew to 10% after six months, but then flatlined. It has not changed for the past four months.	Reach out to community owners and coach them on specifically searching out employees in other offices.
Staff work on office-aligned projects. Only 2% of projects involve staff from multiple offices	*From Measure 4.* Increase the percentage of projects with staff from multiple offices to 30% in 3 years.	After an initial flurry of multi-office activity, projects established from the largest three offices are going back to using only local employees.	Set up discussions with the project leaders at the three offices to explore why they are going back to using local employees. Next steps will depend on what we learn.

Measurements taken in light of the vision can be used to inform management and plan corrective action. If key vision-aligned measures are not trending in the right direction, steps can be taken to understand why and resolve the problem. Such measurements have meaning in the wider context, and link directly with where the firm wants to go.

Alternatively, if the vision for collaboration was tied to process efficiency—which is the first value opportunity noted in *Collaboration Roadmap*—then the measures would include elapsed time and process cost. The intent of using new collaboration technology and approaches would be the reduction of elapsed time and process cost over time. It would be helpful, however, to also consider the impact of the changes on effectiveness and outcome satisfaction. The relentless drive for efficiency at any cost is often too costly.

Principle 3. Make Measurement a Way of Life, Not a One-Off Event

The final principle is to make measurement a way of life. If you are going to measure and evaluate user adoption after the introduction of a new technology or approach, you need to have reliable measures about adoption and value from before the new technology or approach were introduced. If you only have post-implementation measures then your comparisons, conclusions, and decisions about corrective actions will be on shaky ground, and open to attack from adversaries inside your firm who dislike what you are doing.

In the ideal situation, measures and evaluations should be set up in advance to gauge the current timing and cost for targeted processes, process effectiveness, employee satisfaction with the current process, and levels of adoption by staff and other appropriate people. Once the new technology and approach has been introduced, these same measures and evaluations are gathered over time, allowing for real comparisons and effective decision-making about fine-tuning what's happening, or taking a different approach.

Figure 11-4. Comparing the Before and After Process

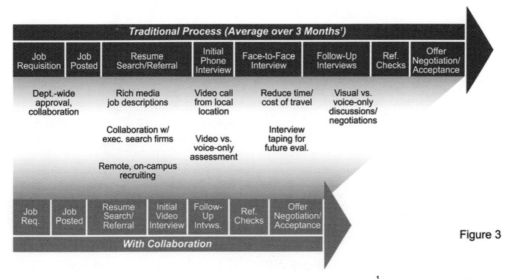

If a firm's hiring process involves travel for face-to-face interviews, there's an opportunity to use video conferencing for remote interviews. This can result in a process time saving of 30%.

Consider Figure 11-4, which shows an example from Polycom about how video conferencing can impact the hiring process.[3] The traditional process takes about three months, and includes a variety of steps. By using video conferencing for job interviews and internal discussions rather than relying on travel, the process time can be shrunk by about 30%. Armed with this data, a firm now has a solid context for the business improvement opportunity ("reduce the process timing by 30%"), as well as a good sense of the benefit of user adoption. If users don't adopt the new technology and approach, this business value cannot be gained.

Summary—Three Principles of Measurement

In this section we have defined three principles of measurement for user adoption. Use these principles to guide your selection of appropriate measures.

Figure 11-5. Principles of Measurement for User Adoption

Regardless of the approach you take to measuring user adoption, be guided by the three principles above. They will keep your work grounded in the business or organizational reality, and prevent a myopic focus on numbers at the expense of meaning.

Approaches to Measuring and Evaluating User Adoption

Building from the three principles we have discussed, there are various approaches to measuring and evaluating user adoption. In this section we consider four approaches to measurement and evaluation:

1. System utilization.

2. Justified and unjustified expenditure.

3. The changing mix of collaboration systems.

4. End-user satisfaction.

Let's look at each in turn.

Approach 1. System Utilization

System utilization is the most basic and easily accessible measure of user adoption. System utilization is a basic (simple) measure because it reports how much usage the system has garnered over a particular period, but doesn't contextualize this within the wider context. It shows a number, not the impact of that number. Measures of utilization are easy to obtain, because collaborative systems usually report utilization counts, and if not, third-party reporting tools can be acquired to perform this task.

While system utilization is a basic measure, it can be used effectively as part of your measurement and evaluation strategy. Here are four key ideas about its effective use:

- *Percentages are more meaningful than raw counts.* Saying that 500 people used the system during March is less meaningful than saying that 10% of employees used the system during March. Percentages are better able to contextualize a number within the organizational context.

- *Trends are more meaningful than single numbers.* If 55% of employees used the system in March, is that good or bad? Utilization in March should be shown in context of utilization over the previous six or 12 months. If utilization of a new system is increasing, then the new system is probably going well. If utilization is decreasing or has flatlined, corrective action will be required, unless there is a clear explanation as to why utilization decreased. See Figure 11-6.

> If 55% of employees used the system in March, is that good or bad?

- *Rolling Averages Smooth Out the Lumps.* The numbers in the utilization and change rows in Figure 11-6 establish the absolute usage, but stark changes in any one month can cause unnecessary concern—such as in March when many employees were on vacation. Using a three month rolling average for utilization and change eliminates these stark changes, and gives a more even view on utilization and change. See Figure 11-7.

- *The trend in context of the opportunity is more meaningful than the trend alone.* Showing the utilization trend in context of the utilization opportunity is more meaningful than just showing the trend. If the opportunity is for 80% of employees to use the new approach, and only 10% are using it, there is huge scope for increasing utilization.

Figure 11-6. Monthly System Utilization by Employees

	Jul	Aug	Sep	Oct	Nov	Dec	Jan	Feb	Mar
Utilization	30%	35%	45%	55%	60%	60%	70%	70%	55%
Change		5%	10%	10%	5%	0%	10%	0%	-15%

System utilization was rising steadily from July to February, but then dropped significantly in March. It dropped to a level not seen since October (five months previous). Finding out why is critically important so that the appropriate corrective action can be taken. The result for March could be an early signal of pending problems, or merely be reflective that many employees were on vacation during March.

Figure 11-7. Three Month Rolling Average of System Utilization by Employees

	Jul	Aug	Sep	Oct	Nov	Dec	Jan	Feb	Mar
Utilization	30%	35%	45%	55%	60%	60%	70%	70%	55%
Average			37%	45%	53%	58%	63%	67%	65%
Change				8%	8%	5%	5%	4%	-2%

Showing utilization by using a rolling three month average gives a more even view of utilization over time. It smooths out the months that have stark changes which can be easily explained and don't need to be highlighted as deviations from the normal range.

In summary, system utilization is a basic but useful measure. Just remember that it doesn't show the impact of adoption. Different measures are necessary for that.

Approach 2. Justified and Unjustified Investment

The second measure involves looking at the investment in licensing costs and adoption efforts that have and have not been justified. In line with the overall vision of improvement, money has been expended to purchase, install, and train people on new collaboration technology and approaches. It is useful to look at the proportion of this expenditure that has already been put to productive use, and compare it with the proportion of this expenditure that has not yet been put to productive use.

What proportion of the expenditure has been put to productive use?

Consider an organization of 14,000 employees that is embarking on the collaboration journey. Its vision of improvement centers on raising the effectiveness of its processes, and some good measures have been established to measure this. The technology costs €185 per employee, and the decision is to progressively roll it out over a three year period. When the technology is implemented for each new group of employees, they will receive adoption support at an average cost of €225 per employee. After three years, while the technology has been licensed for all employees and everyone has received adoption support, actual adoption is only 36% of the employee base.

Figure 11-8. Justified and Unjustified Investment

Technology Cost	€185	per employee		
Adoption Cost	€225	per employee		
	Year 1	Year 2	Year 3	Total
Roll-Out Schedule	10%	30%	100%	
Licensed Users	1400	4200	14000	
Actual Users (%)	6%	17%	36%	
Actual Users	840	2380	5040	
Total Investment	€574,000	€1,148,000	€4,018,000	**€5,740,000**
Investment Justified	€344,400	€650,533	€1,446,480	**€2,441,413**
Investment Potentially Wasted	€229,600	€497,467	€2,571,520	**€3,298,587**

The failure to adopt new collaboration technology and ways of working results in wasted expenditure, missed opportunities, and a reduced chance of achieving the initial vision that drove the investment in the first place. Adoption is critical to success.

There are two sides to keep in mind when looking at the reality portrayed in Figure 11-8:

1. *We need to know the impact of the adoption by the 5040 people.* We know that after three years 5040 people are using the new collaboration technology and approaches to increase process effectiveness. What has this meant for the organization—specifically, which processes have been improved? For example, if we can show that the proposal creation process has been significantly revamped, and that as a result we have increased our win percentage by 35%, and that this has led to incremental revenue of €20 million to the organization, that's a great result. What other processes have been improved?

> The proposal creation process has been significantly revamped, increasing our win percentage by 35% and generating €20 million of incremental revenue.

2. *We need to uncover why the 8960 people have not yet adopted.* What are the root causes that have kept the other people from adopting the new collaboration technology and approach? These root causes can run the gamut from lack of applicability, a poor approach to engagement, no help with adoption (such as how to apply the new technology to current processes), insufficient technical capabilities to support mobile workers, and so on. It could also be that the change involved for these employees is a lot more complex than for the employees who have adopted the technology to date, and that it will take a few more years for the technology and approach to be adopted and justified. By shifting into detective mode and interviewing managers and employees who have not yet adopted the technology, try to work out the root causes.

There are a couple of benefits gained by looking at the expenditure that is not yet in use. First, for the expenditure on a specific project, efforts to increase the amount of usage reduces the amount of wasted expenditure, and increases the likelihood of achieving the value that drove the initial expenditure. Project teams are therefore able to show clear delivery capability for projects of this nature, and will win confidence from executives for future endeavors. Project teams that fail to achieve the advocated benefits and adoption will reap decreasing capability and lower executive confidence.

Secondly, it helps by gathering real-world data on the effectiveness (or lack thereof) of the current procurement approach, so that future expenditures can be managed in a better way. In other words, if the approach to purchasing new technology is fundamentally broken, gathering evidence about what usually happens post-purchase can provide the rationale for changing current approaches.

Approach 3. The Changing Mix of Collaboration Systems

A third measure of user adoption is the percentage share of activity across different collaboration systems, and how this percentage share is changing over time. This measure shows which collaboration systems are being actively used by different groups of people, and how their usage is changing over time. For particular collaboration systems, if the percentage is low when it should be high, or high when it should be low, more effort to change the balance of user adoption is needed.

For example, you could use this measure in the following situations:

- A customer service team in a call center has to quickly respond to inbound customer calls. Customers are usually seeking insight about how to resolve an issue with a new product they have recently purchased. Each customer service team member has previously maintained their own personal question and answer file in an email folder, and will send out broadcast emails asking for answers whenever a new question is asked. A wiki has been introduced to bring the team together. It provides a way to capture frequently asked questions and answers, gives the customer service team a collaborative way of working together, and enables more accurate resolution of customer issues. In this context, the percentage of issues resolved by reference to the wiki is the key measure. If the percentage is low, it signals there is significant room for improvement by including additional questions and answers in the wiki—and getting away from answers hidden in email. This may require hiring extra staff to help the team migrate answers from email to the wiki (including resolving conflicting answers), or alternatively a restructuring of the incentives plan to eliminate the competitive ranking of service agents based on the number of questions they answer during the day.

> A wiki has been introduced to capture frequently asked questions and answers. What percentage of questions are being answered from the wiki?

Figure 11-9. Questions Resolved By Email and Wiki

Resolution	Apr	May	Jun	Jul	Aug	Sep	Oct	Nov	Dec
By Email	100%	95%	90%	80%	80%	80%	80%	80%	80%
By Wiki	0%	5%	10%	20%	20%	20%	20%	20%	20%

After a promising start, the customer service team has flatlined at 20% in its use of the new wiki for answering questions from customers. Most questions are still being answered by looking through personal email records.

- A sales department wants to add greater visibility to its pre-sales activities by creating a single place for all documents and meeting notes for each customer opportunity. This will be used as a go-to-market differentiator when working with prospects on a statement of work—there will be no more confusing back-and-forth of documents by email—and it will also make it easier to transition the customer to a specific service and delivery team once the opportunity has been won. A SharePoint project site will be used for each customer opportunity. The measure in this case is the percentage of active customer opportunities that have an associated project site in SharePoint that is being actively used. We would expect to see this percentage increase over time as an increasing number of sales teams use the new approach with new customer opportunities.

- A product development team has to verify the capability of new suppliers to meet their requirements. This involves collating data from multiple site visits by different people, and comparing-and-contrasting what each learns. This used to be done by sharing spreadsheets by email, but a new system for supplier analysis has recently been introduced. The percentage share in this instance is the number of new supplier verification activities that take place through the new system compared to the spreadsheet.

- A firm of lawyers wants to transition contract authoring away from the current document management system, because it only permits a single author at any one time. The new system allows multiple, simultaneous authors. The share of activity is therefore the percentage of new contracts that are written in the new system, compared to those that are written in the old document management system.

The percentage share of collaborative activity in the targeted system gives insight into what is really happening on a day-to-day basis.

Irrespective of the specific situation, the percentage share of collaborative activity in the targeted system gives insight into what is really happening on a day-to-day basis. If the current reality is different from the desired reality, you will need to increase your user adoption activities. For example, if the percentage share in the new system is lower than it "should" be, you need to find out why. Interview current users to explore what work is happening in the new system, as well as the work that is not happening there. Also interview people who should be using the new system and are not, so as to understand why they are not doing so. If you learn that they don't see the relevance of the new system to their work, investigate how to win their attention. Or perhaps they haven't received any help in applying the new system to their work, in which case you will need to offer assistance through stage three strategies such as facilitated group re-imagining, one-to-one coaching, or an embedded champion.

Approach 4. End-User Satisfaction

End-user satisfaction is a good measure for user adoption. It gives a sense of how satisfied users are with current collaboration approaches and technologies, as well as providing insight into the appetite for new approaches. Statements such as the following can be used to tease out the nuances of end-user satisfaction:

> Measures of end-user satisfaction give a sense of how satisfied users are with current collaboration approaches and technologies, and provide insight into the appetite for new approaches.

1. "The new system helps me to do my job."

2. "The new system provides a better way of working than the previous system."

3. "I think we should use the new system for more tasks and activities in our team."

4. "I recommend the new system to other teams and groups in our organization."

5. "I have the tools I need to do my job."

An appropriate measurement scale, such as a five- or six-point Likert scale, is joined with each statement to uncover the levels of satisfaction and dissatisfaction across a group of end-users.[4] A five-point Likert scale requests end-users to choose one option for each of the above statements. Common wording for the five options are: Strongly Disagree, Disagree, Neither Disagree nor Agree, Agree, and Strongly Agree. It is also good practice to include two other options—Not Applicable (NA) and Don't Know (DK)—so people have a way of not answering questions that don't apply to their situation. Due to the nature of Likert scales it is not appropriate to average the results, but it is fine to report the median —the middle value in a list of results.

Administering an end-user satisfaction survey is relatively easy. It is likely that your existing collaboration technology offers a survey or polling capability, and if so, it's a matter of learning how to use what you already have. The biggest issue will be choosing the right set of statements to tease out end-user satisfaction in your organization. Feel free to start with the list above, or if satisfaction surveys are a regular part of assessing other systems in your organization, talk to your peers who are already deeply into this approach. If your organization does not have survey capabilities, search the internet for a survey service—such as SurveyMonkey (www.surveymonkey.com).

The second biggest issue will be analyzing the results appropriately, and deciding what to do as a consequence of what you learn. This needs to be done across the set of results, rather than taking one measure in isolation. For example, let's assume the five questions above are asked, and the results are as shown in Figure 11-10. For each of the results, a next action is proposed—either as a celebration, or to uncover the meaning behind the number and make plans to improve it. Note that this analysis in done within the context of all five statements and their ranking.

Figure 11-10. From Measuring End-User Satisfaction to Taking Action

Statement on End-User Satisfaction	Median	Next Action
Q1. The new system helps me to do my job	4	Good result, but interview a couple of people with low scores to understand where the new system is failing.
Q2. The new system provides a better way of working than the previous system	4	Mini-celebration! The new system is a clear improvement over the old approach. Good work.
Q3. I think we should use the new system for more tasks and activities in our team	3	Perplexing result. If the new system is better, why are people not overly keen to use it more? Interview some of the employees and the team leader.
Q4. I recommend the new system to other teams and groups in our organization	3	Again, somewhat perplexing. What's holding people back from recommending the new system to other people?
Q5. I have the tools I need to do my job	2	Whoa! Something is clearly missing from this team. Time to find out what it is, and make plans for fixing it.

Measures of end-user satisfaction can be used to plan appropriate next actions for the new collaboration technology and approach. Celebrations are in order for sustained high numbers; interviews and further discussions when the numbers are low.

Finally, it is worth exploring whether there are significant regional differences in the results and why that is happening. For example, if one of the medians for employees in Europe is a two, and for employees in the United States is a four, try to find out why through discussions, interviews, and one-to-one coaching.

Summary—Approaches for Measuring User Adoption

In this section we have looked at four measures for user adoption. These measures are complementary, because they provide insight to the value of adoption from different perspectives. While it is possible to use a single measure for adoption, using multiple measures gives a more rounded picture of the adoption reality, and provides better evidence for planning next actions to increase or decrease adoption.

Developing Your Measurement Strategy

In light of the principles and approaches for measuring and evaluating user adoption discussed in this chapter, your task is to develop an appropriate measurement strategy for your organization. If you have just started on your collaboration journey, the number and complexity of the measures you use will be fewer than if you have been on the collaboration journey for some time. Here's some ideas to guide your thinking:

1. *Focus on Value.* Concentrate the measures you choose on the areas of value your organization wants from new ways of collaborating. The greater clarity you bring to the reason that new ways of collaborating are important, the greater ability you have to design measures to highlight the transition you are seeking. Making the new ways of collaborating real implies that you know how to assess whether you are gaining what you were originally seeking.

> The greater clarity you bring to the reason that new ways of collaborating are important, the greater ability you have to design measures to highlight the transition you are seeking.

2. *Measure to Manage.* Collecting usage statistics and assessing user satisfaction levels should only happen within a commitment to active management. The results gained may give pause for a momentary celebration, but they should always be seen in light of desired future improvements. If everything is going well, ask "How can we improve?" If everything is going poorly, ask "How can we improve?" The question is the same, regardless of the result. If you are not going to do anything with the results, don't bother collecting them.

3. *Start Simple.* Starting with simple measures almost guarantees that you will start. Track the simple measures—number of users, number of projects with an active team space—for six to 12 months, looking at the trend over time. As you gain greater experience with the new tools, and greater insight into the behaviors you want to see, introduce complementary measures to highlight these changes.

4. *Make It Personal.* While it's important to have a sense of what's happening across the whole organization, you should also make the measures of participation and use personal. Managers and team leaders should be able to see how well their individual team members are participating in the approaches to work, and should have the resources they need to encourage greater adoption by individuals. If the new way is going to become the "now" way, individuals need to know how they need to change.

In closing, measurement provides a means for assessing progress, and can be used to prioritize and justify additional investments. Choose your measures wisely.

Summary

We have focused our attention in this chapter on how to measure user adoption. This involved a brief review of three principles of measurement, along with an analysis of four different but complementary approaches to measurement. The most important point to take away is the need to see measurement as a means to an end; the end being more informed management. For example, if a particular measure reveals a low level of user adoption, corrective action will be required to increase adoption to a more desirable level. If it shows a high level of adoption—and that this adoption isn't right for the organization, corrective action to reduce the level of adoption will be required.

> The most important point to take away is the need to see measurement as a means to an end; the end being more informed management.

In our penultimate chapter, we discuss how to work with advocates of the old way of working. They are likely to be the first wave adopters from the previous generation of collaboration technology and approach, and therefore need to be treated appropriately. Various strategies for working with these people are outlined.

[1] Oscar Berg, *Enterprise Collaboration: Focus on Improving Practices*, CMSWire, March 2011. See www.cmswire.com/cms/enterprise-collaboration/enterprise-collaboration-focus-on-improving-practices-010596.php. I've had the privilege of meeting Oscar in person in late 2010 when I presented a workshop in conjunction with his then employer in Stockholm. See also Oscar's blog— The Content Economy—at www.thecontenteconomy.com.

[2] See Chapter 3 in *Collaboration Roadmap: You've Got the Technology—Now What?* for more about collaboration vision. Increasing organizational effectiveness is the third core value opportunity of collaboration technology and approaches, and is discussed on pages 110-111. Find the book at www.michaelsampson.net/collaborationroadmap.html.

[3] Polycom's 2008 white paper, *The Power of Collaboration within Unified Communications: Business Case Considerations for Improving Enterprise Performance*, includes a great figure on page 8 regarding process acceleration for new employee hiring. It makes the argument that the hiring process can be shrunk by about 30% by using video conferencing for some of the interview activities during the hiring process, and offers a visualization of this improvement in Figure 3. Access the paper at www.polycom.com/global/documents/products/resources/ WP_Power_of_Collaboration_Unified_Comm.pdf.

[4] There is an ongoing debate about Likert scales, and whether a five-point or six-point Likert scale works best. A five-point Likert scale allows people to sit on the fence by choosing a middle point. A six-point Likert scale does not permit this, and forces people to indicate their rating on either side of the middle.

Chapter 12.
Working with Advocates of the Old Way

What has been will be again, what has been done will be done again; there is nothing new under the sun. Is there anything of which one can say, "Look! This is something new"? It was here already, long ago; it was here before our time.

Ecclesiastes 1:9-10 (NIV)

When it's time to introduce a new collaboration technology into your organization, some people may actively oppose what you are doing. They are the advocates of the collaboration technologies that your work is going to replace. They won't always fight against what you're doing, but the likelihood is high that they will. If you aren't facing such a situation in your organization, then breathe a sigh of relief and jump to the last chapter of this book. If you are facing this situation, read on.

In this chapter, we will:

- Learn about working with the people who were the advocates of previous ways of working.

- Consider some options for dealing with the collaboration technologies of yesteryear.

- Contemplate various strategies for working with the advocates of previous approaches to work.

- Remind ourselves that while we can make a deliberate effort to work with them, we can't solve all their issues.

Why Will They Resist?

Expecting advocates of the earlier way of doing things to give wholehearted support to what you are doing is naïve. Let's be honest: it's going to be hard to get their support. For IT professionals, they have built their careers, their reputations, and their contributions within your organization around a particular collaboration tool, and you are undermining all their work. For business people, they may have been the executive sponsor and champion for a previous way of approaching work, and your efforts are going to do away with what they see as a hallmark contribution of their career.

> Expecting advocates of the earlier way of doing things to give wholehearted support to what you are doing is naïve. It is going to be hard to get their support.

So what can you do about it?

What Happens to the Technology?

The question about what happens to the older technology is easier to answer than the question, "What happens to the people?" The technology question is easier because you can make some hard-headed decisions about what's going to happen, and as long as you are strong enough to see it out, it is just a technology. It doesn't have feelings!

Here are the various options available on the technology side.

- *Automatically migrate current projects to the new technology*. Depending on the technology you are looking at shifting from and to, there may be migration tools available from the "new" vendor, or from participants in the wider ecosystem. If such tools are available, they can shave significant time and effort off your migration work. You will have to weigh these against the human cost of manually making the transition. For example, there are quite a few vendors who will help you shift data from Lotus Notes into Microsoft SharePoint. There are fewer vendors who will help you shift the application designs though, and custom applications will generally have to be re-developed within SharePoint. While the two platforms are similar for some things, it's not a simple point-and-click migration.

- *Transition with a Bulk Loading Party*. An alternative to automated migration is to work alongside teams so they shift across the documents and data that have ongoing importance. Take another look at the Bulk Loading Party strategy in Chapter 9, which is less about automated data migration, and much more about data migration within a social context.

- *Let current projects finish on the old technology.* Another option is to let current projects finish on the old technology, and start all new ones on the new platform. This means that teams currently using the old technology are able to keep going without being undermined or penalized by forcing them to change mid-way through a project. If they were to change, it could lead to a significant short-term productivity decrease for the team (but on the other hand, if what you are offering is significantly better, and their project still has some years to run until completion, it may be worth getting them to make the transition to the new technology immediately). Note that if you take this hybrid approach, you will have some project members who are straddling the two technology platforms for a while.

- *Let the current platform languish with no support.* In other words, stop actively supporting the old technology, and let people hear that the new stuff is happening elsewhere. If they want to be part of it, they'll have to shift across—and it's their decision whether to migrate their data or not.

There are pros and cons for each approach, but until you start discussing the options with the people in your organization, you won't get a sense of what is the best option.

What Happens to the People?

Now let's come back to the key concern of this chapter: What do we do about the advocates of an earlier way of working?

With the material we've discussed to date, we have been talking about "second wave" people. They have a job to do, but don't feel a great connection to the technology itself. With advocates for an earlier way of working, you are often dealing with "first wave" people from a previous generation. What can you do?

> With advocates for an earlier way of working, you are often dealing with "first wave" people from a previous generation. They feel a great connection to the earlier technology.

1. You can ignore them, and wait for them to leave.

2. You can try to get them on board with the new effort.

If you are going to ignore and marginalize them, take whatever approach you think will work best. You'll make enemies, but that may be a cost you have to bear.

I'm arguing for a different approach: Try to get them on board with the new effort. Given their involvement in earlier efforts, it is highly likely that they know a lot more about the way your organization works than many other people. If you can win their support, you will be much better placed to make a success of what you are doing.

One way to think about winning their support is to use a mixture of reason and emotion.

- *For reason, talk about facts.* The reasoning approach focuses on the facts of the situation. For example, the new tool can do things the old one can't (or can't do as effectively); the decision was made as a consequence of looking at three broad factors; senior executives are actively supporting the new approach. As facts, they can be measured and evaluated.

- *For emotion, talk about implications.* The emotional part talks about implications. As emotions, they can be believed or rejected, but it's harder to put an absolute measure on them. If they support this, their career will be more secure. They have proven their value to the organization over many years, and their support of this new initiative will mean they can continue having a positive impact.

Let's take a look in more detail at seven useful strategies.

Strategy 1. Show Them What the New Can Do That the Old Cannot

The first strategy is to demonstrate what the new technology can do that the old technology cannot. Perhaps it's a particular way of streamlining key tasks within team projects. Perhaps it's a new way of structuring and sharing data among distributed team members. Perhaps it's a new way of forming collaborative groups.

Demonstrate the differences, and be prepared to discuss how the new technology compares with the old. People will have a lot to say about that.

Strategy 2. Discuss the Decision Process

A second strategy is to share how the decision to move to the new platform was made. If it was the result of a 12-month comparative investigation by a cross-functional team with senior executive sponsorship, say so. If there was representation from people who ran the old technology, then name those people. If the evaluation project was divided into three main strands of work—one looking at technology, one at the financial implications of two approaches, and the third looking at strategic factors—bring along a copy of the terms of reference for the project.

> Share how the decision to move to the new platform was made.

Linking your current discussion to the overall decision process, and helping them see that a clear process was followed, may reduce any resistance or desire to undermine your work.

Strategy 3. Get Senior Executive Support

If the decision has already been made, senior executives can be brought into the discussion to lend support for what's happening. It would be inappropriate to take this as a first strategy, but for particular individuals whose support is critical, a clear discussion with a senior executive may be all that's required.

You will need to brief the senior executive you choose on the probable pushbacks ("but our current tools can already do all that") and arguments ("it's a waste of money") that they are likely to hear. They will need good answers—from the factual to the strategic—to get out alive.

Strategy 4. Set the Strategic Direction

Another strategy is to step up the discussion from features and functions to the overall strategic direction. Perhaps it's about rationalization of vendors. Perhaps it's about delivering a more integrated approach to IT tools for collaboration, search and business process management.

Perhaps the decision has been made to purchase a new Enterprise Resource Planning (ERP) or Customer Relationship Management (CRM) application, and as a consequence, there are implications for the messaging and collaboration platform.

> Step up the discussion from features and functions to the overall strategic direction. Perhaps it's about rationalization of vendors. Or about delivering a more integrated toolset.

By switching to a new platform, it's less about features or functions being better or different, and more about delivering an integrated IT infrastructure.

In other words, arguments about "but our current tool can do that" are rendered ineffective because it's not about specific features and functions. It's about strategic alignment—the new tools come from a particular vendor (whereas the current technology does not), the new tool integrates better with another new IT platform (whereas the current technology does not), and so on.

Finally, perhaps it's about shifting away from cutting edge vendors with all the new tools, to more strategic IT vendor partnerships. For example, this could happen within the Enterprise 2.0 market. An organization may decide to replace the incumbent provider of enterprise wiki tools with a vendor who offers enterprise wiki capabilities as part of their broader platform.

Strategy 5. Contextualize Within Industry Trends

If you can, demonstrate the link between what your organization is doing and wider industry "trends"—however you choose to frame your industry and the trends therein. If you can demonstrate that the new technology and approach is necessary to support ongoing competitive positioning, or that strategic business partners are shifting to the new technology and so you need to as well, or that new products or services will be delivered to market faster-better-cheaper as a result of the new approach, then do so.

Strategy 6. Follow the 80% Rule

With all these strategies, keep in mind that you cannot solve all their problems, nor can you eliminate the fact that what they have worked long and hard for is disappearing. You can be respectful in your dealings with them, and can make special allowances to get them on board, but you can't solve all their issues. There will come a time when they have to choose to actively support the new approach or not—but that is ultimately their choice.

> You cannot solve all their problems, nor eliminate the fact that what they have worked long and hard for is disappearing. You can be respectful in your dealings with them though.

Strategy 7. Remember Your Work Will Be Replaced One Day

Finally, remember that there will come a day when what you are currently advocating for will be the "old way." Something new will come along. Someone new will be the advocate for the new way. You will be entrenched in a mindset around what you put in place. You will be seen as the "old guy" or "old gal." When that happens, how will you want to be treated? Whatever you decide is right, act that out now towards the people currently in that category.

Summary

There is another group of people who you will need to work with during your user adoption work—the advocates of the "old way" of doing things—and this chapter has proposed special strategies to use when approaching them. If you can, get them on board. If you can't, give them a gracious way to exit.

Now to our final chapter, where I recap the journey we have taken together, and outline five specific actions you can take in the next stage of your user adoption journey.

Chapter 13.
Final Thoughts

A journey of a thousand miles begins with a single step.

Ancient Chinese Proverb

You made it! Congratulations for getting to this, the ultimate chapter of User Adoption Strategies. We've walked a good journey together, and now it's over to you. The purpose of this chapter is to briefly review our journey, and to preview what comes next. That might mean taking separate paths, or it may mean walking together for some more time yet.

In this chapter, we will:

- Review the main ideas in User Adoption Strategies.

- Discover where to register for more information on User Adoption Strategies, such as additional case studies and examples.

- Learn about the User Adoption Strategies Workshop and Public Masterclass.

- Be pointed to other resources I offer on strategies for making collaboration work.

Recap and Review

The fundamental purpose for this book was to set out everything I have learnt about encouraging second wave people to adopt new collaboration technology and the way of working it encourages. The default approach of "Build It and Throw It Out There" isn't working, and it's time for a revolution in the way user adoption is handled.

I have made the following points in this book:

- User adoption is the main challenge when introducing new collaboration technology into groups and organizations, but is frequently treated as an afterthought, or worse, ignored altogether. There is a high cost in failing to be intentional about user adoption. This was the focus of Chapter 1.

- Work on user adoption isn't an isolated event—it's part of a wider context. Chapter 2 talked about the wider context, and advocated two contextual models that treat user adoption as an integral element of the process.

- The introduction of new collaboration technology requires that people change the way they work—sometimes in big ways, sometimes in smaller ways. Regardless of the magnitude of the change, having an appreciation about what brings about change in people and groups is fundamentally important. Chapter 3 introduced various change models and theories, and Chapter 4 got specific about different types of collaboration technologies.

- There are four broad stages in a user adoption approach—Winning Attention, Cultivating Basic Concepts, Enlivening Applicability, and Making It Real. Chapter 5 introduced these four stages, and Chapters 6 through 9 talked about key strategies that could be used in each stage—including the Executive Support and the Sandbox for Experimentation strategies. Data from a recent global survey on the use and effectiveness of user adoption strategies was also featured in these chapters.

- Taking the ideas, frameworks and strategies outlined in this book, it's ultimately your responsibility to choose how to approach user adoption at your organization. Chapter 10 talked about how to create a User Adoption Approach, introduced the user adoption jigsaw tool, and covered some of the additional considerations you will need to think through. Chapter 11 focused on measuring user adoption, and set the question within a wider framework.

- When new collaboration technology is introduced into an organization, there are usually "implications" for the people who advocated and supported earlier collaboration technologies. Chapter 12 provided some ideas on working with advocates of earlier approaches, and emphasized how getting them on board with the new approach and technology will pay dividends.

Six Additional Resources for Your Journey

I have six additional resources to help you on the continuation of your user adoption journey. These are:

1. My blog, other books, and research reports.

2. The User Adoption Strategies newsletter.

3. The one-day User Adoption Strategies Public Seminar.

4. The two-day User Adoption Strategies In-House Workshop.

5. Consulting services on making collaboration work.

6. A conversation by phone about your journey.

Resource 1. Read my Blog, Books, and Reports

I have written a lot over the past decade, covering many different areas related to collaboration. It may be that some things I've worked on previously will help you—in addition to what you've found in this book.

Check out the following resources:

- I write a blog on collaboration, with a focus on culture, governance, and adoption. Feel free to visit my blog at currents.michaelsampson.net, or subscribe for automatic updates via RSS.

- I write a monthly newsletter on effective collaboration, called *Making Collaboration Work*. See michaelsampson.net/getnewsletter.html.

- I have written other books on strategies for making collaboration work. See michaelsampson.net/books.html for the current list.

- I have created a list of blog posts, articles, research reports, and books about collaboration and related topics. At the time of writing, these resource centers are on Collaboration Strategy, Governing Collaboration, User Adoption, SharePoint for Collaboration, and The Practice of Collaboration. Learn more at michaelsampson.net/resourcecenters.html.

It's all there for the taking. If you can't find what you are looking for, please contact me via my web site at michaelsampson.net/contact.html.

Resource 2. Register for the User Adoption Strategies Newsletter

There's a lot of great material in this book, but it's not the final word. There is much more than needs to be said, and the User Adoption Strategies newsletter is one way of doing that. The newsletter will bring you updates about:

- New case studies and examples of people taking the ideas in this book and applying them for great results.

- Any additional chapters that are written for User Adoption Strategies, and made available for digital download.

- The dates of upcoming webinars with people who are working with the User Adoption Strategies material. This will help you hear from people in the field who are working on similar issues.

- Upcoming public masterclasses—dates and locations—on the User Adoption Strategies material, to help in your strategy work.

The User Adoption Strategies newsletter will be distributed by email. Register online for the newsletter, at michaelsampson.net/useradoption-newsletter.html.

Resource 3. Attend the Public Seminar

There's a time and a place for merely reading the contents of this book, grabbing the opportunity to make a difference with both hands, and running with it. If that's you, go well, and I wish you all my best.

There is equally a time and a place where hearing this material directly from me will add greatly to your ability to implement the ideas in this book. If that's you, then let me tell you about the User Adoption Strategies Public Seminar.

> The Public Seminar is a one-day event that gives you an opportunity to step aside from the busyness of your day-to-day work, and meet with 15-25 other people from your city who are interested in user adoption.

The Public Seminar is a one-day event. It gives you an opportunity to step aside from the busyness of your day-to-day work, and meet with 15-25 other people from your city who are interested in user adoption. During the course of our day together, I work through the User Adoption Strategies material (as presented in this book), and you will have opportunity to discuss, debate and localize what you are hearing through conversations with myself and the other attendees. Given that people from multiple firms attend each seminar, you get to hear what other people are doing too.

Emma attended one of my seminars in London, and had this to say:

> *I had some awareness of the subject from skimming through the book, but it has been REALLY useful to have you go over this and use examples and hear what other people do. The user adoption information was very useful!*

Here's the standard agenda for the public seminar:

09.00am	Opening Comments and Introductions
09.30am	Context and Models
10.30am	Morning Break
11.00am	Winning Attention (Stage 1) - Group Learning
12.00pm	Cultivating Basic Concepts (Stage 2)
12.30pm	Lunch
1.30pm	Enlivening Applicability (Stage 3) - Group Learning
2.30pm	Making It Real (Stage 4)
3.00pm	Afternoon Break
3.30pm	Measuring User Adoption
4.15pm	Your User Adoption Approach
4.50pm	Closing Comments
5.00pm	End of the Public Seminar

See michaelsampson.net/useradoption-masterclass.html to learn more about the User Adoption Strategies Public Seminar. If you subscribe to the User Adoption Strategies Newsletter, I will tell you when and where I will be presenting seminars.

Resource 4. Host the In-House Workshop

As Emma said above, it can be very useful to hear the User Adoption Strategies material from me and learn what others are doing through the Public Seminar. On the other hand, there's a lot of value in having a more focused session just for your organization. That's the role of the In-House Workshop

The User Adoption Strategies In-House Workshop is an intensive two-day session around the material in this book. There's a reason I offer it: people get a lot of value from working through this material in the context of their work and in conjunction with other people from their organization. It provides a forum to get everyone quickly to a similar starting place and to help with creating a shared strategy for user adoption

> People get a lot of value from working through this material in the context of their work and in conjunction with other people from their organization.

Here's the basic outline of the workshop:

- An initial discussion of your collaboration strategy and previous history with collaboration approaches and technology. This sets the scene for our time together.

- A series of presentations on each of the topics in *User Adoption Strategies*, along with the most up-to-date case studies.

- Discussion and debate about the various ideas. The purpose of this is to give you and your colleagues a chance to reflect on the ideas within your context.

- Individual and group exercises to apply the ideas that resonate with your firm, and work out how to implement them.

There is flexibility in the workshop too. For some of my clients, the standard workshop—as above—is all they want. For others, they want something special. For example, they might want me to lead a focus group with one or two of the business teams during the course of the two-day workshop. This gives them opportunity to watch how I engage with the business—thus learning how to do it themselves—and it can also serve as a kick-start to uncovering key areas for investment and focus with business teams. Many of my clients have found that having an external person involved in this way gives credibility and visibility to efforts around user adoption that they can't get by themselves.

The most current information about the User Adoption In-House Workshop is online at michaelsampson.net/useradoption-workshop.html.

Resource 5. Engage Michael for Consulting on Collaboration

As a Collaboration Strategist, I advise end user organizations on making collaboration work. This means I bring expertise and facilitation skills to bear on specific collaboration challenges for clients. The common elements of these are an external viewpoint, the development of capability among internal staff, and review or development of the collaboration strategy.

Here's the type of consulting projects I have worked on during recent years:

> If one of your projects would benefit from my direct involvement, let's schedule a discussion.

- External review of the intranet at a central government department in New Zealand, with recommendations on improvement. The project also involved writing position papers assessing the applicability of various knowledge management and collaboration strategies for the department.

- External input into the collaboration and SharePoint strategy for a law firm, both through position papers and by "holding court" at their premises. For the latter, we meet for a day once a year to discuss and explore their current challenges and issues. I offer my perspective as an interested but removed outsider.

- Strategic audit of the intranet and collaboration strategy at a high-tech organization, and their use of Jive to support different forms of collaboration.

- Facilitation of capability development in the area of user adoption strategies for new collaboration tools and approaches at a risk management firm in Europe, along with drafting the initial strategy.

- External input into the collaboration strategy and decision approach for a new collaboration technology platform for a global professional services firm.

- Development of scenarios for new ways of working based on the availability of new collaboration technology, as input into the collaboration strategy for a global strategy consulting firm.

If one of your projects would benefit from my direct involvement, let's schedule a discussion. It's always a delight to work directly with people around the world, and see them make significant improvements as a result of joint work.

For a longer list of recent consulting projects, see michaelsampson.net/clients.html. To discuss how you can engage me to assist with your collaboration projects, please contact me via michaelsampson.net/contact.html.

Resource 6. Let's Discuss Your Journey

I'd love to learn about your user adoption journey, and how the ideas in *User Adoption Strategies* are helping you. For example:

- What is the context in which your work with user adoption is taking place?

- What types of collaboration technologies are you looking at introducing, and why?

- What strategies are you embracing for your User Adoption Approach, and how effective have you found the different strategies? What's working really, really well?

If you are open to the idea, then maybe your story can become part of a featured case study in the User Adoption Strategies newsletter, thereby providing an avenue for others to learn from your good (or not-so-good) experiences. Let's spread around what we are learning in regards to user adoption, and help others minimize the pain they have to go through.

> If you are open to the idea, then maybe your story can become part of a featured case study in the User Adoption Strategies newsletter.

The best way to set up a time to talk is to contact me through my web site, using michaelsampson.net/contact.html.

Now It's Your Turn ...

Thank you for the privilege of sharing the thoughts in this book with you. I wish you every success in your User Adoption journey, and look forward to meeting you in person.

Now it's your turn to take the next step.

Go and do great work!

Appendix 1.
Detailed Table of Contents

I provided a graphical Table of Contents on page 8—a one-page snapshot of the book to come. Now that you have read the book, here's a full Table of Contents for reference. Use it to find quickly a particular section you want to read again.

Appendix 2.
Table of Figures

Chapter 9. *Making It Real*

Chapter 10. *Crafting Your User Adoption Approach*

Chapter 11. *Measuring User Adoption*

About the Author

Michael Sampson is a Collaboration Strategist. He advises end-user organizations around the world on strategies for making collaboration work. He is the President of The Michael Sampson Company in New Zealand.

Beyond consulting engagements with clients and in-house workshops, Michael shares his research on strategies for making collaboration work through multiple avenues:

- Michael's blog on current happenings in the collaboration world, covering collaboration thinking, philosophy, approaches, and technology. See currents.michaelsampson.net.

- Resource centers on aspects of making collaboration work—including collaboration strategy, governance, user adoption, and the human practices of collaboration. See michaelsampson.net/resourcecenters.html.

- Books on strategies for making collaboration work, with a focus on culture, governance, and adoption. Current titles are *Seamless Teamwork* (2008), *SharePoint Roadmap for Collaboration* (2009), and *Collaboration Roadmap* (2011). This second edition of *User Adoption Strategies* is Michael's fifth book. See michaelsampson.net/books.html.

- Presentations at conferences around the world, both in-person and remotely. Michael has presented at conferences in the United States, the United Kingdom, Netherlands, Belgium, Denmark, Australia, and New Zealand.

Michael holds an MCom with first class honors in telecommunications-based IT from the University of Canterbury in New Zealand.

To stay fit, Michael enjoys cycling, running, and swimming.

Michael lives in New Zealand with his wife Katrina, and their ten children—David, Matthew, Philip, Daniel, Timothy, Susanna, Jonathan, Elizabeth, Joseph, and Joshua. Michael and Katrina home school their children.